POWER

★ ★ ★

Real Estate

★ ★ ★

SELLING

★ ★ ★ ★ ★ ★ ★ ★ ★

Revised Edition

William H. Pivar

REAL ESTATE EDUCATION COMPANY
® a division of Longman Financial Services Institute, Inc.

While a great deal of care has been taken to provide accurate and current information, the ideas, suggestions, general principles and conclusions presented in this book are subject to local, state and federal laws and regulations, court cases and any revisions of same. The reader is thus urged to consult legal counsel regarding any points of law—this publication should not be used as a substitute for competent legal advice.

Executive Editor: Kathleen A. Welton
Acquisitions Editor: Wendy Lochner
Senior Project Editor: Lynn P. Schneidhorst
Copy Editor: Maija Balagot
Interior Design: Miles Zimmerman
Cover Design: Phillip Kantz

©1988 by Longman Group USA Inc.

Published by Real Estate Education Company
a division of Longman Financial Services Institute, Inc.

Printed in the United States of America.

88 89 90 10 9 8 7 6 5 4 3 2 1

Library of Congress Cataloging-in-Publication Data

Pivar, William H.
    Power real estate selling/William H. Pivar
        p. cm.
    Includes index.
    ISBN 0-88462-152-9 : $14.95
    1. Real estate business. 2. Real estate agents. I. Title.
HD 1375.P657 1988
333.33'068'8—dc19   88-9130
                                                                        CIP

To my partner, my pal, my wife

Special thanks to the following people, whose constructive
manuscript reviews contributed so much to this book:
First Edition
Roger Reitzel, Director of Training, Quinlan and Tyson,
Schaumburg, Illinois
Ruth Williams, Director of Training, Byrnes, Barroll & Gaines
Realtors, Inc., Towson, Maryland.
David R. Stipp, Tustin, California
Second Edition
Ruth Blank, Ben Blank Company,
Palm Springs, California
Mary Coveny, President
Career Match Consultants,
Naperville, Illinois

Contents

Introduction

"I did everything right: I took classes and seminars, learned selling techniques and tried to use everything I was taught. Despite all that, I'm still not selling. What went wrong?"

If you could listen to the thoughts that go on in the minds of real estate agents across the country, you'd hear that question asked over and over again. Yet it is a question with a simple answer: These people are using sales techniques that attempt to sell *property*, when what they should be selling are *benefits*. Unsuccessful salespeople think they are just in the property business and never realize they are really in the people business.

This book shows you that housing involves much more than basic shelter, and how utilizing that fact can make you a better salesperson, one who will enjoy the rewards that come with a long list of satisfied customers. The road to success we invite you to explore is called *Power Selling*. Power Selling depends on a basic truth: You don't succeed in real estate by manipulating people—you succeed by helping them recognize their needs and by showing them how those needs can be met.

Power Selling is a carefully planned technique that will help you discover and meet the real practical, financial and emotional needs of your buyers. It goes far beyond just knowing how to make a strong closing.

The technique comes into play with your first prospect contact and continues even after the closing and settlement.

Power Selling leads the prospect to the point where buying becomes the natural thing to do, because the benefits have been made undeniably obvious. Power Selling is *not* pressure salesmanship. Pressure selling tries to force people to buy property they do not feel they want or need. Power Selling shows them how a buying decision will satisfy their real needs. In pressure sales, buyers feel they are being made to buy; in Power sales, buyers feel they want to buy.

The science of Power Selling is built from the successful experiences of many people over many years. This book describes a system of techniques that, properly applied, will help you move into the top ranks of the real estate selling profession. But getting there takes more than just reading. It takes large quantities of a scarce ingredient that only you can supply: good old-fashioned work. So if you're ready with your part of the bargain, welcome. Your journey to success begins on the next page.

1. Preparing: Yourself and Your Profession

If you got into real estate because you thought it would be easy work, you should plan another career. Successful selling is hard work that requires careful planning and mental awareness.

Success in real estate takes total commitment, including dedicated study and practice. People who say, "I think I'll give real estate a try," often find that reaching their goals demands far more preparation and concentration than they'd bargained for. Part-time workers and those with other substantial income usually don't make it in real estate—they have their ace in the hole, so they aren't motivated to expend the effort required for success. Sometimes, though, a strong desire to prove one's worth or to escape an undesirable job can provide powerful motivation. This kind of motivation helps account for the outstanding success women have experienced in real estate, an area in which women have the opportunity to compete with men on an equal footing.

While the desire for self-realization is a powerful motivator, however, it takes more than desire or charm or personality to succeed. You need knowledge applied with hard work. Luck is involved only if you

1

consider luck to be the meeting of opportunity and preparation. Now let's look at some specific factors that will determine how much of that opportunity and preparation you will develop for yourself.

ATTITUDE: EXPECTING SUCCESS

During my first year in college I went to work as a salesperson for a grocery wholesaler. I was to sell canned prune pie filling on commission. After a five-minute pep talk, I set out with a can of pie filling and an order book. Young and innocent, I didn't know I had been given a "dog" product to sell. I started the day calling on small retail stores and sold a few cases of my prune filling. I decided this was too slow, so I made the rounds of chain-store purchasing offices and received two fairly large orders. When I reported in at the end of my first day, I had sold more prune pie filling than all the wholesaler's salespeople had managed to unload in the previous six months. It seems everyone else was "smart." They knew no one would buy prune pie filling, so they didn't try. Being fairly naive, I didn't know I couldn't sell it, so I did. I went out with a positive attitude and kept that attitude.

The negatively motivated salesperson starts work late and makes up for it by quitting early when he or she "knows" there won't be any activity. Afternoon movie matinees and early happy hours are favorite haunts of negatively motivated salespeople. People with negative expectations are seldom disappointed by success.

Some salespeople do well during their first six months and then their results decline. They "burn themselves out." They let their failures negatively motivate them, like baseball players who can think of nothing but the times they struck out. Successful baseball players who reach base only two out of three times don't look at a .333 batting average as proof of failure. They are positively motivated by the successes, which they have—one in every three times at bat.

When you make a closing presentation you go in with even better odds than the ballplayer. Unlike the player, you are not limited in your times at bat. You can keep trying until you succeed. And the harder you work to improve your technique, the more runs you will score.

I learned the power of positive motivation shortly after I opened my first real estate office. I had an 8 A.M. showing and by 8:45 I had an offer. When I returned to the office, I was feeling great—I could do no wrong. I decided to go through my prospect file, calling for appointments to show property.

I set up six showings for the day. Before finishing at ten o'clock that night, I had three more offers and I picked up the fifth the next day. It was then I learned the truth of the old adage, "Success breeds success." It can be a powerful motivator.

Salespeople who consult biorhythms or horoscopes give further proof of the importance of belief in success. Most of them turn out to make more sales when their charts say they will. During these times they expect to succeed and therefore work harder for that success.

The power of expectation can work in reverse, as well. Many real estate salespeople today are suffering from terminal cases of the "blahs." With the blahs you don't really feel like pushing very hard. For a cure you must move away from the status quo. A body at rest tends to stay at rest. It takes a lot of energy to start and constant self-motivation to continue. If you complain that you are in a selling slump, it is likely to become a self-fulfilling prophecy. A dry sales period is usually more closely related to attitude than it is to market conditions. A sales slump must be met with increased effort and not excuses. It is also a time to analyze your sales technique. Some people will press too hard for a sale during a low period. The result can be negative buyer reaction.

Remember, too, that when you first try a new sales technique the initial results will often be negative. If you are going to try new ideas—and you should—commit yourself to giving them a fair trial. Don't allow yourself to be negatively motivated by your failures. When you fully master the new techniques, you can generally expect an upswing in your sales.

Motivation and the People Around You

Sometimes a salesperson gets on a hot roll. He or she has become positively motivated by success and has developed self-confidence, which leads to even greater success. Other salespeople will make excuses for not selling. They blame their customers for not buying, or they rationalize that December is just a bad month: "Nobody buys in December." It never occurs to them that they have failed to meet their customers' needs. Another salesperson who succeeds while they are failing makes them feel inadequate. Rather than strive to increase their own sales, they hope the top producers have a sales decline. They are satisfied working below their capabilities and would like to keep you down at their level. Your success threatens their self-image.

Some salespeople actually feel guilty if they are successful while others working around them are having great difficulty. This guilt trip is often enhanced by coworker attitudes. The result can be unconsciously trying less in order to be liked more. Generally, a successful agent in an office with many unsuccessful agents will fail to work to his or her potential. Basking in the comfortable lethargy of success, a salesperson becomes satisfied being the top salesperson even though it may be far short of his or her potential.

It is difficult to succeed in an office filled with mediocre salespeople. Instead of working with people who can pull you down to their level, work with people who can raise you up. Some salespeople have found that simply relocating their desks to work closer to successful salespeople causes an improvement in their attitudes and results. Salespeople usually increase their productivity when they move to an office filled with top salespeople. Truly successful people serve as positive motivators for success.

Your spouse's attitude makes a big difference in how well you can motivate yourself. You want to enlist the support of your spouse by sharing your enthusiasm, your goals and your hopes. A supportive wife or husband lends positive encouragement and understands that real estate is not a nine-to-five job. The supportive spouse accepts that your time is dictated by the needs of others.

Just as spouses and associates can influence your motivation, customers can affect your view of the chances for success. Don't let customers convince you they shouldn't buy. You cannot help them by agreeing with their excuses. Remember that you believe in your product, which is real estate—not necessarily that a particular property is better than another, but that real estate ownership benefits people. Keep in mind that every piece of real estate has had an owner and will have another owner in the future. There may be bad listings, but there is no bad real estate. Every property is desirable to someone, at some price.

Just as associating with successful real estate people helps you, successful friends also serve as positive motivators. If your friends have self-confidence and are rising in their businesses or professions, they will help you keep a positive attitude. Again, however, friends can affect you negatively if you let them. You have heard people say, "Since they became rich they are stuck up and have forgotten their old friends." The problem is usually not with the successful individual but rather with his or her friends, who can't accept great success from their former "equal." Your success will hurt their self-image, making them feel inadequate by comparison. Your old friends will tell you to take it easy—that you are working too hard. If you should fail, they will rush to help you. Your failure will reinforce their decision to play it safe.

Jealousy

Many agents waste time and energy worrying about and checking on how others are doing. While you want to work to your potential, you should not be concerned about the success of others. Don't worry about office competitions and awards. Your only competitor is yourself. When you fail to develop and/or work to your capabilities you are losing, but when you use your time effectively and carefully plan your presentations you are winning.

Using a Team Approach

One way to maximize the benefits of working with others is to form teams within your office. Team members motivate each other positively and provide mutual aid and support. Three salespeople working for the same broker recently developed an unusual and very successful team approach. They were concerned because their income, while good, was sporadic, so they decided to form a sales team in which commissions would be equally divided. The benefits of this arrangement went beyond just guaranteeing a steadier income. The salespeople have found that their individual efforts have increased now that the whole team is depending on each one's success. The team members positively motivate each other. Customers are often turned over to a team member with greater expertise in a particular area or with a smaller workload. The net result has been increased earnings for all.

The team approach, of course, can have its pitfalls. If a member should become lax because personal goals have been met, other members will suffer. A written contract can help solve the problem by limiting the team's existence to a short period, say three months. At the end of each period the team members can evaluate their progress and decide if they want to sign a new agreement. A salesperson with outstanding production will probably leave a team of lower producing members. Similarly, team members may not keep a member who falls below team performance.

ENHANCING SELF-IMAGE

For many people, the ego gratification that comes with making a sale is more important than the commission earned. A sale improves the salesperson's self-image and the improvement increases confidence, which leads to more sales.

There are other ways to improve your self-image. Dale Carnegie–type courses, as well as some by Success Motivation Institute, are excellent. Joining organizations such as Toastmasters not only provides speaking experience, but reinforces your self-confidence. Good as such inspirational lectures and courses are, however, they provide only short-term motivation. Long-term motivation comes from internal, not external, forces. You must learn to really believe in your own worth.

The Missing Million

You have probably met salespeople with poor self-images. They hesitate to call on doctors, lawyers and other "important people," not realizing that these people are as interested in real estate as anyone.

A supercloser I know who never makes a sale over $100,000 is a case in point. He gets interested prospects all the time, but never seems able to close. His problem is his self-image: his low self-esteem defeats him before he starts. He considers himself competent to work with blue-collar workers and tradespeople, but imagines the "important people" will not listen to his ideas.

If your self-esteem takes a dive, there are ways to revive it. Watch the way you treat yourself. Once a week go out to a fine restaurant for lunch. Buy quality clothes and dress like a successful person. Consider your finery an investment in yourself. If you treat yourself like an important person, you will begin to feel like one. When you see yourself as a person of great worth, others will, too, and this will further reinforce your self-confidence.

Successful nonselling activities can also improve your self-image. Get in touch with service groups such as Rotary Club, Kiwanis, Lions Club, Exchange Club, etc. They are always looking for speakers. Prepare a presentation on some general-interest aspect of real estate and offer your services. Besides boosting your confidence, such presentations can provide you with many valuable contacts.

GOAL SETTING

Goal setting is simply advance planning to reach specific objectives. Chess players know they must follow a plan with their moves leading toward checkmate. Without goals we can move here and there without getting anywhere. A goal gives you direction and motivation. What kind of goals will work for you? Here are some general rules:

- Your goals must express your true desires. If you don't have a strong inner desire to reach a goal, it's unlikely the goal will be met. However, the greater your motivation to reach a goal, the more likely it is to be attained.
- Your personal goals should be *measurable.* You must be able to say, "Yes, a goal was met," or "No, it wasn't met."
- Your goals should be *long-term, short-term* and *daily.*

Long-term goals should describe where you want to be in ten years. They might be financial—for example, to have a million-dollar net worth. Or you might decide you want your own office with at least ten salespeople or your own national franchise operation. Whatever they may be, you should choose long-term goals you want badly enough to work for them.

Your *short-term goals* or interim goals are really a plan to reach your long-term goals. If your long-term goals cannot be realistically obtained after meeting your short-term goals, then your plan is defective. You need either new short- or long-term goals.

Assume a career goal is to have your own real estate office. Here is a sample of the kind of interim goals that can lead you there:

Six months: By _____ I will have completed community college courses in real estate practice, real estate financing and real estate economics.

12 months: By _____ I will have completed community college courses in real estate appraisal, real estate investment and office management.

18 months: By _____ I will have completed the Dale Carnegie course, as well as community college courses in accounting and personnel supervision.

24 months: By _____ I will have obtained my broker's license.

36 months: By _____ I will have completed the requirements for the Certified Real Estate Brokerage Manager designation (CRB).

40 months: By _____ I will have obtained a position as an office manager for a real estate firm.

54 months: By _____ I will have obtained a position as sales manager for a multioffice real estate firm.

72 months: By _____ I will have opened my own real estate office.

As you see, these interim goals point the way a step at a time toward your long-term career goal.

When career goals are reached, develop further goals. A new challenge will keep you moving. We all know brokers who reached success early and then seemed to stop, while other offices expanded and passed them by. The brokers reached their initial goals and were satisfied to remain there.

Your career goals may change. This is fairly common. If so, don't worry about your interim goals being wasted. The steps outlined above provide a natural progression not only for other real estate career goals but even for management careers outside of real estate. Don't continue to work for a goal which no longer interests you. Modify it to meet your needs.

To reach interim or career goals, you need *daily goals* to guide your activities. Daily goals are much more specific than long-term ones. They might take a form like this list:

1. I will telephone at least eight investment property owners to ascertain their real estate needs and interests.
2. I will review my prospect file and call at least six prospects to arrange showings.
3. I will show Mr. and Mrs. Smith the Northridge home at 10 A.M.
4. I will have lunch with the personnel director of Grandview Corporation.
5. I will call at least four personnel directors about employees coming into the area or transferring out. I will contact all prospects by phone.
6. I will write a minimum of ten letters for listings to out-of-the-area owners.
7. I will see Mr. and Mrs. Brown about listing their home.
8. I will check with Jones Realty on what is holding up the Klein closing and contact the Kleins.
9. I will prepare a presentation and make all arrangements for Mr. and Mrs. Sparrow, who will arrive this weekend on a house-hunting trip.

By the physical act of writing out daily goals, you will find that you get a great deal more done each day. As each goal is accomplished, checking it off will give you a sense of accomplishment.

Each night after work, *review* your daily accomplishments. Decide why you did not meet some goals, and whether to try them again tomorrow. Make your list for the next day. If you wait until morning, it won't be finished because of interruptions and calls. Written goals make it difficult to procrastinate. With your daily goal list on your desk top, you won't have time for useless talk; you will have work to do.

Don't keep your interim goals a secret. This makes it too easy for you to change or eliminate them. Let others know what you intend to do. Knowing that your friends will find out your failures serves as powerful motivation to keep on the track.

How can you set realistic daily goals that lead you to your longer term objectives? One aid is the sales activity calculator on the next page. Prepared by Palm Desert, California, broker Don Perfetti, it will enable you to determine the average number of contacts you must make each day to achieve a financial goal for the next twelve months.

THE TRUE PROFESSIONAL SALESPERSON

The true professional salesperson doesn't count commissions until they are in the bank. Instead, the professional worries about how best to meet the needs of others. The true professional has acquired the abilities to meet these needs. If you succeed in helping others to meet their needs, the money will come to you.

Many of us in real estate like to call ourselves professionals. To really earn that title, we must acquire the training and in-depth product knowledge characteristic of professionals.

The usual quickie licensing course is not enough to see us through a career. In good times many salespeople with this minimal training are able to succeed. In bad times, most fail.

The problem isn't any scarcity of training opportunities. Real estate boards, associations and community colleges offer many excellent programs. Unfortunately, not enough real estate licensees take advantage of them, because they don't understand the importance of professional preparation.

To develop the kind of professionalism that brings confidence as well as competence, you need knowledge in two separate areas: salesmanship and real estate. Unfortunately, many people work in only one of these areas and neglect the other. The greatest salesperson in the world will lose many sales if he or she lacks the knowledge to put difficult sales together. A real estate professor I know has tremendous academic knowledge of real estate and related fields. He can tell you a

---

SALES ACTIVITY CALCULATOR

Salesperson's Name _____

Area _____

Manager _____

1. Average earnings per salesperson for our company: ____

2. Your average earnings per sale are: ____

3. How much money do you want to earn in the next 12 months?   ____

4. How many presentations do you make to gain a sale?   ____

5. Divide your earnings per sale (2) by presentations per sale (4). This is your earnings per presentation: ____

6. How many contacts do you make to gain a presentation?   ____

7. Divide your earnings per presentation (5) by contacts per presentation (6). This is your earnings per contact: ____

8. Divide your earnings goal for the next twelve months (3) by 50 (number of work weeks in the year).   ____

9. Divide the results by five or six, depending upon the number of working days. This is your earnings goal per day: ____

10. Divide the earnings goal per day (9) by earnings per contact (7). This is your required contacts per day to achieve your earnings goal: ____

dozen ways to put a deal together. Yet he left real estate sales to teach because he couldn't make a living selling. He lacked basic sales skills—he just couldn't close a transaction. Salesmanship skills are people skills; they depend on the ability to understand the needs of people and what leads them to make the decisions they do. Product knowledge alone is insufficient without these people skills.

The following chapters will show you how to greatly increase your sales skills. To help keep those skills sharp, and to reenergize your motivation, it is a good idea to be familiar with the magazines published for professional salespeople. These include *Specialty Salesman*, *The American Salesman*, *The National Voice of Salesmen* and *Salesmanship*.

Getting Technical Skills

There are also important nonpeople or technical skills to master. For example, your understanding of taxation will enable you to show prospective buyers specific benefits that a property offers them. Financing knowledge will let you show prospects how they can become owners. Professionalism demands that you master not only the people skills of salesmanship, but the nonpeople skills as well. Membership in the National Association of REALTORS® and your local board of REALTORS® offers you the opportunity to attend meetings, seminars and courses that provide basic tech ical knowledge as well as news of the constant changes and innovations you must know about.

Besides courses in appraisal, real estate finance, real estate investment, property management and so forth, courses outside the normal area of real estate study can enrich you professionally and personally. A basic architectural course can help you identify building styles. Trade courses will give you a basic background in construction as well as the ability to identify various kinds of wood and other building materials. Many salespeople find that interior decorating courses give them the descriptive language they need to paint desirable word pictures, and help them overcome decorating problems perceived by prospective buyers. College salesmanship courses will benefit you as well. The basic sales skills taught apply to any product—including real estate.

To find useful courses, check your local community college and adult evening schools as well as your real estate board. Most of the national real estate organizations offer courses which lead to a professional designation. For information about these organizations, courses and designations, check my book, *The Real Estate Career Guide* (Arco, 1981). Belonging to professional organizations, reading their publications and taking advantage of their educational opportunities will help you gain knowledge as well as confidence.

Not all product knowledge comes from books and seminars. Intimate knowledge of your neighborhood also provides powerful sales ammunition. You should be ready to provide information on such items as:

Nursery schools
Montessori schools
Public schools and their districts
Public golf courses
Public tennis courts
Public swimming pools
Parks
Health clubs
Transportation routes
Youth activities
Medical facilities
Senior citizen centers
Religious institutions

As you learn your skills, though, don't let yourself be seduced by the word *professional*. Some publications have begun to constantly emphasize the word *professional* and leave out the word *salesperson*. They do a disservice by leading real estate licensees to think they are doctors who don't have to make house calls. They come to think they are too professional for anything as menial as door-to-door or telephone solicitation. They want the sales without the real labor, but it doesn't work that way. In real estate, as in any other sales effort, the harder you work the luckier you become.

Real estate salespeople should be proud of their work and not say, "I'm in real estate," when asked about their jobs. You don't make a living being *in* real estate; you do it by selling. The answer should be, "I sell real estate."

HOW TO USE ROLE-PLAYING

When playing a role, actors say their personalities sometimes change; even offstage they become the characters they are playing. They have learned to think and react as the characters. This phenomenon can be used toward self-improvement.

Create a character to play. Imagine the perfect, self-assured real estate salesperson, and decide what this perfect person would do in various situations. Going through these mental exercises as you drive, as you bathe and during all your other daily activities, can turn unproductive time into gold. By role-playing not only can you play the role of a successful, self-confident, knowledgeable, caring and happy salesperson—you can become that role.

You can be a reviewer as well as author and actor. Critique in your mind each showing you make. How would Mr. or Ms. Perfect have handled the showing? Would his or her answers have been different? Should a different closing attempt have been made? If so, what? Would objections by the buyer or seller have been handled differently? You can learn from your mistakes if you identify them and find ways to correct them the next time around. Some people refuse to recognize any mistakes. They alibi away failures. Such people cannot learn from their mistakes by role-playing. If you can see the humor in your sales disasters you are likely not only to realize what should have been said, but remember it for the future. By learning from your mistakes, you will actually be turning past mistakes into future successes. Mental exercises like this will prepare you for future sales situations.

Critique your successes as well as your failures. Ask yourself not only what you did wrong, but what could be improved and what you did right.

When you see a home, ask yourself what objections a buyer might have to this property and how the "perfect" salesperson would answer them. Come up with the wildest situations your mind can imagine and let the perfect salesperson inside you work them out.

Imagine buyers making offers. Actually write up offers to reflect what your imaginary buyer wants. Analyze real offers you have written. Consider how you could have persuaded the buyers to make better offers. I like to write an outline of a sales approach I expect to use for a particular buyer with particular property in mind. The outline approach helps organize the sales presentation and reduces the likelihood of forgetting major points to be made.

These exercises prepare you for any situation. The "perfect" person will become you. You will think like this self-assured person who has the answers and is in control of the situation.

Arthur Miller wrote in *Death of a Salesman*, "A salesman is got to dream, boy. It comes with the territory." A salesperson can use his or her daydreams in role-playing to turn wishes into reality. We know that great things can be accomplished with our minds. Golfers who mentally go through hitting the ball, paying attention to their feet, legs, hips, shoulders, head and eyes, hitting mental shots over and over, will show as much improvement as others who actually hit balls. Imagination is a preparation tool.

But we can make use of more than pure imagination. We can practice our role out loud in front of a mirror. I like to prepare presentations before a mirror because how you come across to a buyer isn't based on words alone. Eye contact, a smile and a sense of confidence as well as enthusiasm are also very important. A tape recorder is another useful tool. With it, we learn we don't sound like we think we do. Our voices sound a little weaker, and that person on the tape sprinkles his or her conversation with "Ah...," "Yas," "You know," and so on. Knowing how that person sounds can help you—now the "perfect" salesperson—to even greater improvement.

As you become used to the process of listening to yourself on tape, you can develop the habit of hearing what you sound like. If you turned a tape recorder on to record yourself while you were driving a prospect home, would you hear a voice that tells, and doesn't ask? Many salespeople feel they should have a steady line of senseless chatter like an auctioneer. Evaluate what you said to your customers. Was it necessary? What was the purpose? Should questions have been asked, and if so, what? What should have been said that wasn't?

How things are said can make as much difference as what is said. Did you use three-dollar words? You are not out to "snow" people, but to be understood. Impressing them with your vocabulary of exotic words won't sell them a house.

Watch out for profanity. It does you no good, and offends many people. *Dammit* is not God's last name. Also offensive are sexual, ethnic and religious jokes.

If you faithfully practice your role-playing and learn to listen to yourself, you cannot help but become a more effective salesperson.

CANNED PRESENTATIONS?

A canned presentation is simply a presentation which a salesperson learns and repeats without deviation. Many "experts" say that canned presentations have no place in real estate sales because people have different needs and every property is unique.

I strongly disagree. Each property is unique, but buyers' objections remain pretty much the same. Answers learned in advance can be effective in overcoming most objections. The verbal pictures you paint while showing a property can be better if planned in advance.

Closings are prepared presentations to apply as each situation requires. Even the reasoning to convince owners to accept offers can be canned. Land and insurance salespeople have known for years that their best sales results come from using a carefully prepared presentation with as few deviations as possible. With practice you can be ready for any situation, from the introduction to the closing.

When real estate salespeople abandon their prepared presentations, problems arise because they can seldom think of words that have the force of words carefully chosen and learned. The salesperson also is liable to miss important points which can sway a sale. Ad-lib presentations mean fewer sales than do carefully prepared and learned presentations. This book gives you ideas as well as verbatim language to use in your prepared presentations.

MANAGING YOUR TIME

Have you noticed that the people who never seem to have any time never seem to get anything done? The people who accomplish a lot, on the other hand, always seem able to take on an additional task. The difference is related to time management.

Most people waste a great deal of their lives. Wasting two hours a day in a forty-year working career means throwing away the productivity of ten years. If anything, the average salesperson wastes more than these two hours daily.

Organize

Organization is the key to putting all that time to good use. The time-waster can be spotted by his or her actions. Daily plans are seldom kept. Trips are not coordinated and combined, so much of the day is spent criss-crossing a territory over and over again.

If you want a ready-made plan, look for *Real Estate Professionals' Design-A-Day, Realty Organizers* or *Floor Call Prospect Book.*

Many salespeople and brokers prepare their own plans. The action plan on pages 18 and 19, prepared by Don Perfetti, is one example. Which plan you use matters less than making sure you use it and review your accomplishments daily. A plan goes far beyond just setting daily goals. With a plan you designate specific blocks of time for specific activities. Some salespeople organize their daily activities so they accomplish the most undesirable task first. Then the rest of the day seems easy.

Another timewaster to guard against is chasing possibilities rather than probabilities. Evaluate your prospects and put your greatest effort toward those who are most likely to buy. You have an investment in every one of your prospects, and the only way to get the return on those investments is to close a sale. If the sale isn't likely, stop investing. Put your time into a more likely prospect.

Your floor time and open house time often turn out to be time-wasting commodities that can be turned into assets. Use the time to write letters to out-of-town owners for listings, to call old customers for referrals, and to telephone canvass. When you are on floor time, have all ads for that day and several previous days on your desk under a plastic sheet. Know which property the ads refer to, but have several alternatives in mind for each.

Specialize

Another waste of time comes from trying to handle every kind of property in every area. Specialize in an area or property type, or both. If you have prospective buyers outside your specialty area, refer them to an office that pays referral fees.

Socialize

Your lunch hour will turn into useful time if you don't eat with other salespeople. Eat with people who can help you—buyers, sellers, personnel officers and others who can give you valuable information and leads. Socializing with other real estate salespeople may be fun, but you can have just as much fun with people who might also one day become buyers and sellers.

Many very successful salespeople prefer to be brown baggers when they don't have a business lunch planned. They do this not to save the restaurant costs but to save time. Brown bagging reduces travel, waiting and socializing time which frequently amounts to an hour or more. Eating lunch at your desk doesn't have to interrupt productive activities.

BEING READY: DATA RETRIEVAL

A good data retrieval system gives you the quick information you need for answering phone inquiries and arranging showings. Set up a system that lets you check available inventory quickly for area, price, size and other characteristics. Suppose, for example, a prospect wants a house with good acreage where he or she can keep horses. A good data system tells you quickly whether the property is zoned in a way that allows horses. Then it finds which of your own and multiple listings permits horses.

Before computers, a good system used color tabs on listing books, separating them by sections of the city and price. The same information can be stored on computers, along with much more detailed specifications such as lot size, building material, number of bedrooms or bathrooms and zoning information. With a good program you can find properties instantly that meet any combination of features the prospect wants. And the printout will impress your client with your professionalism.

Data retrieval systems can save time and keep you ready for a sale in other ways, too. When questions arise about financing arrangements for a particular piece of property, you can have sample clauses ready to use in offers to purchase. They can cover such matters as secondary financing by the seller, land contracts, release clauses, loan contingencies and other specific conditions. Having samples that apply to your area, and even to each listing, can save a lot of time and prevent the kind of delays that cool off a hot prospect. Your office file of previous offers to purchase will give you sample clauses as well as an idea of the kind of situations to be ready for.

TOOLS OF YOUR TRADE

You need a *clean automobile*. A four-door, full- or mid-size car with adequate leg room in the rear seat is important. Unless you specialize in the sale of luxurious housing or commercial or industrial property, I don't recommend luxury cars. A Buick, Chrysler, Oldsmobile or Pontiac will convey a solid conservative image. Because every hustler seems to drive a Mercedes or Cadillac, a too expensive car can act as a turnoff. Avoid bumper stickers that express a pet belief, whether political,

ACTION PLAN

Day _____ Date _____

GOALS

Earnings this month $ _____
Month legs* _____
Month presentations _____
Month contacts _____
Contacts today _____

**PLAN YOUR WORK
WORK YOUR PLAN**

8:00	_____
:30	_____
9:00	_____
:30	_____
10:00	_____
:30	_____
11:00	_____
:30	_____
12:00	_____
:30	_____
1:00	_____
:30	_____
2:00	_____
:30	_____
3:00	_____
:30	_____
4:00	_____
:30	_____
5:00	_____
:30	_____
6:00	_____
:30	_____
7:00	_____
:30	_____

HOT PROSPECTS

HOMES TO SHOW

HOMES TO PREVIEW

EXPIRED MULTIPLES

OWNERS FOR SALE

NEW DOORS

NEW PHONE CALLS

OTHERS

*"Legs" is a sales term referring to the number of transactions during a period of time. If someone sold your listing it would be one leg for you and one for the other salesperson. If you sold your own listing, it would be two legs for you.

ACCOMPLISHMENTS	TODAY	MONTH TO DATE
Contacts		
New door calls	———	———
New phone calls	———	———
Expired multiples	———	———
Owners for sale	———	———
Listing call backs	———	———
Motel managers	———	———
Personnel managers	———	———
Tract salespeople	———	———
Personal friends	———	———
Ad leads	———	———
Referred leads	———	———
Notes mailed	———	———
Newspaper leads	———	———
TOTAL CONTACTS	═══	═══
PRESENTATIONS		
Qualified buyers	———	———
Write-ups	———	———
Listing interviews	———	———
TOTAL PRESENTATIONS	═══	═══
LEGS		
Listings taken	———	———
Listings sold	———	———
Sales	———	———
TOTAL LEGS	═══	═══

religious or even environmental. Bumper stickers can lead to discussions that detract from your sales efforts.

After you have made a few sales you should seriously consider a *cellular car phone*. Although prices are likely to come down, current prices are $600 to $1000. As an alternative, lease payments run $30 to $40 per month. Monthly fees vary greatly between systems, but expect a $25 to $50 basic fee. There is a per-minute charge of 20 cents to 50 cents (higher base fees generally mean lower costs per minute). Off-peak rates are considerably lower (8 P.M. to 8 A.M.). For long distance, the charges are added to your per-minute charges. A cellular phone will greatly increase your efficiency. In your sales activity you constantly will see the advantages.

Plastic magnetic car signs are a plus. They should feature your name and home number prominently as well as the name of your firm. The signs will remind people you sell real estate and they will ask questions that could be valuable leads.

The *Realty Blue Book* is a valuable tool to carry with you if you are not proficient in the use of a financial calculator. This book is available in a pocket-size or a full-size format. It contains amortization tables showing monthly, annual and semiannual loan payments and tables of sellers' net based on various commission rates; the amount owed at any future date; true mortgage yields when mortgages are discounted; equity buildup; present value of future dollars at various interests as well as future value of present dollars. The book is available from Professional Publishing Corporation, 122 Paul Drive, San Rafael, CA 94903. This firm also sells *Realty Organizers*, which include prospect cards and floor call prospect books.

An *all-purpose property kit* will include a hand calculator with fresh batteries, a fifty-foot tape measure, "For Sale" signs, nails and hammer, stakes and at least two flashlights with fresh batteries. You should also carry a pair of boots for showing vacant land and maps marked with colored pens to show schools, bus routes, recreational areas and zoning. An umbrella or two and raincoats come in handy, as does a Polaroid camera with extra color film. A tape recorder is a handy way to take notes as you drive. Two other important items are a telephone book and a city street directory to check names of occupants, neighbors and other residents. Extra listing and offer forms in a plastic bag under a seat or in the trunk with extra pens will never leave you with a lost opportunity.

DEVELOPING SUCCESS ATTRIBUTES

Success in real estate selling comes only to those who learn both sales and technical skills. There is still another factor involved, one more difficult to pin down. Even the best-prepared salesperson may fail if he or she neglects to cultivate certain attributes that shape the kind of person he or she becomes. Here are a few qualities you can watch for and develop in yourself. If you study the truly successful salesperson, you will find these qualities well developed.

Genuine Helpfulness

A successful real estate salesperson should honestly like people and want to help them. He or she should view each contact as an opportunity to meet someone's needs.

Courage

A successful salesperson must be courageous. It takes courage to disagree when you must, and courage to press for an offer.

Health

Keeping healthy and watching your weight and diet will give you the physical energy necessary for success. I am a great believer in vitamin and mineral supplements. Whether I just think they help me or they actually help me, the results are positive. Besides being in good physical shape you must also be in good mental shape. Being in top mental condition means more than a positive attitude. You must exercise your mind by constantly planning sales by using role-playing techniques.

Appearance

Appearance is important, but a smile on your face can overcome the worst case of uglies. I know, because my college friends used to tell prospective blind dates, "He has a great personality." That smile is only one of the ways in which you decide what your appearance does for you. Dress to reflect your community's image of a successful person—professional and self-confident. Remember, though, that you are selling real estate, not sex. Eight ounces of gold around your neck or a big diamond on your pinky will inspire suspicion, not confidence. You are not making a pitch in a carnival sideshow; you are helping people to make the biggest investment decisions of their lives.

The Unscent of Success

If you want prospects to trust you with this vital decision, forget cocktail lunches. Liquor on your breath subtly undermines your image of professionalism. If you smoke, try to break the habit. Smoking and the smell of tobacco turn off many people. Many people are offended by the heavy use of colognes, perfumes and even after-shaves. What you may regard as subtle might be overpowering to others, especially when confined with you in an automobile. The less scent the better.

MAKE HAY WHILE THE SUN SHINES

A real estate salesperson can make money in any market if he or she plans the work and works the plan; however, the old adage, "Make hay while the sun shines" does apply to real estate sales.

The real estate market operates in cycles. These cycles generally are directly related to interest rates. When interest rates are low, sales are generally hot and when the market is hot, it is the time to work the ten- to 12-hour days and the six- to seven-day weeks. A truly hot period can shut off quickly because of changes in government policy toward interest rates, and frenzied activity may not be seen again for years.

During a hot period you should be like a squirrel, busily gathering acorns and storing them away for winter, because winter does come to real estate. You must resist rapidly changing your style of living. Consider investments in what you know and understand—real estate—not in someone else's area of expertise. Most people earn their money doing what they know, but lose it in someone else's business.

Now you've seen what it takes to begin climbing the hard road to success as a professional real estate salesperson. With that background always in mind, we are ready to explore in detail the skills and knowledge that will take you through each step of the sales process, from finding buyers to the closing and beyond.

2. Where To Find Buyers

You will often hear it said that 20 percent of all real estate salespeople make 80 percent of all real estate sales. Statistics seem to bear this out. To put it more grimly, 80 percent of the salespeople are left to struggle for only 20 percent of the business. Finding a way into the successful 20 percent requires studying the unsuccessful majority to find out what goes wrong with the way they operate.

As we observe the struggling 80 percent, one quality begins to stand out: Most of them rely on their floor time to provide all their leads. They depend on drop-ins and phone calls because they lack either the ability or the motivation to actively seek out buyers. By relying on their floor time, these salespeople have really given up control of their lead production. When calls and drop-ins are scarce, these are the salepeople who find themselves in serious trouble.

Fortunately, those who are willing to work for success have found a better approach to seeking buyers. These salespeople don't count on floor time for their leads. Some don't even take floor time. They feel they can work more productively on their own instead of waiting around for a buyer to find them. They make use of dozens of pathways to potential buyers. In this chapter we'll explore in detail the active salesperson's buyer-finding secrets.

YOUR OWN FILES

Referrals from satisfied customers provide one of the best sources of business. An advantage of such customers is that they have faith in someone who has faith in you, so they tend to trust your judgment and accept your recommendations.

Buyers as Boosters

Start cultivating your buyers for future business even before the sale is consummated. Stop in for a friendly visit. Keep them informed of closing details. Reassure them on the value of their new property. After closing, stop by to make sure everything is all right.

When people remember you as a thoughtful, capable professional, they will be eager to share their discovery with their friends. Contact former buyers whenever a home becomes available nearby. People like their friends to move to their neighborhood; it reinforces their own good judgment. Every buyer's circle of friends can grow into wider and wider fields of influence for you. Let your former buyers know that you want and appreciate any help they can provide. If a property similar to a property you sold becomes available, tell your former buyers about it. Chances are they have friends with similar needs. The people who bought a home with a few acres for their horses probably have friends who would like more space.

Buyers as Investors

When you qualify a buyer, you learn a great deal about his or her financial situation. Is the buyer in a position to benefit from investment property, either individually or as part of a syndicate? If so, you have the inside track on selling your buyer on the advantages of such a move. Tell him or her about the benefits that apply, such as depreciation, deductibility of interest and property taxes, appreciation and the broader pluses of a hedge against inflation and pride of ownership.

When you have sold your former buyers on the benefits of income or investment property, let them know you will search for property that fits their specific needs. Since you are dealing with people who already have a degree of trust in you, you can expect far greater loyalty than is likely with ordinary prospects. The person who calls on an ad is fickle, using many agents with loyalty to none. Your former buyer is far more likely to listen to your recommendations and act accordingly.

Sellers as Buyers

By contacting the owners of your active listings you often can start a string of many sales. Ascertain the seller's future real estate needs. If owners are unable to buy until they sell their property, an offer could be taken "subject to the sale." Showing homes to owners of listed property increases their desire to own a new home and educates them to become realistic owners who are likely to respond to reasonable offers. If you sell the listers a new property, you have more former owners to work with and can continue a roll indefinitely.

YOUR OWN OFFICE

Sitting at your desk awaiting inquiries wastes your time, but other office activities offer rich sources of leads if you know how to use them. Here's how.

Rental Calls

I often have been in sales offices when rental calls have come in. The routine response is either, "Sorry, we don't handle rentals," or "We don't have anything right now." These calls usually end without the salesperson finding out who is calling, so a valuable lead is completely wasted. Think of rental calls as calls for help in meeting housing needs, however, and their value becomes clear. As usual, when you worry about filling the needs of others, your own needs also will be filled.

Suppose you don't have any rentals. Does that make the call worthless? Here is how you can help yourself by your willingness to help others. Find out the caller's basic rental needs in terms of family size, area preferences and rent payment ability. Obtain the caller's name and a phone number and agree to call back within the hour. Now use your contacts, calling property managers and owners of large numbers of rental units. These calls, too, can be valuable initial contacts for future business. If the rental market is tight, owners will be reluctant to pay a rental commission; but if they have vacancies, they may find it worthwhile to pay a fee.

I don't believe in working for free, but when you help a person find a rental, you can consider it an investment in a future buyer. Call back the prospective renter and make an appointment at your office. This gives you the opportunity to qualify the renter as a possible buyer. If the renter cannot buy at this time, give him or her the information on the rentals you have located. Make sure renters realize that you have gone out of your way on their behalf. If they or their friends get in a position to buy property, you will be the first agent they think of. If they seem to be possible future buyers, enter their names in your files for further contact.

If your qualifying interview reveals that the renters could be buyers now, show them the rentals personally, then show them an affordable house that meets their needs. Point out the many advantages of owning over renting: privacy, no rent increases, no disagreeable landlord, no arbitrary rules, appreciation in value, deductibility of interest and taxes.

The deductibility benefit is especially worth explaining in detail. If you are not absolutely clear on the tax advantages of property ownership, practice the following argument, using various numbers and situations: Because interest and taxes are deductible, a person can afford considerably more for home payments than for rent payments; most renters don't realize this. Assume a couple is paying $600 a month in rent. Their top dollar of income is probably taxed at 30 percent or more (combined federal and state taxes). If they were to buy a home with an $850 monthly payment, their housing costs would be almost the same. Since most of the $850 would be mortgage interest and taxes, the owners would save about $250 in income taxes, making their net cost about $600.

Of all those intending to rent space, the easiest to turn into buyers are former homeowners who intend to rent until they find something to buy. These people usually don't really want to live in a rental. If you show them a house that meets their current needs, you've most likely made yourself a sale.

Your Property Management Department

Your firm's property management department can become a ready source of buyers. Through it, your firm will have built up a relationship of trust with many owners. If they are pleased with your management of their properties, they will likely consider similar ones. Ascertain the interest of these owners in future acquisitions by contacting them on a regular basis. Even if they are not interested, they have friends who might be.

While Canvassing for Listings

When you are canvassing an area for listings, always check as well for buyers. Ask the owners if they or others they know are interested in purchasing real estate. As simple as this sounds, many salespeople canvassing for listings forget that they also sell real estate and that they need buyers as well as sellers.

CANVASSING AROUND A LISTING

For single-family home sales, door-to-door canvassing of the neighborhood around the listing can be very productive. By using a city directory, you can address the owners by name. After introducing yourself, inform the neighbors about the home you have listed. Tell them you thought they might like to help choose their new neighbors. Ask if they have friends or relatives interested in living in the neighborhood. Find out which neighbors are renting their homes. Turning them into buyers might be as simple as showing them how they can finance the purchase. Besides checking the tenants as buyers, check the owner of the house the tenant lives in for a possible listing opportunity.

Another benefit of canvassing the neighborhood of a listing is that when nearby owners find out what the house is selling for they often turn serious about selling their own houses. Either way, it pays to let the neighbors know the details of what is happening. The more people who know about a listing, the greater the likelihood of a quick sale.

In some communities, house-to-house solicitation is so regulated that personal calls on neighbors become impractical. In these cases, use your city directory for telephone contacts.

Owners of Adjacent Land

The old farmer said, "All I want is what is mine and what is next to mine." He is no different from many of us, including me. Since building my summer home, I have purchased three additional adjoining parcels of land and would buy more if I could get the owners to sell. Yet I really don't "need" any more land.

This natural desire to increase a spread can work to the salesperson's advantage. I sold 200 acres of practically worthless swamp land to a farmer by simply pointing out to him that this parcel was all that kept him from owning a complete section of land. Over the years I have sold several farms to adjoining owners and dozens of lots to adjoining home-owners. Once a salesman in my office asked me to put up a "For Sale" sign on an out-of-town lot he had just listed. When I got there I discov-ered a new home on the adjoining lot. Within a half hour I had a full-price offer from the homeowners. I just pointed out that investing in the lot not only provided breathing room, but gave them control over what happened to the lot next door.

The desire to own more property holds just as true for commercial and apartment building owners. Owners of adjacent property are always prime prospects, not just for your own listings but for anyone's listings. You would be amazed by how few listing salespeople actually talk to the owners of adjacent property. Sometimes a sale is as simple as showing an owner how the purchase can be financed.

Neighborhood People

Hot prospects needn't be limited to the people next door. Neighbor-hood people will often be interested or can direct you to buyers. To find a buyer for an apartment building, contact owners of similar apart-ment buildings in the area. If they have found ownership rewarding, they most likely will want to add to their holdings. Point out the man-agement advantages of having a cluster of nearby properties. On the other hand, an owner utterly uninterested in another building could definitely be a listing prospect.

Tenants

Once an angry owner screamed at me when I brought in a full-price of-fer on his property the day after I had listed it. He wasn't angry because of the offer, but because the buyer was his own tenant. He had assumed that the tenant would not or could not buy. This assumption cost him a brokerage fee.

When my family and I first arrived in California, we rented a house. Six months later we decided to buy. We were satisfied with the house and neighborhood and decided to try to avoid the hassles of house-hunting and moving. So we purchased the home from our landlord, as thousands of tenants do each year.

When you contact the tenant of a property you have listed, empha-size that he or she has first chance at the purchase before the ads come out. This creates a sense of urgency and a need to make a decision. You should, of course, show tenants how they can tailor a purchase to meet their individual financial needs.

You don't have to be limited to tenants within the property you have listed. People renting homes in the area should also be contacted. When I first started selling real estate, I would walk up and down the halls of apartment buildings contacting the tenants about homes in new developments. Often after selling to one tenant I would get several more sales from the tenant's former neighbors.

The principle of canvassing apartment buildings still works. Keep in mind that the key to a sale is usually your ability to structure a purchase to the tenant's needs. To canvass security buildings, use a city directory to get the names and phone numbers of the residents. While a telephone canvass is not as effective as canvassing in person, you can contact more owners in the same time than you can by knocking on doors.

Seasonal Resorts

People who patronize seasonal resorts are logical prospects for second homes or timesharing. At one small resort in northern Wisconsin, six cabins were sold. Every buyer was a former summer tenant. Again, be ready to show that the financial benefits of ownership outweigh any attractiveness of renting. Guest lists can become a mailing and phone list of prospects.

ALL AROUND THE TOWN

Outside the office, alertness still pays. The activities and institutions in your community all have clues to finding people who are ready to buy if only someone shows them how.

Mobile Homes

In many areas real estate salespeople can list and sell mobile homes. Should you have a mobile home listing, drive around the park looking for older or smaller coaches. Owners are often interested in trading up to a newer or larger unit. Not only can this selective canvassing locate a buyer for you, but a buyer could mean another listing. If owners are not interested in buying, ask whether any of their friends might be interested in living in their park.

If you have any "own-your-own-lot" mobile home spaces, an excellent time to find buyers is when one of the existing mobile home parks in the area has raised its rates. Be ready to explain moving, setup and financing costs, as well as finance options. You might want to take offers to purchase a lot contingent upon the sale of the buyer's present mobile home. You could then list the unit for sale if this is allowed in your state.

Your sales presentation should emphasize these benefits: no further rent increases; no landlord to deal with; buying something for themselves instead of making a park owner rich; appreciation in value and deductibility of interest and taxes. Even though purchase payments are greater than rent payments, the long-term cost could actually be less.

Churches

When you have a home for sale close to a church—and most homes are—consider using the church membership lists as a canvassing tool. You can call the members and say,

> "[Mr./Mrs.] Smith, I am Tom Riley from Westwood Realty. We were recently asked to sell a beautiful three-bedroom home near the First Christian Church. That is why I am calling you, to see if you or any of your friends would be interested in this lovely home."

This particular canvass is much better than a normal cold canvass because you have a specific reason to call them, and it relates to something that interests them. You will find that the people you call will be both courteous and interested in helping you. A side benefit of these calls could be listings.

Unmarried Couples and Singles

In canvassing an area you will often find two names on a mailbox. Some brokers now realize that unmarried couples are a large, relatively untapped source of buyers. In many cases the arrangements last longer than the average marriage. Usually both parties are working, so the combined income allows for the purchase of real property. In canvassing apartments for prospective buyers, don't dismiss these couples.

People are waiting longer to get married than they did thirty years ago and many women are now electing single lifestyles by choice. These factors combine with a high divorce rate to create a huge singles market. Many singles are very interested in lifestyle. They are ready buyers for condominium developments similar to the large singles complexes where they rented. Mailings, phone canvassing and knocking on doors in complexes catering to single persons can be very productive.

Cultivating Bird Dogs

"Bird dogs" are simply helpers who point out opportunities for you. A bird dog could be a mother or other relative, friend, acquaintance or even a creditor with a financial stake in your success. In *Power Real Estate Listing* I discuss the selection and care of bird dogs in great detail. The important point is that people won't help unless they realize you want help, and know specifically what kind. Let these people know you appreciate their help. Keep them informed of the results of the leads they supply. If a person gets no feedback showing you appreciate the leads, the leads will cease. It isn't necessary to pay bird dogs, but an appropriate gift on important occasions or a dinner invitation will let that person know you are grateful.

FOREIGN BUYERS: UNDERSTANDING SPECIAL NEEDS

One of my friends showed a Korean buyer a new subdivision with most of the parcels still available. After several visits the gentleman said, "I would now like to buy." My friend asked, "Which parcel?" The answer was, "All of them." It was a cash transaction.

Several California real estate firms regularly send out selling teams to visit Hong Kong, Japan, Korea, the Philippines and Indonesia. They have found ready buyers for California desert land. Unfortunately, the firms I know of that do this sell their own inventory at exorbitant prices.

The boom in real estate sales to foreign buyers has captured the attention of the nation and made fortunes for those brokers and salespeople who learned the special needs of foreign investors and the special methods for tapping into this market. The first thing to understand is that motivations may be very different from what you have come to expect with American buyers. To sell effectively to foreign nationals, you will have to study the economic and political situation in their homelands and learn to probe diplomatically for the real benefits they seek from investing in U.S. property.

Politics

Prospects from areas of political and economic instability often have subtle reasons for their interest in U.S. land investments. There have been enough hotel and motel purchases by Indian and Pakistani nationals, for example, to create a miniboom in that specialized market. The story behind the business activity goes back, in many cases, to the fact that these buyers were the mercantile class in much of colonial Africa. With independence, many of them were forced out. They had money and no place to go. Sensing an opportunity, several U.S. business brokers actually went to Africa to sell investment properties in this country.

Were these buyers simply looking for something to do with their money? Apparently not. Owners of substantial property in the United States are allowed by immigration law to apply for visas to manage the property. The owners thus avoid quotas. Americans who work abroad obtain similar privileges when they manage overseas interests for U.S. firms. If you go into this specialty, you will find similar needs among prospects from Asia, Central and South America, Africa and other areas. In addition to immigration concerns, these buyers see U.S. land as the most secure place for their money in an unstable world.

Buyers from other parts of the world may have additional motivations. Nations with little land and high populations often make our property costs look like incredible bargains. Europeans have been increasingly interested in U.S. farmland thanks to the drop in farm values coupled with a weak dollar.

Broker Relationships

The most successful brokers in this area are those who found ways of cooperating with overseas brokers. They actually have traveled to Europe to arrange working relationships. They send photos, slides and even videotapes of listed properties to their cooperating brokers. Generally, the buyers fly to the United States to view the property prior to purchase. The Italian and French buyers like California farmland, while German buyers seem to prefer the Midwest.

One benefit of having a relationship with a foreign broker is direct access to foreign buyers. Brokers with foreign contacts are reluctant to give out details: They have a good thing and don't want more competition. Another benefit of cooperative arrangements is the competitive edge it gives you in obtaining listings. Farm owners feel that foreign buyers mean higher prices and cash.

Japanese buyers make up another prime market. They have already purchased very heavily in California, Hawaii and New York. Low returns on real estate investments in Japan coupled with a weak dollar and U.S. trade deficits that have placed tremendous purchasing power in the hands of Japanese have all worked together to provide a strong Japanese presence in U.S. commercial property investments. The Japanese investors have favored larger properties in major cities. While prices paid often appear high by American standards, Japanese investors plan for a long hold period and the prices seem like bargains compared to similar Japanese property. Many successful commercial brokerage offices have developed working relationships with Japanese brokers.

Due to inflation, many wealthy Mexican citizens have been buying property in the United States. They seem to prefer condominiums in well-known communities. In order to sell in Mexico, you *must* deal through a Mexican broker. Many American developments have had excellent results cooperating with Mexican brokers. Recent Mexican legislation has made these investments illegal in order to stop the flow of hard currencies from Mexico, but I understand that Mexican brokers are still finding legal ways to circumvent these new restrictions.

Canadian buyers have been buying large U.S. investment property as well as Sun Belt condominiums. Our prices are low by Canadian standards. Many U.S. firms advertise in Canadian papers or have relationships with Canadian brokers.

You can obtain the names and addresses of brokers and broker organizations in foreign countries from their nearest U.S. consulate office. You will find most large foreign brokers want to work only with major U.S. brokerage firms, but with persistence you may be able to get a foot in the door by building an understanding with a smaller foreign office.

THE BUSINESS OF BUYING

When thinking about who can become a buyer, don't forget the people who buy and sell property for a living. This section gives you the basic methods for getting a piece of this specialized action.

Speculators

Speculators are buyers interested in selling at a quick profit with a minimum holding period. It won't take you long to locate speculators. You will often run into them when you respond to For-Sale-By-Owner ads. Speculators usually try to handle their own sales to maximize profits.

Speculators should be cultivated. They will welcome you as another pair of eyes and ears. Keep in mind that speculators want below-market purchases, but are often willing to buy numerous properties for ready cash when a quick sale is required.

Having speculator contacts and knowing their interests can be good business for you. There will be times when a quick sale is in an owner's best interests, as in the case of an impending foreclosure. Some real estate salespeople actually specialize in locating and selling property to speculators.

Before you get involved with speculators, find out whether they have real estate licenses. If so, find out if they expect a commission split. Speculators will often spring the fact that they are brokers at the time of an offer and demand a commission split. Forget about dealing with these thieves: They want to steal part of your earned fee for doing nothing. There are plenty of speculators around who will treat you fairly.

We have all had people tell us, "If you come across a really good deal, let me know." Then, when you do as they asked, they refuse to back their wishes with action. If you are willing to invest patience and regular contact in these would-be speculators, you may turn them into genuine motivated buyers. To do so, you'll have to keep at it, impressing them at every opportunity with the need for fast action when something good comes along. Once you get them involved in one profitable deal, you'll find them willing and eager to get into others.

Investors

Investors are a very different group from speculators. Generally, investors are not adverse to paying a fair value, although everyone likes a bargain. They are buying for income, the tax benefits of depreciation, appreciation or a combination of these.

One of the easiest ways to find buyers for investment property is to find who has purchased similar property in the past few years. If they are not interested in a property, ask about their friends who might be.

Another method is to go after people who are not investors but should be. Doctors, dentists, lawyers accountants, airline pilots: Anyone with a high disposable income is a candidate for investment property. Many salespeople hesitate to contact prominent people about a real estate investment, but prominent people, like everyone else, are interested in real estate.

A very well-known broker told me that he called a doctor for a medical appointment. He told the doctor's receptionist who he was and the name of the doctor who had referred him. He was immediately transferred to the doctor. When the doctor realized the call was for a medical reason, he said, "Oh, I thought you had a property for me," and transferred him back to the receptionist for an appointment. Even very busy people will take the time to learn about a real estate investment.

When you go for your annual physical, dental checkup or otherwise visit a professional person, drop off an investment property brief. You will be surprised at the interest real estate investment generates.

Many real estate salespeople build up a relationship of trust with both speculators and investors. I worked for a broker who sold more property than I did, and he seldom left the office. He sold land by telephone to buyers who had complete faith in this able and ethical broker. This kind of trust is earned only by years of faithful, honest service.

Selling to Syndicators

Syndicators simply put together groups of investors to buy real estate. The investors have the protection of being limited partners: They are not liable beyond their investment unless they agree to further liability. The investors are entitled to their share of the depreciation, which can shelter the income from any taxation.

Syndicators usually welcome help in finding suitable investments and will tell you what they are interested in. You can often locate syndicators by their ads for investors. Another source is your local chapter of the Real Estate Securities and Syndication Institute of the National Association of REALTORS®. For information about your local chapter, contact the National Association of REALTORS®.

When you meet a syndicate member, ask who is the general partner—the syndicator. Find out about his or her future needs. An advantage of working with syndicators is that their purchases are usually substantial. Most syndications sell out within about five years to realize the profits. There is always the added possibility of not only selling to the syndicate, but later selling the property again.

Getting into Syndication

Syndication is one of the more lucrative, high-growth areas of real estate, one worth getting into for yourself. In putting together a syndicate for the first time, real estate agents often agree to invest their cash or commission or both. They usually take an additional share for putting the group together. That the syndicator has a financial commitment gives prospective investors an important boost in confidence.

To put a syndicate together, locate a property with exceptional potential and tie it up with an option agreement. Consult an attorney with experience in syndication. Laws vary among states. Be sure to keep the number of investors under the number required for state security registration, as registration can be a costly and time-consuming process. Your attorney will prepare the partnership agreements.

Plan a sales approach stressing the benefits offered and decide who should be approached. Point out that investors in syndicates have their liability limited to the amount of their investment. Along with this financial protection, investors have the advantage of a share in the depreciation. Depreciation can be used to shelter income from the investment, but a tax loss in excess of income can no longer be utilized to shelter other income. Since the Tax Reform Act of 1986, most new syndicates have been structured to generate income, not tax shelters. Because syndicates generally invest in prime income property, they also offer excellent appreciation potential.

Expect your first syndicate to be your most difficult. After you develop a proven track record, your problem will be to locate suitable investment property, not investors. When a syndicated property is sold at a profit, the investors usually clamor to invest again and to bring friends and relatives in on the deal.

If you are currently selling limited partnerships for income property, an excellent source of buyers are investors who purchased limited partnership shares prior to the Tax Reform Act of 1986. Most of these investments were structured for their tax losses. While tax reform has taken away the excess shelter of these tax losses, they can be utilized to offset gains from similar investments. Therefore, such an investor could buy a positive cash-flow limited partnership investment and pay no taxes because of the excess tax shelter of the other partnership.

If you are willing to work for high future earnings that don't come in for a long time, syndication might be worth checking into. To learn more, contact the Real Estate Securities and Syndication Institute of the National Association of REALTORS®, 430 North Michigan Avenue, Chicago, IL 60611.

BUSINESS AND GOVERNMENT

Luckily, the alert salesperson doesn't have to start his or her search for buyers from scratch. Businesses and business groups as well as government offices have already gone through the work of putting together lists of people who have reason to be interested in obtaining property. These lists are available to those who know where to look.

Referral Networks

National referral networks provide you with advance information about people moving to your community. The broker who recommends you is entitled to a commission split if a sale is made. However, this is likely to be a sale you otherwise would not have made. Chances are the prospects have had a favorable relationship with the referring broker, so they will be somewhat presold on you. Buyers you are referred to are usually sellers who have the financial means to buy and, as former owners, they are likely to buy again rather than to rent.

Chambers of Commerce

When I first considered a move to California, I, like thousands of others, contacted several chambers of commerce for information about their areas. Such offices are glad to provide you with lists of people who have made inquiries. This becomes an excellent list of prospects. Send out general information on a wide variety of your listings for general inquiries about your area. Include a data sheet asking specific questions about recipients' needs and when and if they will visit your area.

If any prospects indicate a definite move to the area, phone them in the evening hours. Welcome them to the area and offer to help them with their housing needs. Find out what they are looking for and what they have to work with. In other words, perform a preliminary qualification on the phone. People moving to your area are usually motivated buyers and often will have a large down payment from the sale of other property.

If they are planning to look for housing in your area, find out when they'll arrive and make a definite appointment. Offer to arrange motel accommodations and even to pick them up at the airport. If they are not now planning such a trip, try to interest them in several properties and recommend they come out to see for themselves. You might well have a dozen long-distance phone discussions before you meet your prospects face-to-face.

Moving and Storage Firms

A working relationship and exchange of information with a moving and storage firm can be mutually beneficial. If you recommend a moving firm to sellers leaving the area, you'll be setting up a source of important future leads. While local movers don't usually know about people coming to your area until they arrive, they do store furniture. People storing furniture from another area usually have not purchased a home yet, but are renting. These people are often highly motivated buyers anxious to have their own belongings around them.

Personnel Offices

Personnel offices of large employers know who is being transferred from the area and who is coming in from outside the area. Regular contacts with personnel people mean finding potential buyers among new employees and transferees. Promotions mean greater income and the motivation to own a more prestigious home. One promotion often means a number of people are moving up the line, so being on top of personnel changes can open up a whole series of both listing and sale possibilities.

Contacting and dealing with personnel officers is an art in itself. The companion volume to this book, *Power Real Estate Listing* (Real Estate Education Company, 1988), describes the technique in step-by-step detail.

Franchises

National franchises have a continuing and growing need for locations. Generally, their real estate offices will be very cooperative since you are offering to do the legwork needed to find suitable new locations.

Many franchisors are not interested in buying real estate. They want others to build for them to their specifications and they will sign a long-term lease. If the franchisor has good credit and you can find the right location, finding the investor will be relatively easy. Simply calling the medical doctors in the Yellow Pages will provide you with more investors than you need. Some real estate professionals devote full time to meeting the needs of major franchisors.

Calvin Greenberg's book, *How to Become a Successful Store Leasing Broker* (Prentice-Hall, 1971), provides franchise business addresses, the kind of deals they are looking for and the type of leases they want. While some of the book's information might be outdated, it remains valuable for learning the ropes in this field.

Probate

A few brokers check probate records looking for listings, but they usually ignore probate as a source for buyers. People inheriting considerable cash are natural prospects for homes and investment properties. Even if they own homes already, they are prospects for larger, more prestigious homes. When people who are not accustomed to having a great deal of money inherit sizable sums, whoever gets there first will prevail. Be sure you arrive before the Mercedes salesperson.

Public Housing

In many areas, a person who occupies public subsidized housing must leave the project when his or her income exceeds a set amount. People in that situation can be excellent prospects for low-down-payment housing or even for other government-supported purchase plans. Your public housing authority should be willing to cooperate with you.

Motels and Hotels

Referrals from motel and hotel personnel can be very valuable. Arrange for employees to let you know about people staying in the motel or hotel either on a house-buying trip or as temporary lodging for a permanent relocation. These referrals will usually be extremely motivated buyers. Many real estate offices leave brochures of available listings in motel and hotel lobbies, chamber of commerce offices, restaurants and other places likely to attract people new to town.

HUNTING IN THE HEADLINES

Your local newspaper offers more immediately practical information than the latest political scandal or international incident. Knowing what to look for among the headlines will give you a jump on a whole series of leads.

Birth Announcements

An increase in family size often means a need for new housing. If the address indicates the parents are living in an apartment, they will be excellent prospects for a sale.

Engagements and Weddings

Newlyweds need housing. An apartment is likely to prove too small for a long-term relationship. The combining of two incomes can qualify the couple for improved housing. Some agents solicit the parents of engaged couples and encourage gifts of money toward their first home purchase in lieu of other types of gifts.

Furniture Ads

People selling entire households of furniture often plan on leaving the area. While not buyers for you, they are often buyers for others. They promise referral possibilities if you are a member of a referral service.

Eminent Domain

When a state, municipality or other government entity takes land for public use, the owners receive the fair market value of their property. These unwilling sellers are now potential buyers with cash. Whenever your newspapers announce that property is being taken or will be taken for any public use, contact the owners. Your highway departments and urban renewal agencies will tell you about current and planned eminent domain actions.

USING SIGNS AND ADS

A great number of buyer calls come from For Sale signs. Results per dollar spent can make signs a broker's best advertising tool. Ask your broker if you can put sign strips on signs in front of your own listings. The strip should display your home phone number:

EVENINGS 976-4130

Most brokers will agree to this although you might have to pay for the strips. The benefits will be well worth the small expense.

Consider giving the sign a further competitive edge by using a second strip sign such as:

LOW DOWN PAYMENT

$$\boxed{\text{EXCELLENT FINANCING}}$$

A strip such as this could make your phone number the most important number the prospective buyer writes down and the first one that is called.

Your Home Phone

If your home phone number is not included in your firm's newspaper listings ads, ask your broker to include it. Having a person answer an inquiry after business hours is far better than having a machine take a message. Many people refuse to leave messages with an answering machine. If you are going to be gone in the evening, get your own answering machine. I recently called a broker and received the following message in a very pleasant feminine voice:

> *"Hi, I am a machine, but I am a very friendly machine. I work for Tom Hendricks of Sunshine Realty. If you will leave a message after the tone, I will have Tom return the call. Honestly, would a machine lie to you?"*

With a message like that, I couldn't just hang up. I left my message.

Consider getting a second home phone for your business calls so that prospects will be able to reach you and you will know how to answer that phone. A second line is especially desirable if you have teenagers. You should also consider call-waiting and call-forwarding phone features.

COMMUNITY INVOLVEMENT

Getting involved and recognized in the community pays dividends in both your personal and business life. There are many good ways to get started.

You have undoubtedly read about con artists who joined clubs and other organizations and persuaded many prominent individuals to invest millions of dollars in bogus investments. What these con artists had in common was that they were super salespeople. They targeted prospective buyers and went after them. While I certainly would never suggest you commit fraud or misrepresentation, you can still learn from these charlatans. Joining the proper organizations gives you the opportunity to meet buyers in a positive nonbusiness environment. A lodge, health club, sports organization, religious group, charity and so forth all provide contacts. Specific groups can be more valuable for specific types of desired contacts. As an example, collecting money for a worthwhile charity could give you access to many potential investment property buyers.

Disaster Aid

Disasters offer a unique opportunity to help others and to build a community image that will eventually mean more sales for you.

Any disaster such as fire, flood or tornado that destroys housing, gives you a chance to be of service. Since you are an expert in housing, what better person is there to handle the housing needs of those left homeless? Offer your professional assistance. Contact the people who lost their homes or the Red Cross, as well as property owners with vacant units. Often apartment owners will allow people to move in without charge for one month when there is a disaster. Because you have volunteered your efforts for a charitable purpose, you can be very forceful in dealing with owners and they will not resent it. You will find that helping in an emergency can be contagious. All it takes is someone to take charge and get things organized.

You might request donations of clothes and furniture to be left at your office. Your local radio stations and newspapers will be only too glad to help pass the word. Enlist the help of local service clubs.

Besides feeling good about yourself, you will build a positive community image. You will open many new doors for future business dealings. People like dealing with people who take a strong community interest.

Public Speaking

You can receive good personal and firm exposure by preparing talks for local service clubs. Organizations like the Rotary Club, Optimists, Kiwanis and Exchange Club are always looking for speakers. Topics can include:

Creative Financing in Today's Market
Is It a Good Time To Buy Real Estate?
Investing and Our New Tax Laws

Many state REALTOR® organizations and national real estate groups offer monthly publications that will provide you with many more speech ideas, as will general magazines such as *Business Week*, *Forbes* and *Fortune*. Keep in mind that people are especially interested when you talk about topics that affect their pocketbooks. Before groups of professionals, you can never go wrong by including some ideas on the tax shelters that are still available.

A good presentation can sell you as a real estate professional and assure that any future contacts with members of your audience will not be cold contacts.

Seminars

A number of successful real estate salespeople obtain a great many leads from free educational seminars. Sometimes these seminars are run in conjunction with a community college or community organization. Others are run by the real estate firm using a hotel meeting room. Typical topics would be:

How To Buy a Home with a No or Low Down Payment
Evaluating and Buying Investment Property
Real Estate Investments and the New Tax Law
Real Estate Syndicates—Advantages and Dangers
Real Estate and the Small Investor
Fixer-Uppers for Value or Profit
How To Choose Your Home
Buying and Selling a Home

Seminar titles should appeal to specific potential buyers. The seminar must be well prepared and informative. Handout material is desirable, such as loan amortization tables, financing explanations and so on. The seminar should not include any sales presentation about you or your firm, although your affiliation should be clear. Attendees should have an opportunity to ask questions.

Some prospective buyers will contact you directly at the seminar and others will call you later. However, you should not limit yourself to those who contact you. You should have a roster of all attendees. Call each attendee and thank them for having attended. Ask how you can make future seminars more valuable. (People like to be asked for help.)

Ask about their specific needs. Ask that they stop by at a specific time to discuss those needs as you may have some ideas.

The seminar established you as an expert. Prospective buyers are likely to pay special attention to your recommendations and are less likely to stray to other agents than prospects from other sources because of the special student-teacher feeling.

Teaching

Teaching a real estate course at a local community college or adult education school offers a very special opportunity. Many of your students will have extensive real estate holdings and will be taking the course for additional personal knowledge. The student-teacher relationship that develops will place you in an advantageous position for future dealings with your former students.

A Newspaper Column

Small local newspapers usually will be happy to run a column on your area's real estate if you offer to write it. Chances are they won't pay, but the column will win you great recognition, especially if your photo becomes part of the heading.

The column should cover topics that will enhance your image as a property expert. It should educate readers as well as stress the benefits of real estate ownership. Here are just a few of the kinds of subject matter that will fulfill both your readers' needs and your own:

1. An explanation of specific financing techniques and the benefits of each.
2. The possible effect of legislative acts on interest rates.
3. Local trends and factors influencing value.
4. The effect of deducting interest from taxes on the net cost of home ownership.

Once your face and name become known through the column, you will find that most people give you a much friendlier reception than they might have if they'd never heard of you. The boost to your ego will in turn increase your confidence. It's great being a celebrity, even on a small scale.

WHERE TO SELL BUSINESS OPPORTUNITIES

Selling a going business requires special expertise. I don't recommend that salespeople in general real estate brokerage get involved in business sales. Specialists in these sales say their three best sources of buyers for a business are employees, competitors and suppliers.

Employees

Business owners often don't approach employees because they know their employees can't afford to buy the business. But employees frequently have relatives and friends who could. Employees know what a business is actually doing and often have ideas about what it could be doing. In addition, purchasing the business assures that their jobs will not be lost when the new owner takes over. In some cases brokers put a group of employees together to form a corporation to buy the business. A furniture store was on the market for $500,000. Three salespeople refinanced their homes and obtained the substantial down payment.

Owners are often more willing to carry part of the purchase price when the buyers are employees, because the owners realize their employees have a greater chance of success than strangers would.

Competitors

Competitors will often buy a successful business. It can be more economical to buy a business with established goodwill than open a new location and develop it. Competitors who buy an unsuccessful business not only eliminate a competitor, they get the chance to hold a going-out-of-business sale. Competitors' employees are also excellent prospects as buyers of a business.

Suppliers

Suppliers and their employees know what a business is actually doing. Even when a supplier is not interested in buying, they may have a monetary interest in the continued success of the business. Suppliers can locate prospects for you in similar businesses. Make sure they realize the new owner will feel an obligation to the supplier for finding the property.

Suppliers are also an overlooked source of financing. Rather than see an owner retire and go out of business, a major supplier often will finance a buyer through actual loans or—more likely—through excellent credit terms for the purchase of inventory.

Let Your Fingers Do the Evaluating

To help in evaluating who can use nonresidential property, I recommend you use the Yellow Pages. Simply start with the *A*'s, going through the various listing categories. Ask yourself if the property would be suited for use in each of the categories. You can then canvass everyone listed in each of the applicable categories. It is a time-consuming process, but can be extremely productive. I know agents who have successfully used this technique for years to lease and to sell. After just a few months you will know the specific needs of dozens of prospective buyers or renters.

This method proved its value when I listed a beautiful suburban home on several acres of land. It had a dog kennel with 24 inside compartments and outside runs. I went through the Yellow Pages and called every veterinarian, dog groomer, dog boarder and pet shop owner I could find. In just three days I had a full-price offer plus a backup.

WHITE ELEPHANTS?

If you list a vacant property with very limited appeal, approach investors and speculators about it. Ask what they would do about this problem property. People are usually flattered when a real estate professional asks them for help. Often they will want to see the property. If one of them comes up with a solution, he or she is most likely your buyer.

NOT YOU

Buying your own office listings can lead to unhappy sellers, lawsuits and a poor public image. If you buy, even with full disclosure at a fair price, a later sale for a profit could subject you to claims that you took advantage of an owner. Because of these problems, many offices will not allow their agents to buy office listings. The National Association of Estate Agents, an English trade group, considers buying from a principal to be an unethical act. They don't believe an agent can properly fulfill his or her fiduciary responsibility to the seller while acting as the buyer.

YOU

When you feel that property listed by *another* office is a good investment, consider buying it. In any offer, reveal that you are a licensed real estate agent. If you have faith in your own judgment, unlimited earnings are possible. A salesperson can make a good living on brokerage fees but can become wealthy by buying and selling in his or her own name.

If you buy a property and receive any part of the sales commission, chances are you will be considered a subagent of the owner. This could mean that you would have a duty of full disclosure, which could include why you are buying the property, and what you intend to do with it. If you fail to do so, a court might determine that you breached your agency duty of full disclosure and to give the owner the benefit of your expertise. Because of the inherent conflicts in dealing both as a principal and an agent, many licencees deal wholly as principal when they buy properties and refuse to share in commission splits.

If you lack the courage to invest, investing with a partner for your first few purchases will serve as a crutch. After a few purchases you will have the courage to invest on your own. When you sell your own property, be sure any purchaser understands that you are a licensed real estate agent. You don't want to take any chances with your reputation. Always be completely open in your dealings. In the long run it will be to your advantage.

ICING ON THE CAKE

This chapter started with a warning not to rely on floor time. Because you have no control over the calls that come in, don't rely on them to fill your work load. Treat the leads you get during floor time as icing on the cake, and use the Power techniques in this chapter to actively hunt for buyers. The next chapter takes you through proven ways to turn inquiries into sales.

3. Power Telephone Techniques

You don't sell real estate by telephone. What you can do by telephone is get information and set up appointments where you will have the opportunity to make sales.

I recently called a broker about an ad for investment property. When I described the ad, the broker said, "I'm sorry, but that property has been sold. Thank you for calling Sunrise Realty." Then she hung up on me. Not only did she fail to find out anything about me or what I was interested in, she didn't even find out who I was. She had squandered a valuable opportunity.

Many salespeople have never stopped to figure out the cost, much less the value, of each phone inquiry they receive. If you divide the total number of buyer inquiries in your office by the total promotional budget, you'll find that every inquiry costs good money. Direct promotional costs to bring in a telephone inquiry can range from $5 in a small community to $50 or more in metropolitan areas. Office costs can double that figure.

If salespeople considered every call money, from a ten-dollar bill to a hundred, perhaps they would stop throwing them away. A poorly handled phone call throws away commission dollars as surely as it wastes money spent.

GET THAT NAME

Every call should end with your getting a name and phone number and either a definite appointment or a future contact. The broker I called could have said, "I am Ruth Rogers. What is your name, please?"

Don't be shy about asking the caller's name. Most people will give a name if asked. If not, don't make it into a big deal. Some brokers refuse to discuss anything unless the person gives a name, thinking it might be just a nosy neighbor. The fact is, though, that many people resist giving a name for fear of being harassed by a salesperson. Anyway, even nosy neighbors buy and sell property or know people who do. A nosy gossip can help you make sales.

When a caller initially resists giving a name, don't worry; you can get it later. Here is one way to do it:

> "I've prepared some information on that property as well as several other properties that might interest you. I'll put a packet in the mail to you today. How should I address it?"

People are not going to feel threatened by receiving something in the mail: They like to receive information without a salesperson influencing them. Of course you follow up with a personal visit. Your mailing was simply a door opener.

A caller might indicate that he or she does not want to be bothered by real estate agents. You can get the name and phone number of the caller with this approach:

> "One of our salespeople expects to bring in an extremely desirable property in the _____ area [where the caller has inquired about]. She thinks the price will be less than [price range the caller inquired about]. From what you have told me, I feel it will be perfect for you. This property will likely sell very fast. Would you like me to call you as soon as the property becomes available?"

There is never any need to fabricate a story for this approach. Every office has salespeople who always "expect to" bring in super listings. Chances are that you will be working on several yourself.

As soon as you have the caller's name, ask, "What is your phone number, [Mr./Mrs.] Schmidt?" Usually the caller will give it without hesitation. If the caller wants to know why, I use the following effective and truthful reply:

"I have been having a great deal of trouble with my phones and have been cut off in the middle of a number of conversations. I have a feeling the phone company doesn't like me. In case I get cut off again, I would like to call you back."

PREPARING FOR THE INQUIRY

Keep all your firm's current ads as well as ads for the last few days on your desk. I like to use clear plastic covers to hold them or place them under a plastic sheet on the desk top. Have the addresses and basic information so that you know which property each ad refers to. Be ready with alternative or substitute properties for each one advertised.

For calls on signs, have an index by street or a map showing your office listings and identifying them. The map is better because people often give the wrong street but are in the general area. Nothing is more frustrating than to have a call on a sign and not know what property the caller is inquiring about.

HOW CALLERS BECOME CUSTOMERS

Keep in mind that you are not going to make a sale over the telephone. All you want to do is to interest the prospective buyer enough so that you can get an appointment. Keep calls fairly short and end them when you have an appointment.

Hold the Details

The more you tell the prospective buyer, the less chance you have of making an appointment. People will buy homes in spite of features they don't really like, but only if they see the property's good features on a personal visit. Mentioning the negative features on the phone deprives them of that chance. Here are better ways to handle specific types of questions:

• If a caller asks if a property is on a corner lot, you could ask:

   "Do you want a corner lot?"

- If the caller wants to know how long a property has been on the market, answer:

  "I don't know offhand. How long have you been looking for a home?"

- If the caller wants to know if a house is of a particular architectural style, say:

  "People describe property differently. When we go to see this property, you can point out styles which interest you and I will be better able to meet your needs."

- If your prospective buyers want to know why the owners are selling, avoid getting into details:

  "I don't have that information right now, but I will be able to let you know when I meet with you and [Mr./Mrs.] Jones at 6 P.M. By the way, how long have you been looking for a home?"

  You have switched the conversation to the caller.

- If a caller asks how much the down payment is, your answer should be:

  "Normally, we can arrange the down payment to meet individual needs of the buyers. How much of your savings did you intend to invest?"

This response flatters the prospects by your assumption that they have more than just the down payment and will use only a portion of their savings.

How To Get More Than You Give

One of the greatest salespeople I ever knew had a degree in industrial psychology. He was a master on the telephone and taught me how it should be used. He seldom gave out more information than the ad contained but managed to average five or six appointments for every ten calls.

The method was really very simple. For every bit of information he gave out, he asked a question. He also asked questions without giving any information. An ad, he said, is simply a teaser, a means of creating interest. A telephone conversation is a chance to turn that interest up into an appointment. While he knew every home advertised, he wouldn't pull out the listing and start to recite the data. Lot size, taxes, age and amenities don't sell homes. Homes are sold because they fulfill needs, both practical and emotional. He wanted to meet the prospects, find out all he could about them, sell them on himself and then sell them on a house. To do this, he had to get them into the office. Suppose an ad read as follows:

Lovely 3BR, 2-bath ranch home in Willow Springs. Reduced to $89,500. Owner financing available.
Oasis Realty 976-4132

My former mentor would probably have handled an inquiry like this:

"My name is Howard Young. What is your name, please?"

"Yes, that is a lovely three-bedroom home. How large is your family, [Mr./Mrs.] Jones?"

"What are the ages of your children?"

That home is available now. When do you need a new home, [Mr./Mrs.] Jones?"

"Where do you live now?"

"Do you own your present home?"

"Is your home currently for sale?"

"That home is in one of the nicer areas of Willow Springs. Is that the area you are interested in?"

"Are there any other areas which you are considering?"

"That home is priced at $89,500. Is that the general price range you are interested in?"

"The owners indicate they are willing to handle the financing and are flexible as to down payment. How much of an initial investment were you interested in making?"

"I can arrange to show this lovely home as well as another home that I think will interest you and [Mr./Mrs.] Jones at 5 P.M. today, or would 6 P.M. be more convenient for you?"

Notice that the choice is in time, not in whether or not they want to see it. If your prospective caller indicates neither time is convenient, ask when it would be convenient to show the property.

If the caller indicates he or she is not free at all today, you should state:

>*"Let's set it up for tomorrow at 5 P.M. I'll meet you and your spouse at my office."*

If the caller doesn't object, you have a definite appointment. Whenever you have an appointment for the next day, call the prospects in the morning to remind them of the appointment. When you call, be enthusiastic and tell them you have several other properties you feel they will also be interested in. This will reduce the "no-shows."

As you see, asking questions gives you control of the conversation. You get an appointment without giving out too much information and without undue delay.

By mentioning another house to Mr. or Mrs. Jones you probably perked some interest and set the stage for alternative properties if necessary. Now say:

>*"I will see you and [Mr./Mrs.] Jones at my office at 5 P.M. Do you have a pencil and paper handy? Our office is at 1911 Elm Street across from the Security Bank. Are you familiar with the area? [If not, give specific directions.] Again, my name is Howard Young. I look forward to seeing you."*

Your question is about their knowledge of your office location, not where you will meet them. You are telling, not asking the place of the meeting. You can ask another question if you have been unable to get the caller's phone number:

>*"In the unlikely event I get tied up for any reason, what is your home phone number?"*

When you know who Mr. or Mrs. Jones is, and their home phone number, then the chances of a no-show have been decreased significantly.

Improving your ability to get appointments can have a significant effect on your earnings. Assume you are making $30,000 per year selling an average of one and a half homes per month out of 15 prospective buyers shown each month. If you can triple the number of prospective buyers per month to 45, you should also triple your sales and your gross to $90,000. That's without even improving your sales presentation.

Locking in the Prospect

Often when a prospective buyer gets on the phone, he or she will continue to call about other ads even after making an appointment with you. You don't want your prospects to have a four o'clock appointment with another broker when you don't get them until five. Here is a Power technique to prevent this:

> *"If you have the time, [Mr./Mrs.] Jones, go through the classified ads and circle any other properties which interest you. You can bring the ads with you and I'll be happy to provide you with information on any of the properties advertised, as well as arrange for you to see any of those properties if they appear to meet your needs."*

What you have done is to take your prospective buyer off the phone. You can bet that the prospect would have otherwise continued to call other offices. You have simply offered to make the task easier. You want to be "their" salesperson, not one of many of the prospects they are dealing with. You want to set the stage for a close personal relationship.

While there is no contractual obligation, many buyers develop enough trust in a salesperson that they do not consider dealing with another. That salesperson has shown real interest in fulfilling their needs.

End the conversation with an assurance that you can locate a property that will meet their needs:

> *"[Mr./Mrs.]Jones, I look forward to meeting you and your husband. I feel certain you will be delighted with the home[s] I will be showing you. Ask our receptionist for me, Howard Young."*

With this closing you will have further reduced the likelihood of a no-show by reassuring Mr. or Mrs. Jones and reminding them of your name.

After you have an appointment and have ended the conversation, consider possible alternative properties, keeping in mind that people generally end up buying more expensive properties than they inquired about.

If the property the prospects inquired about doesn't suit their needs and you don't have a suitable property for them, set up an appointment at their home. Often a lengthy discussion will reveal needs which differ radically from those discussed on the phone.

POWER PLAYS FOR CLIENT COMPLICATIONS

"My Spouse Won't Be Coming Today."

Keep in mind it is essential to show to both spouses. Enthusiasm often dwindles, so having one spouse ready to buy when the other still has to be consulted won't give you a sale. If one spouse wants to see a house without the other, you can say:

> *"I believe house-hunting is too important a task for you to do alone. From what you have told me, I believe I have the house for you. This home has been receiving extraordinary activity and I am afraid delay could result in your losing the opportunity for this exceptional property."*

If it is physically impossible for the other spouse to view the property, tell the prospect:

> *"If you find that the house is right for you, I would strongly suggest you put in an offer at once, subject to the approval of _____."*

With this Power technique you change the caller's thoughts from looking alone to actually buying alone.

"How Much Will They Take?"

Expect the unexpected on the telephone. I have had prospective buyers who hadn't even seen the property ask me, "Will the owner take $50,000?" or "Will the owner reduce that price?"

Here is how I handle this advance chiseling:

> *"[Mr./Mrs.] Collins, could you hold on just a moment? I want to make sure that the property is still available as we have had a great deal of activity on it the past two days."*

I put the prospective buyer on hold for thirty to forty seconds. This should make the prospect nervous and fearful that he or she may have lost a nice deal. When people feel they may not be able to have a property, they want it more.

Now, tell your prospect:

> *"The property is still available, but I suggest we set up an appointment to view it as soon as possible. Would you and [Mr./Mrs.] Collins be able to meet me at my office in 45 minutes?"*

The above statements will put the prospective buyer in a more realistic frame of mind about price. I do not consider it unethical to use urgency in this situation. You are dealing with a person who has larceny in the heart and wants to steal before having even seen what he or she is stealing. The only way to get this sort of person to be realistic is to use a Power technique to create urgency. Never say, however, that you have a nonexistent buyer. Let the buyer make his or her own assumptions.

If this type of buyer makes an offer when the feeling of urgency is present, the offer is more likely to be fair to both buyer and seller. Here's another Power approach to use when a caller wants to know if the owners will reduce the price:

> *"I don't know, would you be interested in buying it if they would?"*

The answer will generally be positive, so you should immediately follow up with:

> *"Then you should see it right now. How soon can you be at my office?"*

"What's the Address?"

Prospective buyers at times resist your taking control. They want the address so they can drive by or meet you at the property. I learned my lesson by waiting in my car in below-zero weather for prospects who never showed. Prospects often arrive early and drive by the property, then decide it isn't, or doesn't appear to be, what they really wanted. So they leave without bothering to cancel the appointment. Don't give out addresses.

Even if prospects do meet you at the property, they have their own car. You might wish to show them additional property, but they can drive away any time. When customers meet you at a property, you have no control.

One way to avoid giving out an address is to state:

> *"I have several other properties that I also believe will meet your needs. I would like to brief you at my office on what is available."*

or,

> *"It wouldn't be fair to you to give you the address. Driving by would not reveal what this home has to offer. A 'look-see' driving by could cause you to miss what I feel could be the house you have always wanted."*

Those approaches are better than the traditional:

> *"I would be happy to provide you with the address but my contract with the owner specifies that we not allow anyone to view the property [or that we not give out the address] if they are not escorted by one of our salespeople."*

The problem with the above approach is that your prospective buyers might argue that they won't bother the owner or no one will know.

"I Have a Broker."

If a caller indicates that he or she has a broker and is only calling to get the address, I recommend you counter with the following:

> *"I would be happy to call your broker and give your broker the details concerning this exceptional property, or if it is more convenient for you I would be glad to show it to you myself. Would 2 P.M. or 3 P.M. be more convenient for you?"*

Notice that with this Power answer you are not asking if you should call the other agent. You said you could, but that isn't one of the choices you are offering.

WHEN THE HOUSE IS SOLD

If an advertised property is sold, don't waste the telephone inquiries. Check alternatives not only from your own office but other offices as well. You can then tell callers that while an offer has been accepted on the inquired property, you would like to show them the property anyway. Perhaps they might want to place a back-up offer should the purchase fail for any reason. Have an alternative property or properties to tell them about. Ask for an appointment. Give minimum details on your alternative property. Again: The less you say, the less chance you have of providing negative information.

"I SAW YOUR SIGN"

Inquiries from prospects who have seen your signs put you a step ahead. To start with, you know more about the caller:

1. The caller likes the area or would be satisfied with it.
2. The caller likes the exterior of the property or would be satisfied with it.
3. From the exterior, the house appears to meet the caller's needs.

An important point to keep in mind is that people often call about property beyond their financial means. After hearing the price the prospect might pretend interest in order to avoid admitting he or she can't afford it. Calls on For Sale signs also provide a good reason for not taking overpriced listings. You never want to be apologetic in giving a price.

Before you give the price, find out what the buyer really needs. Then you can say:

> *"That property is competitively priced at $89,000. Is that within your general price range?"*

Even if the prospective buyer indicates it is, I would continue with the following Power switch:

> *"I also have another fine home in the same Westwood area in which you might be interested. It is priced at $68,000."*

For the possible alternative property use a home priced significantly less than the first property. If the price you quoted on the first home was actually too high, the caller will want information on the lower-priced property. By having a lower-priced property to change to, you avoid a wasted inquiry. When you meet with your prospective buyers, you can qualify them properly and decide if you want to show them the property they called about.

THE POWER OF NEW LISTINGS

When you get a new listing that you really feel suits one of your prospective buyers, call your buyer and be enthusiastic. If you have developed a warm relationship, a call like this might be proper:

> *"Our looking is over. I have the house for you. Grab your checkbook and be in my office in half an hour. This one won't last long!"*

Here you leave no doubt that you have found the property your buyers are looking for. You are talking about buying, not looking, and you are expressing a sense of urgency as well as excitement. A call like this spreads your excitement and creates a mood to buy. Be certain of your prospective buyers' needs before you make such a Power call. You will lose credibility if the property is not suited to your prospects' needs.

In cases where you have yet to build a strong personal relationship with the prospective buyers, I suggest a less powerful approach:

> *"I've found the house we have been looking for. It's a new listing and I don't want anyone else to snap it up. Could you and [Mr./Mrs.] Schneider meet me at my office in a half hour?"*

If your buyers are at work, suggest they take off an hour because this property won't last. You will be surprised how readily buyers drop everything when you show enthusiasm.

At least once a week—or better, every day—review new listings against your prospect cards. If you file your prospects' needs under the same categories you use for your listings, matching up property with prospects will be very easy. Closely check all the new listings, then call possible buyers to tell them about something new. Give them the barest details and set up a showing.

PRICE AND NEED

If you feel that a property is overpriced or a little high for your prospects, don't mention the price. When asked, you can respond:

> *"Price alone doesn't mean anything. First let's see the house. I will tell you that you can afford it, and you are not going to pay one dime more than it's worth."*

Prospective buyers often tune out the possibilities of a property above a certain price but end up buying one just as expensive. What the buyers offer is their personal decision; they are not going to offer too much. Get your prospects to consider their needs first. If the property does not meet their needs, any price is too much to pay; but if the property meets their needs and gives them shelter and enjoyment, no price can be called excessive.

4. Qualifying Buyers: Setting Up the Sale

Selling is not enough. You must sell to qualified buyers.

A qualified buyer is one whose interests and needs have been ascertained and who is not only interested in buying property, but can afford to. Most real estate licensees waste their time either showing the wrong property to prospects or showing property to prospects who lack the motivation or the ability to buy. Spend the bulk of your sales time on probabilities rather than possibilities. The qualifying process helps you decide on your level of effort.

Generally, sales that fail due to financing are directly related to an agent's failure to get proper financial information from the prospective buyers. Just ten additional minutes spent qualifying prospective buyers will save hours of showing unsuitable properties and working on impossible sales. Generally, the entire qualifying process should not take more than 45 minutes.

The qualifying process goes far beyond simply determining a prospect's financial condition, however. Properly conducted, qualification lays the groundwork for the sale. It sets the direction and strategy you will take as you follow the selling process to a closing. This chapter explains how to get the information that enables you to recognize and meet your prospect's needs, and how to use the information to begin the planned activity that ends in a successful sale.

WHO, WHAT, WHERE

Everyone Needs Qualifying

Don't judge prospects by their cars or clothes. Repossessors' warehouses are crammed with Cadillacs, Mercedes and Rolls Royces. Many millionaires look as if they do their apparel shopping in the nearest alley, while the fashion showplates may be wearing their net worth on their backs. Prosperity is evidenced by a balance sheet, not clothes, car, speech or manners. Always qualify buyers.

One of my students told me her clientele is the very best, so she doesn't have to qualify. She thinks asking these people questions on financial ability would be an affront. That is utter nonsense. The only people who resent financial qualifying are those who are not what they seem or who are not serious buyers. I am sure she showed many movie-star homes to people who lacked the ability or motivation to buy and only wanted to satisfy their curiosity.

Then there is the other extreme: One of my former students went to work for a broker who specialized in raw acreage. While my former student was working on floor time with a more experienced agent, a very grubby-looking gentleman drove up in an old pickup truck. The more experienced agent, whose turn was up, excused himself and told my former student to handle this one. The grubby-looking gentleman was a major developer and the result was an eight-million-dollar sale. The lesson—don't assume anything.

Where To Meet

Generally, there are only two places to meet your prospective buyers for the first time: at their home or your office. There are times when you will pick up prospective buyers at the airport or their motel.

Some salespeople prefer to meet and qualify prospects in the prospects' home. They feel the security that prospects feel in their own environment makes meaningful communication possible. The salesperson also gets a chance to see the present home and furniture, and thus be in a position to point out the comparative advantages of a new property. Knowing the prospects' furniture, the salesperson can later help his or her clients visualize their lifestyle in a new setting.

> *"The shutters and maple woodwork look like they were made for your colonial furniture."*

> *"Your beautiful dining room set would fit this home perfectly."*

or,

> *"It's rare to find a family room like this that has room for your Ping-Pong table."*

Another advantage of meeting the owners at their home is that it eliminates no-shows. Nothing is more aggravating than waiting for prospects who never come after you have set up several showings.

Despite these advantages, I prefer having prospects come to the real estate office for their first qualification, then picking them up at home for a later showing. Your office provides a professional environment you can control. Use that advantage by holding calls and other interruptions so you can devote full attention to your prospects.

Acquainting prospects with your office gives you a chance to show them it is a nonthreatening environment. This will make it much easier to get them to come in to discuss a property after a showing. Qualifying at your office also makes it easier to change initial showing plans based upon your interview.

One broker I know always qualifies in a closing room. He sets up coffee cups and provides coffee, tea or hot chocolate for his prospective buyers. He feels that this private closing-room atmosphere encourages prospects to open up. Providing coffee sets the stage for a relaxed conversation. Being in the closing room during a nonthreatening process also reduces the buyers' apprehension about being taken to a strange place after a showing. A closing room either should not have a phone or, if there is one, it should have its tone disconnected to avoid interruptions. You should appear to have only your prospective buyers' interests in mind. They must feel they are receiving your undivided attention.

Take notes during the qualifying process. Remember, what your prospective buyers tell you is important and must seem important to you.

How To Get Names Right

Most people have difficulty remembering names. Have you ever been introduced to someone at a party and two minutes later you've forgotten the name—but the other person knew yours? Chances are good the person you met made an effort to remember. I probably have had as much trouble remembering names as anyone. I've even started to write up offers and drawn a complete blank when it came to *Buyer's Name.* I realized I had a problem. By borrowing ideas from memory experts, I developed a three-part memory plan that really works. Many of my students have also used it successfully.

1. Upon being introduced for the first time, repeat the person's name to yourself three times.
2. As you converse, use the person's name each time you talk to him or her.
3. Think of someone else you know who has the same or a similar first name. By identifying the person you're meeting with someone you know, you can remember the person's name the next time you meet.

Using their names will help you build personal relationships with your prospective buyers. People like to hear their names used; it indicates you care. The same goes for children. Don't talk about their "kids," use names.

Getting the name right is as important as getting it at all. No one likes to hear his or her name mispronounced. If you are not sure about the pronunciation, ask. Never ask for the derivation of a name. Many people feel it smacks of prejudice.

THE QUALIFYING PROCESS

The qualifying process involves much more than finding out "How much do you have?" or "How much can you pay?" or "What do you want?" The qualifying process is a mutual exchange of information. Besides finding out about your prospective buyers, you should be selling yourself as a professional who is interested in them and shows empathy with their needs and desires.

The qualifying interview often involves counseling, especially with first-time buyers. The counseling process provides an opportunity to gain the prospective buyers' confidence, a step that puts you halfway to a sale. Many buyers don't really know what they want. Your job is to take general desires, needs and resources into account and help them recognize what they want. You do this through questions. It is not enough to ask questions; you must listen to what the prospective buyers actually are saying. The qualifying process normally extends to showing property and getting the reaction of the prospects. You often will find that what people say they want isn't what they really want at all. What they say may be based on practicalities, but what they really want is influenced by their hearts. Prospective buyers might say they want a fairly modest home; however, they really might want a showplace but think such an expenditure isn't wise. Unless you discover their secret desires you have little chance of making a sale. Keep in mind no one has ever been sorry purchasing too fine a home when it was within his or her financial ability.

As an introduction to your questioning, explain that you have many homes to show, but just rushing out to look would waste the prospects' time. By understanding their needs and abilities, you can select properties suited to them.

At this point, keep your attention on your prospects' motivation. Have they sold their home with a deadline to find a new one? Are they being transferred into the area or forced to move for some other reason? If so, their motivation is probably very high. On the other hand, if they must sell their present home before they can buy a new one, they are probably less likely to buy now.

Some people have no intention of buying at all. They simply want to get an idea of the value of their own property or to pick up some decorating ideas. Keep your greatest efforts focused on motivated buyers.

How To Get Information

Many real estate salespeople feel embarrassed asking financial questions, but misjudging the prospect's financial limitations will cause more embarrassment if you show properties beyond their reach.

One saleswoman I know tells her prospects:

> *"I am going to be asking you some personal questions. I want information you haven't given even to your best friends. It's not that I am nosy, but to help you I must know a great deal about you."*

Explain that many of the questions you ask will be the same ones lenders want to know. Most sincere buyers will understand that you need full information if you are to help them find the property that meets their needs. A prospect who balks at giving you information is probably not a buyer.

In order to protect yourself against a possible charge of discrimination, develop a set of qualifying questions to be used for every prospective buyer in the same manner.

When the prospect is comfortable with the idea of answering your questions, have a plan ready to guide the interview. Filling out a form like the one on the next two pages helps you make sure you get all the facts. It also assures prospects they are dealing with a professional. Make the heading on the form large enough for the prospects to see it clearly while you're writing. Seeing that it is *Confidential* will help the prospects answer your questions fully and honestly. The word *buyer* gets your prospects thinking of themselves as planning a purchase instead of just looking.

What the Answers Tell You

All the questions on the form have a definite reason for being there: They will become part of the selling process. Let's look at the questions and see how they can help you lead the prospects toward a buying decision.

Size of Family. This, plus the children's ages, indicates the present and future property needs. The names indicate sex, which will also help you determine the ideal size and arrangement of the house. (For example, older children generally want their own rooms for privacy, and boys and girls want separate rooms.)

Referral Source. If the prospects were referred to you by a friend, you may be in a very strong position. They will regard you with trust based upon their friend's recommendation.

Status of Current Property. If buyers must sell their own property before buying another, they are less likely to place an offer even if you find the perfect house. If they have not listed their home for sale yet, either go for the listing yourself or refer the owner to another broker.

If the prospects are renters, you want to ask:

> What is your current rent? $ _____
> When does your lease expire? _____

If the prospects have ten months to go on a one-year lease they are unlikely to buy unless they have the right to assign the lease. In this case you not only will have to find a home for them to buy, but also a tenant to take over their lease.

CONFIDENTIAL BUYER INFORMATION

Name _____

Current address _____

How long there _____

Size of family _____

Names and ages of children _____

_____

_____

Initial contact with your firm was because of: (advertisement, sign, referral, etc.) _____

Do you presently own your home? _____

Must you sell your home before you buy? _____

Would you prefer to sell your home before you buy? _____

Is your home presently listed for sale? _____

Will anyone else, such as a friend or relative, be helping you make your purchase decision? _____

If so, who? _____

Your reason for relocating _____

_____

_____

_____

How long have you been looking for a new home? _____

_____

Employment or profession _____

Employer _____

How long in your present position? _____

Current annual income $ _____

Anticipated annual income in 3 years $ _____

I would be interested in a total investment price for a home up to $ _____

I would be willing to allocate $ _____ for my initial investment.

I would be willing to make monthly investment payments up to $_____

What, if anything, don't you like about your present home? _____

_____

_____

_____

What features do you like about your present home? _____

_____

_____

_____

What are your minimum size requirements for a home?_____

_____

_____

What are essential features for any home?_____

_____

_____

_____

What are the desired features for any home?_____

_____

_____

_____

Do you currently own all your own appliances?_____

Areas or locations in which you would prefer to live _____

_____

_____

_____

Would you prefer to be close to a particular school or church? _____

_____

_____

Special hobbies or interests _____

_____

_____

Have you been looking at homes before today?_____

Have you found any home that you like? _____

Why haven't you purchased the house? _____

Helpers. Anyone else helping the prospects decide will be another person you have to sell. Most people won't admit that others are involved in their decision. Once they make this denial in writing, it becomes harder for them to back out of a sale because of another person's opinion.

Parents who help young couples with the down payment often insist on approval before they provide the cash. In this case, suggest that your prospects tie up the house they want with an offer. Parents are far more likely to approve a house purchase after an offer has been made. Without one, they may suggest ridiculous offers or want to look at other houses, forcing you to begin the sales process all over again.

Reason for Relocating. The reason the prospects are moving affects the likelihood of a sale. If they are looking for a place to retire a few years hence, they are unlikely to make a prompt offer. Chances are great they just want to get an idea of what their money will buy in your area.

Looking? People who have been looking for a home for a long period of time either are poor prospects or have never run into a professional salesperson.

Employment or Profession. This information tells you what kind of area will be most likely to appeal to your prospects. If your prospects can relate to others in the area, your chances of success are enhanced.

Income alone is not a gauge of what a person can afford. Keep in mind that white-collar people usually allocate a greater percentage of their incomes for housing than do blue-collar workers. Knowing both the income and profession of your prospects is more meaningful than either of these separately.

Also, people with higher educational levels generally spend a higher percentage of their incomes on housing. What people can afford is relative to what they are willing to afford. Many buyers will make great sacrifices to live in a particular area. Find out how flexible your prospects' limits really are.

In driving around your city you will see modest homes with expensive motor homes, cars and boats on the property. You will also see homes of twice the value with more modest automobiles. Priorities determine what a person can afford.

By knowing how lenders are currently qualifying buyers in your area you can ascertain how much of a loan your prospective buyers can qualify for. You might have to lower your prospective buyers' expectations or limit your search to owner-financing and assumable-loan situations.

Often buyers will indicate a price range that is far beyond the purchasing ability based on what the buyers consider their payment ability. In such cases education of the buyer becomes necessary.

Find out about prospective purchasers' debts (car loans, credit cards and so forth). Advise prospective buyers that debts reduce their home-purchasing ability. Strongly suggest they refrain from major credit purchases until after they have purchased their new home and closed the sale.

Anticipated Income. The buyers' income in three years is very important. If their income is rising, they will stretch current finances, knowing payments will become easy in a short time. If the buyers' income is rapidly increasing, an adjustable-rate mortgage with a low initial rate might meet their needs. Financing should be explored prior to spending a great deal of your time.

Investment. You are asking for total investment, not *purchase price*. *Investment* has a positive connotation, while paying a price has a negative one.

Payments. If new financing must be obtained, what the lender allows becomes more important than what your buyers are willing to pay. Again, you must fully understand local lender requirements. Lenders are conservative and will not make a loan if they think the buyers can't handle the payments. They don't want to repossess homes.

Make sure your prospects understand you can often tailor financing to meet their individual needs, but that you must understand their needs if you are to help them.

Keep in mind that people generally pay more and make higher payments for a home than they say they will. Don't get so technical that you confuse your buyers, but offer extensive counseling in the realities of what they can afford.

Present Home. What your prospects like or don't like about their present home gives you an insight into their interests as well as ammunition for the closing.

Minimum Size Requirements. If you ask what size home they want, buyers tend to choose one beyond their financial reach. Learn to ask why a couple wants a three- or four- bedroom home. Often a den or family room is all they really want. If an older couple says the home must have three bedrooms, ask, "Why?" By simple inquiry you can broaden the inventory that meets the prospects' needs.

Features. Find out why a feature is called *essential*. Often it is only a desire and not a need. A buyer may react favorably to a home with several desirable features even though one of the "essential" features is absent.

Appliances. Don't ask if they want a house with appliances. This will unnecessarily restrict you. If prospects don't own any, asking the owners to leave appliances can be a strong sales strategy.

Area. Never ask where the prospects want to live. Again, this precludes other equally desirable areas. Only ask preferences. If a prospective buyer says the home must be on the West Side, ask, "Why?" When you show property outside the preferred area, refer to it as "an area very similar to. . . ."

Churches and Schools. By asking about church and school preferences, you come up with a very effective reason to canvass an area for listings. *Power Real Estate Listing* deals in detail with how to use this information effectively.

Special Hobbies or Interests. These provide an area for small talk. People like people who share their interests. Hobbies can sell features of a home, as well. If a prospect is interested in oil painting, a house with a sewing room or sun-room could be the perfect studio. A prospect with a craft-type hobby will be halfway sold if the home being shown has a workshop.

Rejected Houses. Knowing why prospects rejected another home tells you about potential problem areas to avoid or overcome.
 Other information you should ask your prospects:

> *"When would you like to move?"*
>
> *"Why?"*
>
> *"If we were fortunate in finding the ideal home for you today, would you be prepared to make an offer today?"*

Ask questions to find out if there are any conditions that must be met before your prospects can buy. Examples would be:

1. The prospect must be offered a new job.
2. The prospect must get an expected promotion.
3. The prospects must get the down payment from their parents.

In qualifying buyers, don't ask limiting questions, such as:

"Do you want a colonial home?"

"Do you want a fireplace?"

All these questions do is to limit you from showing what might be the dream home for your prospects. Amenities lose importance when prospective buyers see the home they "love."

Many agents *tell* and *ask* but don't really listen. To make certain you fully understand what the prospective buyers are saying, summarize the needs and desires of your prospects and ask them if it is accurate and complete. Ask if there are any other requirements for a home purchase. The qualifying approach includes listening to what the prospective buyers are saying and not saying. Customer reactions when properly observed will help you find the home they will buy.

Educating the Buyers

Besides getting information you should be giving information during the qualifying process. The buyers should understand that they, not the seller, determine what price will be paid. However, if they believe a property is priced fairly, they should offer full price to ensure that they don't lose the property to someone else during the negotiation process. If they feel a price is too high they are free to offer what they consider to be a fair price.

Explain that the seller has three alternatives to any offer:

1. Acceptance.
2. Rejection.
3. Counteroffer.

Explain that if there is a counteroffer from the seller, they can accept it and have a binding agreement or say no and get their deposit back or give a counteroffer to the counteroffer—the choice is theirs. Explain that while you will be happy to offer advice, you are the sellers' agent.

If during the qualifying process you have a number of interesting properties with attractive financing, you should explain the relationship between interest and price.

> *"When you talk about price, you are really concerned with your monthly investment, isn't that true, [Mr./Mrs.] Jones? If you could find a home with a monthly investment you can afford, it really isn't that important what the price is. What I am talking about is below-market-rate financing. A higher-priced home*

> *whereby you can assume a below-market-rate loan or where the seller will provide below-market-rate financing will mean a lower payment to you. Therefore, it is possible that a higher-priced home could cost you no more to buy than a lower-priced home.*
>
> *"While I don't know if we will find such a home for you, if we do, don't be too concerned about the price. The payments are really what count."*

You could use an amortization table to further explain the price-interest relationship if your prospective buyers do not understand.

The earnest money deposit should be explained to the purchaser during the qualifying process.

> *"When we find the right home for you, [Mr./Mrs.] Smith, with your offer to purchase you will be making a deposit. This deposit will be a check payable to the trust account of Clyde Realty and will be held uncashed until your offer is accepted.*
>
> *"In the event the sellers decide not to accept your offer, the deposit will be returned to you in full. The normal deposit would be from 5% to 10%. In the case of a home in the $100,000 price range, which you have expressed an interest in, that would make the deposit from $5,000 to $10,000.*
>
> *"Should you be making an offer at less than the price set by the seller, an even larger deposit could be helpful for you. A large deposit shows you're sincere and sellers hesitate to say no when there is a significant deposit.*
>
> *"Do you have any questions? If we were very fortunate and found your future home today, would you be able to make a deposit today?"*

A brief discussion of loan costs for new financing is appropriate. You don't want a complete surprise at a later date.

The qualifying process can include a general indoctrination into financing, but avoid too much detail because it can be confusing. Assure the prospective buyers that you will be there to provide financing guidance.

Make certain that prospective buyers fully understand your agency role and your duties. Misconceptions are likely to lead to lawsuits. Clearly explain the agency relationship. As an example, the following could be used if you are going to be acting in the capacity as an owner's agent:

> *"[Mr./Mrs.] Henderson, I want to explain how real estate agents work and what our responsibilities are.*

"I am a seller's agent and am paid by a seller for successfully completing a sale. As a seller's agent, I regard you as a customer. I do not represent you in negotiations nor can I act in any manner inconsistent with the interests of the sellers I represent.

"However, I have duties toward you as well. I must make honest and full disclosures. If I know of anything that is detrimental about a property, I must fully reveal it to you. I will not deceive you in any manner. I will do my best to find you the home that I believe best meets your needs. I will answer any questions you may have about an area, property, financing or closing. I will point out benefits of particular properties. If you wish to place an offer on a property, the decision as to price and terms are yours, not mine, and I have a duty to present any offer I receive to the seller.

"Do you have any questions?

"Is the arrangement satisfactory with you?"

The above agency disclosure would be modified by special state requirements or if you were a dual agent or a buyer's agent. Because agency representation is such an important issue, I strongly suggest you read John Reilly's *Agency Relations in Real Estate* (Real Estate Education Company, 1987).

When you have obtained and clarified all the information, use it to find appropriate properties, but don't take the prospects' stated requirements as the last word. Sales are based as much on emotional desires as on rational need fulfillment. Buyers will give up an amazing variety of desirable features for something that appeals to them emotionally. If you check the prospects you failed to sell in the past, you will usually find that the house they finally bought had no more "needed" features than the ones you showed them. But something about the house, or something the salesperson said, struck the right emotional chord.

Your qualifying interview will give you the initial direction for beginning the showing process, but always remember that what your prospects say they want and what they end up buying won't necessarily match. You will be further qualifying prospects at every showing. *The qualifying process continues until the sale is closed.*

As a general rule, if prospective buyers indicate few preferences and very vague requirements, they are not strongly motivated to buy. Prospects who are open to anything rarely become buyers.

BEFORE THE SHOWING

Before you show your prospects any homes, tell them:

> *"After we have viewed the properties I have selected for you, we will come back and discuss them. Only by fully understanding your reactions to these homes can I help you. It is really as important to know what you don't like as it is to know what you do like."*

This sets the stage for a sit-down discussion and either a chance for a closing or an opportunity to build a relationship with your prospective buyers.

I like to give prospective buyers a blank *Offer To Purchase* form which I fold and place in an envelope. I then tell them:

> *"[Mr./Mrs.] Jones, when we find the home that is right for you, the purchase procedure is to use this* Offer To Purchase *form. I want you to look over this form when you have a chance, so you will be familiar with it and the purchase procedure when we find your home."*

This Power technique starts your prospects thinking about actually signing a purchase agreement early in the sales process. It will make their decision to sign a lot easier, since the form no longer seems threatening. Prospects are less likely to object to any provisions at the time of an offer if they have had a copy in advance, though few prospects actually study the form.

I like to continue with:

> *"When we find the right home for you [be very positive], I want you to know that buyers often get very nervous. A home purchase is an important decision. Some people are actually unable to take control of themselves and make a decision. These people remain renters all their lives. What I am saying is that apprehension is normal, and if you get nervous, you are normal, so relax."*

Talking about buyer jitters in advance reduces the chance that your prospects will revoke an offer prior to acceptance.

Guard Your Listing Book

It is not a good idea to let your prospects go through your listing book. Many real estate salespeople do so hoping buyers will find something they like. The only advantage to this is that when prospects do find something, they are likely to feel they "discovered" the property and now must go through with the purchase.

However, having prospects look through listing books is more likely to confuse them. Too many choices will result in their going elsewhere. Don't relegate your job to your buyers. You are not selling from a catalog.

Most multiple-listing services consider their material confidential for subscribers' use only. By letting prospective buyers have direct access to this material you could be breaching your duty of confidentiality.

Don't Sell until the Showing

Some offices have elaborate slide and video displays that let prospective buyers preview properties. This is a poor practice: Sales won't be made from these presentations, but if the pictures reveal something the prospect doesn't like, he or she won't want to see the house. Pictures that reveal a poor decorating scheme may turn off a prospect, and you'll miss the chance to point out advantages that overcome the objections. Even without a display, just talking too much about the houses could kill a sale if you mention a feature your prospects see as a negative.

MAKING THE APPOINTMENTS

When you think you fully understand your prospects' needs and desires, set up your showing appointments. Chances are good you've already made some appointments based upon your telephone discussion. If they are still applicable, show them; if not, cancel them. Your qualifying process might suggest additional properties you think will interest your prospects or properties you think are better suited for them. Call to make these additional appointments.

Agents who accept client limits as gospel in setting up appointments usually end up seeing other agents making the sale because they haven't shown the prospects what they really wanted. Most buyers end up buying a home costing more than they initially set as a limit. Even if the limits hold, your prospects' limits are *buying* limits—not *listing* limits. The listings of many agents are at the upper edge of the value spectrum while actual sales are likely toward the lower edge of the spectrum. Therefore, the home listed at $115,000 might be the perfect home for the prospective buyer who set a $100,000 price limit. While an offer of $100,000 might be rejected, a counteroffer in the $105,000 to $110,000 range could be irresistible to your buyers. Naturally, you should consider financing because below-market financing could have the same net effect as a price reduction.

You must know your inventory if you are going to efficiently set up showings. See every home you are going to show in advance. The qualifying interview might reveal that the homes the prospective buyer called you about will not meet your prospect's needs and a new choice of homes must be made quickly. If, when you caravan new listings, you take notes, those notes can help you quickly recall details. If your office has a computer you can plug in requirements and get the listings available. This often favorably impresses prospective buyers. Be careful to use requirements broad enough to encompass the house the prospective buyer will likely buy. Often homes purchased do not include features, such as a fireplace, which the prospect had said were "essential."

If an owner on one of your own listings has indicated a minimum down payment beyond your prospects' reach, but you think your buyers will like the house, call the owner.

> *[Mr./Mrs.] Knight, this is Tom Sanborn from Olympus Realty. I have a young couple in my office. He is a teacher at South High School and she is an associate professor of zoology at State University. They have one daughter, six years old. I feel your home would be perfect for them; however, there is a problem. They only have $6,000 to put down and you indicated a minimum of $10,000 down. They would be able to make the payments required. Do you want me to show this couple your home?"*

Prior to this call, your owner was thinking in generalities. Now you have real human beings as potential buyers. Does the owner want to turn these buyers away? If the owner tells you to go ahead with the showing, then he or she is in fact accepting the possibility of a lower initial payment.

Having obtained the concession, you have shown the prospects your willingness to go out of your way for them. You have created a feeling of obligation as well as trust, and in the process tremendously increased your chances of a sale.

If the listing is with another office, do *not* call the owner directly—call the agent.

If the owners indicate they won't accept the $6,000 down payment, ask if they will reduce their down payment requirement and, if so, to what amount? Let the owners decide. Even if they refuse to change terms, you will have shown the owners that you are working on their property and the prospective buyers that you want to meet their needs.

Never use this technique for a price reduction. It will alienate the owner. Price should not be negotiated on the phone and certainly not for a prospective buyer who hasn't even seen the property.

Before leaving your office to show homes, ask your prospective buyers if they would like to use your office restrooms. This is especially important if you have served coffee or if they have brought along small children. Many buyers have ended showings for reasons that a restroom would have solved.

WHOSE NEEDS—YOURS OR THEIRS?

Be very careful not to substitute your own feelings for those of your prospects. A house that looks horrible to you could be someone else's dream-come-true.

When I first began selling real estate, I inspected a very old house in poor condition. When I came back to the office I started to tell everyone what a dog the property was. My broker cut me short and taught me a lesson. "There are no bad properties," he said, "although there can be bad listings." The listing on this house was competitively priced and he considered it a good one. All the house needed was the right buyer. "Every home has had an owner in the past and will have other owners in the future," the broker pointed out. Three days later the house was sold.

The lesson was reinforced for me several years later when a couple walked into the office I was managing just at closing time. I was the only one there. They were well dressed and had brought along their ten-year-old daughter. They had seen the following ad:

CHOICE CHAPMAN AREA
3BR, Large Garage
$10,000—$500 down—$85/month

As you can see, this was long ago, but even then the ad looked too good to be true. I had just returned from vacation and so had not seen the property. Because it would be dark shortly, I decided to skip qualifying the prospects and show the property immediately.

When we arrived, I saw why it was so cheap. In contrast to the new homes around it, it looked a hundred years old, an old farmhouse with imitation brick siding. The large garage was really a small decrepit barn. Inside we found a dank, dark disaster area with ancient wallpaper, small rooms, a damp basement and a bath with rotten flooring that exhaled the unmistakable odor of ancient urine.

The couple looked through the house without saying much, but I could imagine what they must be thinking. When we got back to my car, I said the kindest thing I could, "Well. It certainly has possibilities."

The husband answered, "Yes it does."

Hiding my surprise as best I could, I quickly pointed out that they would never again have the opportunity to buy a home in such a desirable area for such a price.

Well, I sold the house. I later found out they had wished very much to live in the area because of the schools, but had been unable to find anything they could afford. The man was a disabled veteran on a pension. He did a great job of fixing the place up and they were delighted with their purchase.

Experiences like these emphasize the importance of not confusing your needs and wants with the needs and wants of your buyers. The purpose of the qualifying process is to determine the *buyers'* needs and wants. If you regularly show properties unsuited to your prospects, you will lose credibility as a professional with good judgment.

5. Making the Showing Work for You

The time has come to take all the information you gathered in your qualifying process and apply it to finding and showing properties you believe suit your prospects. The showing involves much more than just driving people around to look at houses; it will challenge your instincts, knowledge and sales skills. This chapter takes you step-by-step through the showing process, explaining Power techniques that will help you move smoothly through the showing and toward the closing. Chapter Six shows you how to deal with specific buyer objections.

CHOOSING THE PROPERTY

For the salesperson the showing begins before his or her clients have looked at a single home. The real start of the showing process is deciding what kind of property to show, based on the answers to your qualifying questions.

Is It Realistic?

Keep the homes you show restricted to ones your prospects can afford. Otherwise you just create expectations you can't fulfill and end up with clients who will never be satisfied. Prospects who have just toured the "superhouse" will not be happy with anything they can afford.

A recent Los Angeles newspaper cartoon showed a prosperous-looking buyer sitting in a real estate office, saying, "I just sold my place in Arkansas for cash and I want a really nice four- or five-bedroom place with ocean view, pool and if possible a tennis court. I am willing to go up to one hundred thou!" Now this customer may have had such a home in another area, but you probably couldn't satisfy his wants in the Los Angeles area without going close to the million-dollar mark. Before such a buyer can be sold, he or she must be reeducated to the realities of the marketplace.

Can You Deliver?

Getting offers on homes you cannot deliver wastes a lot of time and good will. Expect effort spent on nonexclusive and verbal listings to be wasted. People who won't give a legitimate listing are usually trouble. If a property is the only one you feel meets a buyer's needs, get a one-day, exclusive-right-to-sell listing for that buyer. If the owners refuse, forget them and their property.

Is It Overpriced?

Your first criterion in choosing homes to show to prospective buyers should be meeting the needs of your prospective buyers as you perceive them. Next, the property must be priced realistically based on market value. If a property offers exceptional financing, that would be a plus factor that could be considered to effectively reduce the price. An overpriced property should be shown only when realistically priced properties that meet the buyers' needs are not available, and then only when the owner is highly motivated.

Overpriced homes owned by speculators and real estate agents are poor choices to show. These owners tend to be difficult to deal with when you have obtained a fair offer. Generally, they are not highly motivated and want more than what is fair. You could waste a great deal of time and even lose a good prospective buyer.

Many salespeople choose their showings based on self-interest more than buyer interest. They show properties offering greater commissions or office listings before they show listings of other offices. Or, they may show one of their own listings to please an owner. Placing your own interests above prospective buyers' interests is a good plan if you desire failure. When you show properties that don't meet customers' needs, you can expect to waste an exasperated customer's time and have a customer who will likely defect to another agent at the first opportunity.

DECIDING THE SHOWING ORDER

Don't try to show prospective buyers every home you have listed. Your prospects need only one. The more homes they see, the more confused they become. Finally they forget which house had what features.

Your qualifying process should have given you a good idea of what houses to show. After you've chosen the most likely, pick out several alternates as well, so you'll have something to turn to in case your first notions of your buyers' needs prove mistaken.

Often prospective buyers view many homes with many real estate salespeople who show them what they say they want. They are finally sold by a salesperson who shows them what they really wanted all along—a home in a higher price range.

The average buyer chooses a home costlier than the one he or she initially inquired about. My own last three homes have exceeded my limits by at least 25 percent, and my summer home went over budget by 300 percent. So plan an alternative showing of a home that will meet your clients' needs with a price ten to 20 percent above their maximum price.

The Three-Homes Approach

The three-homes approach to showing property is the most widely used showing technique and one of the most successful. It consists of saving the most appropriate house for last.

Saving the best for last and pressing for a closing can be very effective. Some licensees use overpriced houses, houses in poor repair or properties in undesirable neighborhoods for their first two showings. They think this will make the house they want to sell seem better by comparison. Some licensees have an ulterior motive in showing their overpriced listings. They go back to the owners and say they showed the home x times and all the buyers thought it was overpriced. Their purpose in showing the home is to cut the listing price, not to sell it. I consider these tactics deceptive and unethical. I believe you should pick homes which best meet the needs of your prospective buyers and allow fair, unbiased comparison. You can, however, show the home the prospects inquired about, even if you don't think they will buy it.

The Best First

One successful broker defies the conventional wisdom with an approach all his own. He first shows the house he feels best meets the needs and desires of his buyers, then goes to other homes. He likes to show more than three. If he thinks the first house still best meets his clients' needs, he ends his showings by returning there. If another house has impressed his clients more, he returns to that house instead.

This unorthodox showing approach makes sense and should be considered. The second visit reinforces first opinions and provides an excellent comparison tool.

The Experienced Looker

The one-two-three approach is for prospective buyers who have not done much serious house-hunting. If your buyers have previously seen a number of homes, go right to the house you want to sell. If you think your choice was good but you are unable to close, that is the time to show several more properties, then return to the first house. This gives you a second opportunity for a closing. This is really the best-first showing method used in a different situation.

Adjusting to Buyers' Reactions

A favorable reaction on a home may make it unnecessary to show every home on your schedule. It may be time to go into a trial closing instead.

On the other hand, your prospects' reactions to the first two homes may tell you the last showing you planned is wrong. If so, stop for coffee and make a call setting up a different third showing.

Set Buyer Anticipation

When you have previously shown homes to prospective buyers it is easy to create a strong degree of anticipation for another showing. A telephone call such as the following will set the proper stage for a showing:

> "[Mr./Mrs.] Smith, I will be checking on a home today that has just come on the market. It appears almost too good to be true. I

will verify the facts and view the home. If it is as it appears I will call you right away for a showing, because I anticipate this home will be sold quickly."

You are creating anticipation. During the second call for the appointment, say you were right. The prospects should be excited and in a buying mood. The house must fit their needs as well or better than anything they have seen, or it will end in great disappointment.

THE DRIVE

For your clients, the showing process begins when you leave your office with them. Walk directly from the office to your car. If the prospects want to follow in their own car, tell them:

"I want to use the driving time to tell you about the property and to discuss a few thoughts I have."

If the prospects still insist on driving their own car, tell them:

"There's no sense in taking two cars; I'll ride with you."

Don't let yourself be separated from the prospective buyers. If they voice objections, you must be present to overcome them. You must understand the prospects' feelings if you are to help them. Ride in the prospects' car if you must, but try to drive them if at all possible. This way you are in control and don't have to worry that the prospects might not like the look of the house and drive right by. You also control the timing: You decide how long the showing will be, and you can pull in for a coffee break if your strategy demands it.

Drive slowly to a showing. Fast driving makes many people very nervous. If you appear relaxed, your attitude will help make your prospects relaxed and receptive.

If one or more prospects are in the back seat, set your inside mirror so you can see their reactions and they can see you. Ask the prospects about themselves and their work. Be interested in them. A short discussion showing your interest in their work or hobbies will open the door to better communication.

The questions you ask your prospects will help you further qualify them. Ask about specific homes and areas they have seen and their reactions to them, positive as well as negative. Your questions might lead you to change your planned showings, so consider carrying keys for alternative properties. Avoid giving very much information on the property you will be viewing. You don't want to touch on a feature that prospects consider to be negative. They might change their minds about seeing a home or get negative mind-sets even before entering the house. If the feature had been left unmentioned, then positive features would have a greater likelihood of outweighing the negative one. Often the general ambiance of the initial impression can overcome the absence of "must" features and the presence of "don't-want" features when the customers don't have preset negativism.

The Route

Pick a pleasant route to each showing. As you get close to the property you are showing, point out the homes of prominent people. This reassures your prospects about the neighborhood's desirability. Be certain your prospects know about recreational features such as tennis courts, fitness clubs and parks. Point out comparable listings and homes that were recently sold. Be certain to give only accurate price information and then only if the property you are showing compares favorably.

While a pleasant route can set a good mood, I do not believe in taking a route to avoid what you may consider a negative feature. This would be concealment. Failure to disclose is fraud as much as a false statement. If you know anything negative about a property or the area, let your prospects know. If the zoning was changed to commercial a block away, or an office complex, service station or glue factory is planned for the area, say so. Your duty of full disclosure includes telling buyers any facts that could reasonably affect their decision making. Never pretend ignorance about negative facts.

The fact that people of different racial backgrounds live in the neighborhood is not negative. In fact, mentioning this violates the Federal Fair Housing Laws. Steering prospective buyers toward or away from an area because of race is a violation of Title VIII of the Civil Rights Act of 1968.

No Smoking

Don't ask customers if it's all right to smoke. Out of politeness they may say they have no objections, but your smoking could distract them from what you are saying. Smoking bothers many people, especially when cooped up in an automobile. It also permeates their clothing.

Don't smoke in your car even when you don't have customers. Also, ask passengers (including buyers) to please not smoke. A great many people hate the smell of stale tobacco smoke. Psychologically, taking this approach puts you in control of the sales process.

Skip the Syrup

Many people are turned off by strangers calling them "Dearie" or "Honey." Use of expressions such as these strike most people as phony. After you get to know your prospects, ask if it is all right to call them by their first names. Don't use common nicknames unless they tell you to. Once I showed property to an English gentleman I called "Sid." He indignantly told me his name was Sydney.

Don't be apologetic to prospective buyers. Keep in mind that you are helping them. No matter how important a person is, you are the expert.

The Buyer Gets the Spotlight

Your prospective buyers may love to tell you about their grandchildren, but chances are great they are not really interested in yours. Let your prospects have center stage. A salesperson who tries to top his or her clients with smarter grandchildren, a more serious illness or a more traumatic experience had better have another source of income—because that salesperson will starve in real estate.

Avoid political or religious discussions. If your prospect brings up a controversial subject, ask, "What do you think?" or try to change the subject. Many people are unbending on certain issues and voicing your opinion could make any meaningful discussion of property impossible.

Useful Talk, Useless Words

Most people talk too much. Some salespeople are proud that their mouths never stop moving, but constant chatter can make people nervous, especially when you are talking fast. Fast talking calls up pictures of shady salespeople and prevents trust. It implies you are nervous, and your customers will respond by becoming tense themselves. If they feel that you "must" sell them, they will be afraid of you. Keep the relaxed attitude that you are showing property as a service, not for possible rewards.

Learn to slow down your speech and to keep quiet when you have nothing constructive to say. Ask questions so that the prospects do the talking. Learn to listen; it's not easy for some of us, but nobody learns anything by talking.

There is a time to be excited. When prospective buyers are excited about a property, your excitement will reinforce their feelings. Otherwise, try to remain calm. Your voice level should, however, convey your convictions.

Don't be the Howard Cosell of real estate. Use understandable language with a minimum of technical and legal terms. Try out those new words you learned on your spouse, not a prospective buyer. If your prospects don't understand you, they are not likely to buy from you. Your job is not to impress prospects, but to sell them.

Don't use abbreviations. Many people don't know that BLM means Bureau of Land Management. They haven't the vaguest idea who this Fannie Mae is that you keep talking about, or what she has to do with their buying a house. If the person who formed the first acronym had been shot, we might be able to understand each other today.

Great diction or enunciation isn't as important as your choice of words. If you can make yourself understood, you can sell. Many great salespeople butcher the language, but buyers know what they mean.

Never interrupt your prospects. To them, what they are saying is important. Treat it that way.

Never talk down to buyers no matter how stupid or aggravating you feel they have become. People know when you are being condescending and they don't like it. People are not about to spend money with someone who fails to respect them.

Smile

Several years back I did a series for educational television on real estate. After my first few shows my wife started drawing happy faces ☺ on my scripts and writing *SMILE* on each page. I found that this helped me. We often forget that people like pleasant people.

STAY WITH YOUR PROSPECTS

Lecturers at real estate seminars often tell us not to show more than three properties a day. I still remember when I learned that this rule has exceptions, too. After showing a couple several homes in one day, I made an appointment for the next day to show them more. The prospects called me later that day to tell me they had purchased a home—one I had planned to show them the next day.

If you have motivated buyers who are ready to buy in the near future, stay with them. After a few showings, stop for coffee. Have the prospects talk about the most desirable of the homes they have seen, and its good features. Next, show another group of homes and repeat the evaluation process. Your prospective buyers will be a little confused after viewing ten or twelve homes, so go back to the best homes in each group and have your clients decide which is best for them. Keep in mind that positive reactions signal that it's time for a closing presentation, no matter what the time of day or what point you have reached on your schedule.

This process can use up several full days. When you have out-of-town buyers with only a few days to look for a home, this is the approach to use. If you take them back to their motel after a few showings, you can bet they will be calling other brokers. In these situations, stay with your prospects during all possible waking moments.

If you feel a particular house has impressed your buyers, but you have been unable to get an offer, make a point of driving the prospects past that property at every opportunity. This will help them get more of a feel for the area and give you additional opportunities to close the sale.

If you stop for lunch or coffee, don't let your prospective buyers pick up the check. If your prospects pay they may feel they have fulfilled an obligation to you. Psychologically you want your buyers to feel obligated: This reduces the likelihood of their straying away to other agents. Also, when you are making a closing presentation it doesn't hurt if buyers feel an obligation toward you.

The lunch problem also can be solved by suggesting you take a 45-minute to one-hour break for lunch. You must have a definite appointment for after lunch. The advantage of a break is that it gives the buyers a chance to talk privately. They are likely to firm their opinions. A word of warning: If you give your prospective buyers a break of more than one hour, there is a good chance they will use the break to contact other agents or owners.

CURES FOR PROBLEM PROSPECTS

Any experienced salesperson could keep you busy for months listening to stories about the unique prospects they've dealt with, and how they made the sale anyhow. No one can predict what your next buyer might say or do, but this section describes some basic types and lets you in on tested ways of handling them.

The Talker

The talker knows everything and lets you know it nonstop. The best way I have found to deal with talkers is to compliment them on their keen judgment. The talker will discover that you are a keen and discerning person, perhaps even worth listening to. People like people who think as they do.

The Chronic Complainer

Some people, upon arriving in heaven, would complain they had to wait too long at the pearly gates. There is something for such folks to find wrong in any situation. Yet these difficult prospects do buy homes, and the agent who knows the right techniques will make the sale.

The important goal here is to lead the disagreeable buyer into discussions of a property's positive points. If all else fails, show a house that totally fails to meet the buyer's needs, and use that as the negative comparison with a more suitable property. Your prospect then gets a wonderful opportunity to point out everything wrong without hurting the eventual sale.

Some disagreeable prospects use antagonism as a defense measure. Such people often warm up if you get them to talk about themselves. Ask the prospect's opinions on a few topics and agree with his or her conclusions. Use these opinions to lead into questions more related to the property at hand.

Never get into an argument with this type of prospect. Even if you win, you lose: Being shown up in an argument is not the experience that sweetens an antagonistic disposition, nor does it put a prospect in the mood to buy a house from you. Rather than defending a property against the prospect's attack, agree with the objections. Then try to turn them to advantage:

> *"[Mr./Mrs.] Thompson, if this were your home, what would you do to solve the problem of. . . ?"*

If this fails, your prospect may be the ideal candidate for the reversal approach to showing described later in this chapter.

The "Expert"

The neighbor, friend or relative who comes to a showing unexpectedly can ruin the sale. The prospect usually takes the third party along because of imagined expertise, or for moral support. No matter how absurd the "experts'" comments, don't let yourself be drawn into an argument. "I haven't found that to be true in this area," is about as strong as you can get.

If the expert downgrades the first house, find points to agree on. You must get the expert on your side. Treat the expert as a real expert. Ask for his or her opinion. I like to discuss matters beyond the expert's limited knowledge:

> *"Of course, you will agree we should consider a loan assumption rather than a wraparound loan in order to take advantage of the attractive interest rate."*

This kind of statement forces the expert to either agree or expose the limitations of his or her knowledge. If you have the expert agreeing, he or she can become an ally who reinforces your opinion.

The Group

Selling to a group such as a church or club presents its own special problem lems. Each member will react differently to your presentation. The person who asks the most questions may not be the person to please.

Try to find out from the group's leader in advance how a decision will be made. Normally one or two people actually make the decisions and the others follow.

Ask the committee chairperson questions to clarify the group's needs. If another person answers, this is probably the person who will influence decisions. Otherwise, keep your attention on the chairperson.

The Dominant Spouse

Listening to a husband and wife will usually indicate which one really makes the decisions. Marriage isn't always an equal partnership, so knowing who gets his or her way tells you which needs will take priority and whose needs to emphasize in a closing.

The Changing Mind

If prospective buyers en route to a showing indicate they don't want to see a home, tell them something like this:

"I called the owner and it really wouldn't be fair not to view their house. They are prepared for the appointment, and we owe them at least a walk through. Besides, I would like your comments. By knowing specific features you like or don't like I will be better prepared to meet your needs."

WHEN YOU ARRIVE

When you arrive at each showing, park across the street or at least on the street rather than in the driveway. This allows your prospects to see the house in its full setting. Let your prospects know why you are parking this way. You can then ask them to turn around slowly to get a 360-degree view. This helps your prospective buyers appreciate the area and make each individual home seem more important.

As you walk toward a home with exceptional curb appeal you might state:

"Just imagine your name on the mailbox."

When you return to your car, stand outside for a moment and discuss the home from the favorable vantage point. Many sales are closed while viewing the exterior of the home after a showing.

If a home has excellent interior features but lacks positive curb appeal (considering the price range), pull right into the driveway and park as close as possible to the front door. This allows the entire home to be viewed without an initial negative reaction.

The Presale

After you have shown prospective buyers several homes and you think you now know what your prospects want, a good technique as you stand looking at the outside of the house would be to say:

"I believe you are going to agree with me that this home is perfect for you. It has the large split plan you liked in the last home, but it also has a much larger fenced yard and rear-facing kitchen window so you can keep an eye on little Tony. Be prepared for a preview of many happy years."

This approach helps the viewers to consider buying rather than looking. They will be more likely to imagine the home as *their* home.

Respect the Property

Salespeople who sell expensive jewelry treat each item with near-reverence. The way a property is handled affects its value in a customer's eyes. The same holds true for real estate. Treat it with respect, regardless of its dollar value. Wipe your shoes before entering a home and your prospects will do the same. Your owners should have prepared the house for showing to create as favorable an image as possible. The details of preparing a house to produce the maximum favorable effect are discussed in *Power Real Estate Listing*, the companion volume to this book.

The Owners

If the owners are at home, introduce them to your prospects. Ask owners to be absent when you arrange a showing. If this is impossible, ask them to remain in the background and not volunteer any information. Owners who are poorly instructed or ignore your request have high potential for ruining a sale with uncalled-for comments and information.

If owners decide to tag along, excuse yourself from your prospects and talk privately with the owners. Explain that buyers are nervous in the presence of the owners and won't ask the questions they need answered before they decide to buy. Ask the owners to remain in one place while the showing is going on, and promise to let them know how the showing went immediately afterwards.

The Children

Children can turn a showing into a nerve-wrenching sideshow if the house is furnished and the children are on the wild side. One large brokerage firm installed a children's room in their office with a pile of comic books, a television and a pinball machine. The room gave parents a place to leave their children while they looked at homes. If children have been a problem, suggest that the parents get a baby-sitter so they can evaluate a home without distraction and tension.

If your prospects do bring a small child to the showing, consider carrying the child or taking it by the hand. This frees the parents to concentrate on the house. Where there are several active children, they can remain in the car while you show a property. You can't really sell a home with children running through the halls and rooms.

Older, well-behaved children, however, can become your allies. Asking questions such as, "Which room would be yours, Alice?" can result in the child selling the parents on the house.

Be in Control

As an agent you must maintain control of the showing. If you lose control, the only chance of a sale will be if the prospects sell themselves, because you will not be selling them. In addition, if an owner is present when you fail to control a showing, you will damage the professional image of yourself and your firm.

Keep your prospects together during a showing. When they separate and peek through the house, you can't give a meaningful presentation. Even the best property won't sell if you don't present it properly. When one spouse wanders off, you can say, "[Mr./Mrs.] Brown, I think this will interest you." Make a mental note of what they were looking at so you can point out features or ask questions as applicable.

Take Notes

Take notes on prospective buyers' reactions to negative and positive features in each home. Put this data on the prospects' file card with a record of which homes were shown and when, and every contact made with the prospects. When a prospect has commented that a home lacks a particular feature, you will know this feature is one to emphasize in future showings.

From your notes you can decide in advance the features to emphasize, as well as what will go into an effective closing presentation.

Buyer Safety

If a prospect is injured during a showing, you may be held responsible. So be alert for areas of potential danger where buyers might trip, fall or otherwise injure themselves. Provide the necessary assistance for elderly and disabled prospects.

Even though prospects are injured in their own automobile, you could be held responsible if they were following you and it was held that your negligence contributed to the accident. Safety is another good reason prospects should travel with you in your car and be under your close control at all times.

You should, of course, carry high limits of personal liability insurance for your automobile. In addition, your office should have a high-limit, general liability coverage policy that protects both you and your broker for injuries to others resulting from any negligence on your part.

THE ROUTE THROUGH THE HOUSE

Experts disagree on which features of a home to show first. I don't think different showing patterns have much effect, but I do recommend that you start with a strong feature and end with a strong feature—for example, walk around a house to view the garden area before you enter the home and end up in the living room or family room.

In a furnished house, I like to sit down with my prospects in the living room after the showing and suggest that they sit where they get the most favorable view and impression of the property. An attractive patio or garden can also provide a nonmenacing atmosphere in nice weather.

Then I talk about the house, asking more than telling. Seated in this relaxed atmosphere, the prospective buyers can imagine themselves as the owners.

If the conversation brings favorable reactions from the clients, I go for a very relaxed closing right then and there with trial closing statements or questions.

> *"This could be habit-forming. Don't you agree it's a very relaxing room?"*

> *"How would you like to own this fine home?"*

(See Chapter Seven, *Trial Closings.*)

SELL THE BENEFITS, SELL THE HOUSE

People don't really want to buy real estate; they want to buy the benefits real estate ownership offers. Point out all the benefits a property offers without worrying about repeating yourself. Repetition drives home the point. Here are some specific points to make, and ways to make them lead toward a closing.

Sell Features in Each Room

It isn't necessary to make statements such as, "Now this is the living room" and "This is the master bedroom." Your prospective buyers have been in homes before. A far better approach is to point out positive features in each room.

> *"I like living rooms that open onto the backyard. They provide a much more private and homelike atmosphere."*

> *"There is plenty of room in this bedroom for your king-size bed."*

"If we ever move again, I will insist on well-lighted, walk-in closets like these. I never seem to have any room in mine." [Invite your prospective buyers to walk inside the closets.]

"Notice that your dishwasher and washer/dryer are all Maytags. They reflect the quality that has gone into this home."

"The way the home is oriented, the morning sun will light up the kitchen. A sunny kitchen is a pleasant way to greet the day."

"[Mr./Mrs.] Thomas, how would you use this workroom?"

"With a rear kitchen you will be able to keep your eye on Jimmy when he is playing in the backyard."

"Isn't that a fine workbench? Perhaps we can convince the sellers to leave it. I doubt if they will have room for it in their new mobile home park."

"Would you use this room as a study or as a spare bedroom?"

"I imagine this would be John's room?"

"Whose bedroom would this one be?"

"I hadn't noticed before but this is real wood paneling. Today a lot of what you think is wood is just a photofinish on Masonite hardboard."

If a couple has small children or are planning on a family, you might mention:

"This fenced backyard will provide a safe place for your children to play."

"There is plenty of room for your camper [or boat] beside the garage."

If prospects don't have a camper or boat, point out the feature anyway. It could be that getting a camper or boat is a strong goal for them, and seeing a space to park it will make the house a lot more attractive.

Don't ask prospective buyers if they want to see any feature. Assume that they do and lead them.

"You will want to see this large dry basement."

By selling the small amenities, you end up selling the house that contains them.

You can often overcome negative features, such as a very small kitchen, by making them seem like benefits.

"[Mr./Mrs.] Liszkowski, I know you will appreciate this step-saving kitchen."

"I thought you would be interested to see how easy it will be to maintain this [small] yard."

Don't enter smaller bedrooms and baths with your prospects. All of you together in the room will make it seem smaller than it actually is.

Put Them in the House

Whenever you can, talk as if the prospects already owned the house.

> *"Your [son's/daughter's] new school is only two short blocks away."*

If your prospects have children or grandchildren and the house is on a cul-de- sac, point out:

> *"Because your home will be on a cul-de-sac, you won't have to worry about fast traffic and the safety of your children."*

> *"This quiet cul-de-sac will provide a safe place for your visiting grandchildren."*

Involve the Entire Family

Many buyers get very nervous when they finally find a home they want. In the case of married couples, you can use each spouse to support the other. You can also use children for emotional support to go ahead with the purchase. You can accomplish this by addressing questions that will elicit positive responses to each spouse and child (if applicable) separately so they all realize that the purchase is a mutual decision.

Examples of these positive-response questions include:

> *"[Mr./Mrs.] Jones, don't you love the old-world character of this richly paneled dining room?"*

> *"[Mr./Mrs.] Jones, how do you like the idea of having your own paneled den for work or just to relax and watch a ball game?"*

> *"[Mr./Mrs.] Jones, wouldn't this large, open basement make a great rainy-day playroom for the children?"*

> *"Sally, how do you think you will like having your own private teen suite with bath?"*

Sell the Location

Every location has some positive feature. For example:

> *"This home is in the _____ school district, which, as you probably know, has the reputation of being one of the finest schools in the city. Are schools an important feature for you, [Mr./Mrs.] Jones?"*

If the prospective buyers have school-age children, you can be certain such a statement will evoke a positive response.

For a house close to a freeway you might say:

> *"This home is well located in relationship to freeways to avoid lengthy commuting."*

If the house is some distance from a freeway:

> *"An advantage this house offers is that it is away from the noise, dirt and smell of the freeways."*

In selling a location, utilize your specific knowledge of the area:

> *"[Mr./Mrs.] Jones, do you know Alfred Hicks? He also works at T-Bar in engineering. He purchased the home three doors away last May. Perhaps the two of you could work out a car pool."*

> *"Timmy, from your Cubs cap I see you are a baseball fan. We have an active Little League in the neighborhood. They practice only two blocks away at McArthur Park."*

Paint the Scene

Try to create pleasant visual pictures for your prospective buyers.

> *"Wouldn't you love to entertain your best friends in this room?"*

> *"A swim in that pool would be a welcome relief after a hard day's work."*

> *"When I was a child we all gathered around our fireplace and popped popcorn on cold winter nights. Those are some of my most pleasant childhood memories. You'll have to get one of those long-handled poppers for Alice and Ted."*

> *"Don't you love a natural wood fire on a cold night?"*

> *"There is enough space in this family room for a family reunion with all of your grandchildren."*

> *"When your grandson comes to visit, I bet he would love this room."*

> *"Right here under this tree would be a great place for a barbecue and picnic table."*

> *"There's plenty of room over here for your swing set."*

> *"These trees are perfectly spaced for a hammock. Now that's the way to spend a lazy summer afternoon."*

If the prospective buyer is a good gardener, you could ask:

"What could be done to improve the landscaping?"

"Where would you put your vegetable garden?"

Choose your words carefully. Words like these convey positive images: *estate-size lot, patio, lanai, garden room.*

In describing colors, call light colors *refreshing* and dark colors *rich.* Both of these words convey positive feelings.

Whenever possible, tie in your statements with hobbies or special interests. Appeal to all of your prospects' desires.

Good Neighbors

In listing, most salespeople fail to get information about neighbors, even though this can be just what you need to close a sale. Ask about the neighbors when you call the owners for an appointment, looking for specific points related to your prospects' needs.

If prospective buyers send their children to a private school across town, for example, having other children nearby who attend the same school is a definite plus. It can mean great convenience to a parent who has to drive the child to school. Other areas they looked at might have contained many students from the same school, but the salesperson has to know this at the time of the showing or the fact is useless.

Knowing about children in the neighborhood of the same age as the prospective buyers' children is another bit of positive information.

Some buyers will be highly impressed if you mention some important people living in the neighborhood. The fact that well-known bankers, doctors, attorneys, politicians, professors, retired military officers, authors and other prominent people live in the area can help you make a sale.

Teachers, small-business owners and tradespeople can help sell a blue-collar neighborhood to a factory worker or tradesperson.

The people you mention should be at or above the social and/or economic level at which your prospects view themselves.

Privacy and Safety

When your prospective purchasers are currently living with a relative or in an apartment, push the element of privacy that a home offers.

Some buyers place high value on security. You can probably assume this is true of people living alone, people in high-crime areas and those with barred windows, burglar alarm systems or large dogs. In these cases you should emphasize the safety of the neighborhood and security features of the house such as door peepholes, solid-core doors, strong window locks, deadbolts and so forth. For many buyers, one hundred dollars' worth of security hardware will make the difference between purchasing a home and looking elsewhere.

The Lower Down Payment

If you are showing a home that can be purchased with a significantly lower down payment than the prospective buyers indicated they were willing to spend, state:

> *"An advantage of this property which might interest you is that this home can be purchased with an initial investment of $5,000 less than you indicated you were planning to invest. Is there any new furniture you would like? I imagine there are a lot of nice things you could get with $5,000."*

Financing

If there is attractive assumable financing or seller financing, show the benefit:

> *"The nine percent assumable loan offers a wonderful opportunity for you, doesn't it, [Mr./Mrs.] Smith?"*

Using your amortization book and your calculator, you could have prepared in advance the following Power advantages of assumable loans:

> *"[Mr./Mrs.] Smith, do you realize what a $90,000 assumable loan such as this, at two percentage points less than the present market interest rate, means over the 30 years of the loan? It amounts to more than $48,000.00. That makes this home truly a·bargain."*

Status

Many homes are purchased more for their effect on others than for the living comforts they offer. In other words, the home is purchased in large part to impress others, just as a Rolls Royce may be more important for its impact on other people than for its comfort and luxury. Ego gratification is an important human need.

People new to wealth are usually eager to show others that they now have money. In showing the house to status-conscious prospects, emphasize the effect this house will have on friends and relatives. Statements such as the following would likely appeal to prospects with newly acquired wealth:

"This dining room is big enough for a family reunion. What do you think your relatives would think of this house?"

"Wouldn't you like to entertain your best friends at this poolside patio?"

Any time the house you are showing is a vast improvement on the prospects' present housing, this approach can work well. Wealth is, after all, a relative value, not an absolute.

Architecture

A knowledge of architectural styles can help sell higher-priced homes. Injecting architectural statements adds an additional element of desirability.

"This home is a classic example of French Provincial. It looks as if it had been transplanted from an estate near Lyon."

If a luxury home's architect is prominent, or was a student of a well-known architect, you may have found the key to the sale. Even if the architect is relatively unknown, mention his or her name and a prominent design.

"This home was designed by Thomas Kenyon, who also designed the new Colonial Shopping Center. Kenyon's designs are very much in the style of Royal Barry Wills. I feel he has captured the classical beauty of early New England colonial architecture. Don't you agree, [Mr./Mrs.] Jones?"

If you specialize in luxury homes, knowledge of local architects, their styles, works and reputations will give you excellent sales ammunition. You will enjoy learning to spot the architectural style of a property and to guess with fair accuracy the building's date and architect.

The Decorator

If a home is being sold furnished and was professionally decorated, be sure to comment on the decorator.

"The home was professionally decorated by E. Wilson Byer, who also did the home for Thomas King, the president of United Consolidated."

Mentioning the decorator's well-known clients may be snob appeal, but it is highly effective in making buyers feel they are getting the best.

MORE POWER SHOWING STRATEGIES

The Question Method

The question method is the opposite of talking too much. To use it, you say nothing but, "What do you think about. . .?"

While I prefer positive statements, painting visual pictures and making the prospects think like owners, the question method has its advantages. It forces prospects to constantly reveal their reactions.

I have effectively used the question method for my first two showings in order to get reactions and then have gone to a positive approach on the home I expected to sell.

When showing a prospect property for the first time, you are never sure of your selection. If you are to help the prospect, you need feedback. Instead of making statements, ask questions. Find out what the prospect thinks of the neighborhood—is it satisfactory? Ask questions about the house such as, "Which features do you like the best?" or "Are there any features you wish this house had?"

Some customers say very little. These silent types are difficult to draw out. You must constantly question them. If you can get the silent types to talk about a hobby, job or anything else that really interests them, you can often open the route to good communication.

Your talking doesn't tell you anything. If, like many real estate salespeople, you are in love with your own voice, force yourself to let the buyers express themselves. While you can never *know* too much in real estate, you *can* talk too much. Silence is an art and you have to learn to do it. Only by your silence will you be able to listen.

As previously stated, be careful not to substitute your own feelings for the feelings of your prospective buyers. What you imagine they want could be different from what they really want. A home that you don't like could be their dream home. Keep in mind every home will have a future owner. Someone will love it. By asking questions and evaluating your feedback you can determine what prospects really want. Unsuccessful agents fail to listen to what buyers are saying.

Watch Body Language

Watch your prospects. Their movements can tell you a great deal.

- Crossing and recrossing legs may mean your prospect is either bored or in need of a restroom.

- Glancing at a watch indicates your prospect wants to end the showing; however, it doesn't necessarily mean you should do so.
- Arms folded across the chest is a defensive posture, usually meaning the prospect is not at ease with you yet or has not been receptive to a property or a presentation.

One, Two and...

When a house offers several benefits, say:

> "This home has three very important features. The first is _____
> _____. The second is _____."

Don't say what the third is. Wait until the prospective buyers ask. If they don't ask right away, repeat:

> "Those three features I feel make the property very desirable."

When the prospective buyers ask what the third feature is, explain a very strong and positive point:

> "Oh, didn't I tell you, the owner will finance the property with 20 percent down at only nine percent interest."

Touchee-Touchee

You don't have to limit your showing to the sense of sight. Involving other senses will enhance a property. My students call my approach "touchee-touchee," as I exhort them to touch the property and get their prospective buyers to touch it as well. If you touch something and comment on it your prospective purchasers will normally follow your lead. If they don't, you'll have to get them involved.

Bending down, you can run your hand over plush carpeting and make a comment such as:

> "Just feel this quality carpet!"

If there is a solid-core wood door, knock on it and observe:

> "Now listen to that sound of solid wood. Today many builders try to cut corners and use hollow-core or foam-filled doors that can be opened with a can opener."

Lath and plaster walls invite a similar treatment:

> "Now that's the sound of solid construction. Not much real lath and plaster like this is used anymore. Most builders today seem interested in how cheaply they can build a house, not in its quality."

Slide glass doors and windows open and comment:

"Feel how easily these sliding doors open."

You can hold your hand to a heating or cooling vent and say:

"Feel that heat [or cold air]. That will keep you warm this winter [or cool this summer]."

If there is ceramic tile in a bath or kitchen, rub your hands over the tile and say:

"I like ceramic tile on the walls. Besides its beauty and durability, it reflects quality."

For fine woodwork, rub your hands over the wood and comment on its beauty.

If there's a brick fireplace, rub your hands over the brick. Chances are good your prospects will do the same.

If a house has a brick or stone exterior, touch the outside wall and say:

"To me there is something solid and lasting about a brick home."

For homes with wells, turn on the water for a few minutes until it is nice and cold and fill glasses for your clients. Ask them to taste the water and then comment on its quality.

"After drinking chlorinated city water, good well water is certainly refreshing."

If there are dimmer switches, turn them on and adjust the light levels. If there is an automatic garage door, open and close it.

On unfenced property, walk the lot pointing out the boundaries. Walking the property seems to emphasize the size of a parcel favorably.

In the garden I like to bend down and pick up a clod of dirt and rub it between my fingers. Usually my clients will do the same. I don't say anything, but the action seems to have a very strong favorable effect. If you say, "Looks pretty good," your prospects will usually agree with you. If there is any fruit on the trees, pick one and cut it into slices with your pocket knife. Eat a slice and give slices to your prospective buyers.

In showing a home, don't just observe the backyard through the windows, walk out into it. Give your clients a rear view of the home. I recommend you walk completely around the house. You want your prospects to feel the property and to think of it as their own.

By involving all your prospects' senses in exploring the house and lot, you impress favorable features upon them much more effectively than is possible by sight alone. In addition, touching helps to create the desire to own. It can be one of your most effective showing techniques, yet is used by only a few real estate salespeople.

How To Quote Prices

Never be apologetic about quoting prices. When you say, "It's listed at $98,000," your voice can make the price seem fair, low or excessive. If you say, "The home has an $87,000 assumable loan, but it's at 12 percent," the 12 percent loan sounds like a negative feature. If, however, you say, "The home has an assumable $87,000 loan at only 12 percent," it is presented as positive.

Should prospective buyers not want to see a house because they feel the quoted price is high, consider this:

> *"Forget the price for a moment. Houses sell at market value. Market value is actually determined by buyers, not sellers. What is important right now is not the price but rather how this house meets your needs."*

What you are trying to do is set the issue of price aside for the time being. If the prospective buyers like the house, you can then try to close at list price or as close to it as possible.

Here is a similar approach for an overpriced listing when the prospective buyers want to know the price:

> *"Let's not worry about dollars for a few minutes. The important thing is that the house meets your needs. I will tell you, however, you won't pay one dime more than this house is worth."*

If the prospects knew the price they would likely react negatively to the house. Once they are sold on the house, then it's time for a closing at the highest price possible. Notice that you do not suggest or invite low offers. This would not be fair to your owners.

The Negative Showing

Overemphasizing a negative feature before a showing can be effective. Suppose you are showing to prospects who answered an ad for a "fixer-upper." On the way to the showing you make it sound much worse than it actually is. When the prospects see the property, they get a pleasant surprise.

The same technique works on a single negative feature that the prospects find is nowhere nearly as bad as you painted it. You might warn that the yard is awfully small or too large, or that the kitchen is too small and so on. The negative feature you choose should be a minor fault or one not likely to be viewed as really negative by many buyers.

While showing the property, bring up the negative feature: "Except for _____, the house would really be perfect for you." Now ask your prospective buyers what they think of the property. You could be ready for a closing.

Because you appear to be taking a negative position, buyers often feel that they have *discovered* the property and how to cure its faults. To use a variation of this approach in the three-homes showing, give details of the first two homes in advance but don't mention the third. Let the customer ask about it. Answer, "Perhaps it isn't right for you," or "I don't think you need that large a house." After you have shown the two homes, say, "We might as well see _____."

The negative approach is especially effective for difficult or argumentative prospects. Telling them they don't want or don't need a property can goad them to prove you wrong and in the process sell themselves.

Take a Picture

Carry a Polaroid camera with color film. If your prospects are excited about a part of the house, take their photograph there. Give the photograph to your prospects. If they buy, the photograph will reinforce their purchase and they will be less likely to cancel out before closing. They will show the photograph to all of their friends.

A major land developer gives each prospect a Polaroid camera to use while he or she is taken on a tour of recreational property. The prospects are encouraged to take photos of themselves in beautiful settings. The developer has found that the few dollars for film has resulted in many sales.

ANSWERING QUESTIONS...SOMETIMES

Never jump to answer a prospective buyer's question. What you might feel is a positive selling point could look negative to the buyer. If a prospective buyer asks you whether the refrigerator stays, you might happily answer that it does, only to find that your prospects already have a fine refrigerator and are upset at the thought of paying for something they don't need. However, if the refrigerator is better than the one they presently own, they might feel that they are getting it ''free'' if it is included in the sale of the property. Until you know the situation, your best answer is a question.

"Do you want it to stay?"

If they don't, then you can tell the buyers either that it isn't included or that the owners would likely deduct an appropriate amount from the price if they don't want the appliance. If the prospective buyers want the refrigerator, tell them either that it is included or that the offer can be written to include the refrigerator.

The Opinion Trap

It is much better to ask prospective buyers their opinions than to volunteer your own. Suppose you are showing a couple the last, and to your mind, best, of three homes. Should you say something like this?

"This house is obviously the best value of the homes we have seen. While the second house has some fine features, you wouldn't want to live in that neighborhood."

Not if you want to sell a house. If your prospects were very much interested in the second house, your unsolicited opinion may well have lost the sale. A far better approach would have been:

"Of the three homes we have seen, which do you feel best meets your needs?"

This way you would have been in a position to reinforce the opinion of your prospects.

How Big?

Unless you are positive about the square footage of each home you show, avoid talking about it. Should your estimate prove too high, you could be successfully sued and assessed the value of the additional square feet you said were there.

Another problem about giving quotes is that customers will try to compare houses by price per square foot. This is comparing apples and oranges because costs vary tremendously with quality of construction. Should a prospective buyer state that a house is too expensive per square foot, you could reply:

"I can show you less expensive homes. We have some very nice tract homes."

If the prospective buyer is interested in a luxury home, the use of the word *tract* would make such homes seem common and less desirable.

When a customer specifically asks how many square feet a house contains, here is one good answer:

> *"The listing says_____square feet. However, listing figures are often supplied by the owner and could be inaccurate. If you like, I have a tape measure in my car and we could compute the actual square footage."*

If the prospects want to measure the house, there is an excellent chance that you will make a sale.

Have the prospects get involved with measuring and figuring. Let them give the dimensions while you hold the zero end of the tape. Let the prospects check your figures. If the actual measurements are less than anticipated, say:

> *"Either we made a mistake or the architect did an excellent job of space utilization, because I would have thought the house contained at least_____square feet."*

How Much Are Taxes?

If you stick to the absolute truth, you need never worry about what you said yesterday. Too often salespeople try to make the truth more palatable and end up getting into trouble. If a prospect asks you about taxes, anything but a straight answer is unethical and will lose you your credibility. Creating a feeling of trust requires complete honesty, and is the only way you can look forward to a long career in real estate.

If you don't know a tax answer, give an estimated range, but tell the prospective buyers you will get the exact figures and let them know within_____days. It isn't fair to guess when actuals can be obtained. Give an estimate only if you have enough expertise to know that it will be fairly accurate. Even then, make sure the prospects understand it is only your estimate.

TYING UP THE PROSPECT

If you let prospects run around to other brokers and answer sale ads on their own, you are wasting your time showing them property. You must attempt to tie them to you so you become their one channel to the real estate market. Be careful, though, not to try to tie up buyers before you have won their confidence by showing your interest in their needs and wants. Premature attempts to tie up prospects will be viewed as pushiness and drive your clients to less threatening competitors.

After you have shown your prospects a few homes and feel you have gained their trust, take them to your office. Get a commitment with this Power technique:

> *"I prefer to work with just a few serious buyers. I dedicate my efforts to finding them a property that best meets their needs. Usually I'm able to meet the needs of my buyers in just a few weeks. I am willing to work for you and concentrate my efforts on your behalf if you are serious buyers. At times buyers don't really have the down payment they say they have, or for some other reason are not in a position to buy. Are you serious buyers?"*

Your buyers can be expected to assure you that they are serious. Continue:

> *"If you are willing to let me take over the exclusive responsibility of finding the home you want, I will use all my efforts to locate the property that meets all your needs. If you see an ad that interests you, if you drive by a home you like, or even if you see an open house sign, call me about it. If another broker contacts you, tell that broker to call me and I will cooperate with him or her. If you are willing to work with me, I am willing to go all out for you. Does this seem fair?"*

The answer will usually be positive, and most people will live up to the agreement. Further, when you find a house that meets their needs, committed buyers will likely feel obligated to put in an offer when they might otherwise have procrastinated.

False Urgency

Many agents create a false sense of urgency by setting appointments for their listings at times when other agents have indicated they will be showing the property. They do this so that they will "run into" other agents and their prospects at the property. By telling their own prospects the home has had unusual activity and will probably sell quickly, and then having this reinforced by meeting another agent, the sense of urgency is enhanced. When buyers feel there is competition for a home they are more likely to make a reasonable offer. I feel strongly that this practice is unethical because it is based on deceit. There are plenty of ethical ways to sell real estate.

SELLING THE NEW HOUSE

A new home gives you some special benefits to explain:

> "A home is the only thing you can buy where new doesn't cost any more than old. Think about it. Your car can be practically new, but if you wanted to sell it you would take a terrific loss. The same holds true for used furniture and clothing, regardless of condition. But when you buy a new home, not only can it be resold for what you paid, you can usually make a profit. In addition, new means lower maintenance expense and the pleasure of owning something still fresh and clean."

Stop and Visit

If you see a friend or former buyer in a new subdivision that you are showing to prospects, stop and talk for a few moments. Introduce your prospective buyers as "possible new neighbors." Ask the neighbor how he or she likes the area and new home.

People who buy in new subdivisions will be very positive about their home and area. They are really justifying their own purchase and will be eager to help you sell others. Ask your prospects if they have any questions. Answers and opinions by a prospective neighbor will be accepted much more readily than if you had provided the information yourself.

Builder Concessions vs. Price Cuts

Often tract builders won't consider cutting prices or accepting lower-than-list offers because they fear trouble from other buyers who already have paid full price. They will sometimes agree to include extras instead, however. Buyers may find such extras more tempting than cash discounts.

> "The builder has agreed that for sales made this month [he/she] will include the G.E. refrigerator that's in the model home—the one that dispenses ice cubes and cold water. [He/She] will include the built-in Litton microwave oven as well."

Some people like luxury items such as fancy refrigerators and microwaves, but feel they can't buy them because other priorities should come first. Getting the special products "free" relieves them of this sense of guilt, and so may be a better sales point than a price reduction.

MANAGING THE OPEN HOUSE

Open houses serve a number of purposes. First of all, they are great for owner relations. Owners like open houses. They are something they can readily understand. They show the owners you are actively trying to sell their house.

Many serious buyers will attend an open house including people from other areas who are interested in relocating. Going to open houses seems less menacing to them than contacting a broker.

Open houses sell many homes at the first visit or later, and they also provide you with leads for listings. Because people don't feel committed when stopping at an open house, you will get many visitors who are thinking about a new home but have not yet placed their own home on the market. At this stage, this viewer is more a listing prospect than a buyer.

In choosing homes for open houses, give preference in the summer to homes with air-conditioning and in the winter to homes with natural fireplaces.

Preparing

Instruct the owners to have the house ready: The baths and kitchen should sparkle; the lighting should be checked (put larger bulbs in fixtures if needed); all drapes should be opened and all lights turned on, including outside lights. A house that appears as bright as possible seems larger and puts buyers in a better mood. In winter, a fire in the fireplace is a good idea. On hot summer days the air conditioner should be on, set a little cooler than normal.

One broker brings sheets of cookies and loaves of bread dough with her. She bakes during the open house, and the aroma of fresh bread and cookies says that this house is a home. The house becomes a very desirable place to live.

If you have an unfurnished model, consider plastic runners for the carpets. It shows respect for the property.

You might want to furnish the model. Often local stores will furnish it at no charge if your ads and signs show that it came from them. Even cooperative ads can be arranged, with the furniture store paying part of the cost. You can also provide an option to buy the property furnished.

Arrows and signs can be used effectively in model homes. An arrow at a light switch that reads *Silent Switch* or a sign in the laundry area stating, *Both 220 wiring and natural gas* helps make sure visitors notice all the desirable features.

Keep television sets off, but a radio turned low to an FM music station can help create a pleasant mood.

Of course you want the owners, children and pets gone during the open house.

Generating Interest

Use flags and signs. Arrows should direct traffic from the closest major street. Before you put up an arrow on someone else's lawn, stop and get permission. This is also a chance to give out one of your cards and make a new contact.

Go through your prospect file and call every prospect who might be interested in the property. Invite them to stop by. Some offices blanket the area with postcards telling residents about the open house. Besides helping to generate traffic for the open house this also shows owners the effort you place on marketing and aids future listing efforts.

Canvass the area an hour or two prior to the open house. Tell the neighbors about your open house. Ask if they have friends interested in relocating to the area. Be sure to leave a card with every contact.

If your office will have a number of open houses in the area, hand out a mimeographed map showing the route to each open house from the others. This directs traffic attracted to one house to several more open houses.

I knew the cheapest broker of all time. He never advertised open houses but was always holding them. He waited until Saturday afternoon when the early edition of the Sunday newspapers came out. He would find large open house ads, then make last minute arrangements in areas where he had listings. Then he used signs and arrows to divert traffic going elsewhere to his open house. Actually, if an open house is on or close to a well-traveled street, ads are not essential. The arrows and signs can generate a lot of traffic.

In areas where signs are not allowed for open houses, brokers put magnetic open house signs on their cars and park them in the driveway. Check first to see whether your municipality allows such signs. Some communities require every sign to be registered and a fee paid.

Turning Visitors into Clients

A registration book by the front door is a must. Some brokers bring along a stand to hold the registration book. The book should call for name, address and phone number. Rather than using just a registration book, ask people to complete the following evaluation card.

HOME EVALUATION

	Positive	Satisfactory	Negative
Home Size	☐	☐	☐
Area	☐	☐	☐
Floor Plan	☐	☐	☐
Price	☐	☐	☐

Special features I like _____

_____

_____

_____

Comments _____

_____

_____

☐ I expect to buy a home within the next six months.
☐ I am not in the market for a home.

Name _____
Address _____
Phone No. _____

People will fill in the information if you ask them and if it is easy. Be sure to supply a pen with the card. The information you get back will give you not only prospects, but a good picture of how people rate the house.

One way to keep people from running in and leaving quickly is to have a full coffee pot and plastic cups on a table. People who take a cup of coffee will be yours for a few minutes of questioning.

"Do you own the home you are living in?"

"Have you placed your home on the market yet?"

"How long have you been looking for a new home?"

Also ask questions on price range, size, area and other qualifying information.

Some people have their phone calls transferred to the open house number. I don't like this because a call could interrupt at a crucial time. Take the phone off the hook to prevent interruptions.

When a number of prospects arrive at once, give them your card and tell them you will be with them in a few minutes.

People will tell you, "We're just looking," even though they are serious buyers. They are afraid of being hassled. Let them look but have them fill out an evaluation card.

In order to increase the percentage of lookers who will sign your guest book or will fill out evaluation cards, use the would-you-be-offended technique.

> *"Would you be offended if I asked you to please complete our guest registry?"*

It is a good idea to call your open house visitors the following day. Ask them for their "frank opinion." People like to give opinions. Follow up with some qualifying questions and an appointment to see other homes or to further discuss—this means *buy*—the open house.

SHOWING SPECIAL PROPERTIES

Not all showings take place in average homes, but Power Selling methods work in any situation. This section tells how you can apply them to a variety of special cases.

The Fixer-Upper

Before showing a fixer-upper, be sure your buyers are specifically interested in this type of property. When showing, consider a statement like this:

> *"I wouldn't show this next home to many people. You see, most people look at property the way it is now, not the way it could be. They lack the imagination to visualize the changes that paint, carpeting and a few minor repairs can create. Because most people want everything done for them, this home offers an exceptional opportunity for people with both imagination and willingness to do a little work."*

What you have done here is pictured the buyers as they picture themselves.

During the showing, ask questions about how the prospects would deal with the house's problem areas.

"Would you tile the family room or carpet it with the rest of the house?"

"Can anything be done about the front yard? All those plants look so shabby."

"How much paint do you think it would take to paint the house inside and out?"

When you get the answers, say:

"Then, if the paint cost $10 a gallon, for only $_____ you could have the home completely repainted inside and out."

What you are doing, of course, is having the buyers visualize how they will fix up the house.

Here is another Power statement for such situations:

"You know, I just realized there is a big advantage to buying a home that needs everything. When you are through, you'll have a house that reflects you, not some previous owner. I know that when I purchased my present home I wasn't happy with the new interior painting, but since it had been recently done, I lived with it for four years before I got around to repainting the way I wanted it. That was four years of being unhappy with a color I hated. You won't be stuck with the taste of a previous owner."

Point out that while it is difficult, a buyer who can visualize the house as it might be will have a unique opportunity. You are not asking for a low offer, but prospective buyers will realize that because of the way the house shows it will not readily sell unless the owners make concessions.

The fixer-upper approach can also be used for homes that are not fixer-uppers but simply victims of horrible decorating. Beautiful homes may need new paint, carpeting and even different tile because of the very individualistic taste of a previous owner. Again, you must get the buyers to visualize the house after they've changed it to suit their taste. The same holds true for homes furnished in Neo-Ugly or Salvation Army Modern. Emphasize that few people are able to visualize the changes, but if they can, they have a unique opportunity.

Recreational Land

In showing recreational land, point out:

"We are experiencing an increase in population and an increase in leisure time. State and federal park systems are overloaded. They can't meet the needs of the people. In addition, many of the camp-sites are overcrowded and dirty. If you want a place away from

crowds and pollution where you and your family can relax and enjoy nature together, you are going to have to buy recreational land now. With the increased demand for good recreational land, the prices in a few years could make the purchase prohibitive. Whether it's for weekends, vacations, retirement or for your children and grandchildren, now is the time to buy."

While showing recreational property, a statement such as either of the following can be effective:

"Can you imagine living among this beauty?"

"Every time I come up here I hate to leave."

When selling California recreational land, I had a huge map that had to opened on the floor. I would lay it on the carpeting and get down on my knees, showing the exact location of the parcel and its relationship to recreational areas of interest. I found that usually the husband would get down on the floor beside me and often the wife as well. This mutual involvement would go a long way toward setting the proper attitude and relationship for the sale.

The Expensive Home

In selling a very expensive home or a second home, don't overlook investment potential. Often people want to buy, but they consider the home a luxury they can't justify. You can help them get what they want.

Statements like the following will generally result in a negative response:

"How have you done in the stock market over the last few years?"

Now, continue with:

"What has happened to the value of your real estate in the same period of time?"

"Do you know anyone who today is sorry they invested in real estate twelve years ago?"

"While stocks have yo-yoed or gone sideways or plunged, values in real estate have tripled or more. Because of the leverage possible, many owners have made over 1,000 percent on their investments in just those few years. Pension plans have turned to real estate because they realize that in the long run it's safer than stocks."

"A home today [or second home] is a lot more than shelter. It's a forward-looking investment that will provide you with future se-

curity. It's an integral part of your total investment package. The pleasure your home ownership gives you is just an additional bonus the investment offers."

Retirement Housing

When showing homes in a mobile home park or retirement village to buyers interested in a retirement home, first stop at the activity center or clubhouse. Point out the recreational activities. When prospective buyers see people they can relate to busy doing things, it sets a positive mood. They can imagine themselves living there. If the development has a daily or weekly activity sheet or newspaper, go over it with your prospects. If there is a list of clubs and organizations in the development, have one available for your prospects. Chances are good one or more will be of interest to them. You can presell the way of life offered by the development.

Income Property

Income property buyers are normally more sophisticated than home buyers. Be fully prepared to answer their questions. Have expense and income figures as well as a pro forma statement showing estimated future income. A five-year projection is an excellent selling tool. It gives a buyer an opportunity to analyze your projections. Many buyers are very interested in income property—even when the property's present income provides a substandard return on equity—if the anticipated future earnings meet or exceed their desired return.

While showing income property, if access is not available to all units, make certain the units shown are representative. Features to be emphasized besides tax benefits and spendable income include the rental history of the property and area, low maintenance features, management, presently raisable rents, future likelihood of significant rental increases and lack of rent control.

Setting Up Your Own Investment Syndicate

You probably have had many people tell you, "If you ever come across a really good investment be sure to let me know." When you do let these people know often they will look and hesitate. Although they may be interested in a real estate investment they are also afraid of a real estate investment. An effective way to harvest these would-be investors is with a simple phone call stating:

> *"You indicated you were interested in a real estate investment if something exceptional came along. I am putting together a small group in which I will also be an investor to buy an exceptional property. Could you have $10,000 to invest this Saturday?"*

Give no information on the property over the phone. All you want to know is if he or she can invest $10,000 on Saturday. If you receive an affirmative answer, continue with:

> *"We are meeting at my home at 2 P.M. on Saturday to discuss the property. Can you be there with your checkbook?"*

Because you have said nothing about the property, your contact will be intrigued. You have an excellent chance of bringing him or her to the meeting if they can afford such an investment.

At the meeting after everyone is introduced, discuss the property and its benefits. Go to the property in several cars for a viewing and then return to your home. Ask those who are not interested to please leave while the rest discuss the property further.

Your share should be approximately 25 percent of the net after the return of investments plus a ten percent per annum return for investors. In addition, you should receive five percent to ten percent of the gross (if it's an income property) for management. Your cash investment should be treated like any other investor. Be certain you fully reveal that you will also receive a commission for the purchase of the property and its eventual resale.

This type of syndication allows small investors to get a piece of a prime property. It reduces the fear of investing because other investors act as a crutch for each other. The fact that you are investing yourself will give credence to the quality of the investment.

Naturally, if you are licensed as a salesperson rather than a broker, this arrangement will have to be approved by your broker. Have an attorney prepare all contracts and review offering material. In small offerings it is possible to avoid security registration. (In some states syndicates with a small number of investors, such as ten or less, are exempt from state security registration. Your attorney can advise you as to your state law.)

In this type of purchase you would be the general partner and other investors would be limited partners.The beauty of syndication is that after one syndicate has been successful, the same investors and their friends and relatives will be eager for further investments. Further syndicates can then be put together easily with or without your direct cash investment. Your return would then be purchase and sale commissions, management fees and profit upon resale.

Lots

Although you can view many lots right from your car, don't do it. Walk the lots with your clients. A Power sales technique is to actually stake out a house so your prospects can visualize its setting.

> "How large a home do you think you would be building on this site, [Mr./Mrs.] Jones?"

> "Would your home likely be one-story or two-story?"

> "A 2,000-square-foot home with an attached garage would likely be about 60 feet by 40 feet. Is that about the size home you envisioned?"

> "Let's roughly stake out the lot so you can envision how the home would be sited on your property."

With stakes and a hammer you can measure or pace off the structure. Get the buyers involved in the process. Once they have staked "their" house you will have significantly increased your likelihood of getting an offer. By staking the house the lot also appears larger.

Raw Land

Raw land often looks unimpressive. You can take advantage of this fact.

> "Now, raw land looks just that, raw and undeveloped. Most people lack the foresight to see what will happen on this land in just a few short years. People with vision have made tremendous fortunes on land such as this."

In selling a farm or orchard to an investor, consider:

> "This is more than just a farm which produces food; it produces another crop year after year: tax deductions. This is a tax farm."

> "Ronald Reagan found that puttering around the ranch was the source of his greatest relaxation. It's a lot better than Valium, and your income will be sheltered by tax deductions."

A different approach would be:

> "People may not buy new cars from Detroit, but as long as we have people, we will need food. Food-producing land is the surest investment you can make."

THE NONBUYER

People who are not really buyers can waste a great deal of your time. These people may simply want to check out an area as to possibly relocating or retiring. In such a case they will be unlikely to buy even the perfect home for them until they first make the relocation decision. Other people are looking because of a possible job or job transfer to the area, in which case the job is a condition precedent to any decision—the job could be some time away. Other people are simply out for decorating ideas for their own homes. They won't tell you these things, of course, because they want you to show them around. Ways to spot people who are not buyers or who are not yet ready to buy are:

1. They generally are quite positive about the homes. They like the homes they see, but want to keep looking.
2. They view homes fairly quickly.
3. They ask about several other areas.
4. They resist trial closings by asking to see more homes.
5. They are not specific about their down payment or earnings or both.

If your prospects have four out of five of the above characteristics, chances are good they're not buyers.

WORD PICTURES

For descriptive terms that can help you provide desirable verbal impressions of a home, turn to *Words and Phrases of Power Selling*, which begins on page 219.

6. Overcoming Buyer Objections

How you handle buyer objections will determine whether the selling process moves to a closing or ends in wasted time and effort. The successful salesperson views objections not as events to be feared and resented, but as opportunities to bring the prospect nearer to making a buying decision. Through the use of role-playing exercises, this chapter leads you through proven responses to objections you will meet in actual sales situations. You will learn to use your imagination to regularly turn objections into sales ammunition.

The Power Selling approach to dealing with objections makes use of a simple idea: Once a prospect tells you what is wrong with a house, he or she is also saying "If it weren't for this feature, I'd be ready to buy." Your job is to emphasize that connection in the prospect's mind.

> *"Now if I understand you correctly, the reason you don't wish to purchase this house is* _____*."*

The buyer will usually agree. If you overcome the objection, you could be ready for a closing.

Often prospective buyers will seem unresponsive to your presentation. If they resist, they probably have an objection. The way to uncover objections is simple—ask questions:

"Is there something I haven't fully explained?"

"Is there something I should know?"

"If you were building this home today, are there any significant changes you would make?"

Try not to misread your buyer. If the buyer is not interested in a property, don't try to force a sale. The probable result will be that someone else will end up selling your buyer.

THE WHY APPROACH

If an objection is unclear or unsubstantial, you can use the children's winning one-word argument: "Why?" Asking why often clarifies or eliminates objections. Asking why can reveal that "I don't like the living room" really only refers to the decorating. This, of course, can be overcome.

Rather than responding, "Why?" to a specific objection, you could answer:

"What exactly is there about the _____ that you don't like?"

If the objection were the backyard it could be the size, fence, flowers or just a particular tree. If you don't know exactly what the objection is, you cannot overcome it.

Asking questions like "What if you _____?" or "Couldn't you _____?" allows a prospect to solve a problem without feeling that you have done the persuading. When that happens, the prospective buyer moves a step closer to seeing himself or herself as the property's owner.

When prospects solve a problem, compliment them on their successful effort:

"You are absolutely right. All that is needed is paneling for the one wall. I had thought the entire room would require replastering. It is obvious, [Mr./Mrs.] Parker, that you have had quite a bit of experience in interior designing."

EXCUSES VS. OBJECTIONS

Often what is presented as an objection will turn out to be an excuse to avoid a decision or to slow down a transaction that threatens to develop too fast. The buyer might be interested in the property but feels threatened by normal buyer fears.

If you think an objection is really just an excuse, you can suggest:

> *"I would like to set that aside for just a few minutes and we will get back to it a little later."*

If the objection *is* merely an excuse, chances are good the prospective buyers will not bring it up again. If the prospects do raise the objection a second time, it has to be answered.

Never belittle a prospective buyer's objections. If you make a prospect look silly, the prospect will never develop into a buyer, at least as far as you are concerned.

ANTICIPATING THE OBJECTION

If you feel certain that an objection will be raised or a problem noticed, raise it yourself and then overcome it, treating it as a minor detail. If the living room carpet has a burned area several inches wide, tell the prospects:

> *"I have checked with Collins Carpeting. They can replace the burned section with carpeting from the hall closet. They will then tile the hall closet floor. Because of the pattern, Collins Carpeting guarantees that the patch will not be detectable. They estimate the total cost will be under one hundred dollars."*

DON'T LOSE BY WINNING

In dealing with buyer objections, don't be argumentative. It's hard to make a sale after you have won an argument. Instead, be understanding and agreeable:

> *"I understand how you feel, but _____."*

> *"You are absolutely right, but have you considered _____?"*

> *"I am glad you mentioned that. You are certainly discerning. I was going to explain _____."*

NEGATIVES TO POSITIVES

If you turn a negative feature into a positive one, you've moved a step nearer to obtaining an offer. If the buyers solve the problem themselves, the outlook gets even better. When [Mr./Mrs.] Jones says, "Oh! This bedroom is way too small!" you might respond:

> *"[Mr./Mrs.] Jones, perhaps you could help me. If this were your home, whose room would this be?"*

or,

> *"How would you use this room?"*

Should [Mr./Mrs.] Jones's response be, "I guess it would have to be Tim's room," you could ask:

> *"How would you furnish and decorate this room for a seven-year-old boy like Tim?"*

If the prospective buyers can come up with a solution, they will have solved their own problem, and in the process begun to see themselves as the owners decorating and furnishing the room. The buyers' own solutions are much more valuable than ones you suggest.

If a prospective buyer doesn't know how a small room should be furnished, and from the family size you know a small room isn't needed as a bedroom, offer a solution yourself.

> *"[Mr./Mrs.] Jones, am I right in assuming that this room would be used as an office or guest room?"*

Suggest it could be furnished using a convertible sofa, so that the room could be used as an office for daily use and converted to a guest room when needed.

Should there be an objection such as, "I don't like the decorating!" this response will help the buyer solve the problem:

> *"[Mr./Mrs.] Kaiser, perhaps you can help me. I have been in your home and you have excellent taste. If this were your house, how would you recommend decorating it?"*

As [Mr./Mrs.] Kaiser tells you what he or she would do, he or she will end up looking at the house in a different light, eager to start the redecorating.

Objections You Can't Fix

Some objections will be difficult or impossible to overcome. Treat such objections as excuses and set them aside. If the objection is brought up again and you cannot overcome it, try to outweigh it with positive features. Get the prospects to make a chart listing positive features in the first column and negative ones in the second. When you study the result together, emphasize how many more positive features your buyers have listed.

POWER RESPONSES TO BUYER OBJECTIONS: THE HOUSE

The objections you encounter while showing a property will prove as varied as the buyers' personalities and the quirks of each house. Nonetheless, the vast majority of objections can be predicted in advance. What follows is a handbook of common objections and specific remedies to use in overcoming them. First, objections to the property itself.

"But There's No..."

What if a house meets the prospects' needs in all but one point? If the lacking feature could be added easily, there is no problem. If not, you can outweigh the lack with a Power approach like this:

"You wanted a three-bedroom, two-bath home on the South Side. This is a three-bedroom, two-bath house on the South Side.

"You wanted a rear-facing kitchen. This house has a rear-facing kitchen.

"You wanted a fenced yard. This house has a fenced yard.

"You wanted a double garage. This house has a double garage.

"You wanted room to park your camper. This house has space to park your camper.

"You wanted a family room. This house has a family room.

"You wanted a brick home. This is a brick home.

"You wanted a home under $90,000. This home is priced under $90,000.

"Doesn't the fact that this is a three-bedroom, two-bath home on the South Side with a rear-facing kitchen, fenced yard, double garage, room for a camper and a price under $90,000 far outweigh the fact that it does not have a fireplace?"

Treat this as a rhetorical question and continue with:

"Doesn't this house meet your needs more than any other house you have seen in this price range?"

"This House Doesn't Have a Pool; I Told You I Wanted a Pool."

Once again, the objection can be made into an advantage.

"That's exactly why I am showing you this house, [Mr./Mrs.] Borden, because of its pool-size lot. We can arrange to have a pool included in the mortgage. With a new pool you needn't worry about leaky valves and costly repairs. I have an estimate for a thirty-two-foot, kidney-shaped pool with a hot spa, gas heater, pool light and three feet of cool decking for under $12,000. The home is listed for $82,000, so with the pool it is still well under the $100,000 you indicated as your limit. Doesn't having a brand-new pool make sense to you?"

"I Don't Need a Furnished House."

"Comparing the price of this home, including furniture, with comparable unfurnished homes, I don't think you are really paying for the furniture."

or,

"I don't think you are paying more than $_____ for the furniture."

"I would suggest that after the purchase, you donate the furniture to one of your favorite charities. Not only will it be appreciated, but you will get a tax benefit that could end up making your purchase of this house a bargain."

If your purchasers are fairly sophisticated, suggest that the purchase offer price the furniture separately. Your buyer would want to maximize the furniture costs to set as high a cost basis as is realistically possible for a donation to charity. If the buyer plans to rent out the property, a high value on the furniture will help with depreciation deductions. Don't underestimate this special tax appeal.

"It's All Wrong for My Furniture."

Suppose a prospective buyer stated, "Oh, this home won't do! We just purchased a new formal dining room set and it would be out of place in this dining area."

An appropriate response would be:

"Aside from the dining room, does the home otherwise meet your needs?"

If the answer is positive, you could state:

"I have an idea. Perhaps the owner could use your dining room set. If the owner would be willing to accept your dining room set at its full value as part of the down payment, would you want to buy this home? What did you pay for your dining room set?"

"It's Rather Small."

As a response you can make this a positive attribute:

"That's one of the reasons I wanted to show you this house. It has excellent utilization of space, which provides not only convenient living, but also results in realistic heating and cooling costs.

"Because of higher energy costs, we have designed automobiles such as the Cadillac Seville and the Mercedes into smaller luxury packages. The builder did the same thing for this home; [he/she] packaged luxury living in a convenient and efficient manner that avoids wasted areas."

"I Didn't Want a Two-Story Home."

This objection will probably be raised as soon as you arrive at the house. Again, you can turn it into a sales point.

"I want you to see this house because I regard it as special, and I think after seeing it you will agree with me. Of course, from a practical viewpoint, two-story homes offer much more economical heating than a one-story home of the same square footage.

"I am sure you will agree after seeing this house that it offers a lot more home for the money. Personally, what I like about a two-story house is that it provides a solid feeling, a feeling of prestige that single-story homes seldom seem to have."

This response gives some practical reasons and finishes with a little "snob" appeal. The prestige approach has sold many colonial homes to buyers who set out to buy a ranch home.

"I Didn't Want an Older Home."

Your first response to this remark should be to ask, "Why?" To counter objections, you must know specific reasons. Here are some of the points in favor of older homes:

"The old notion that new is better than old doesn't apply to housing. Older housing doesn't mean less desirable housing. Buyers who can afford to buy any home often seek out older homes."

"This isn't just another boxy tract home. This house expresses its own individual character in a way that's rare today."

"Craftsmanship like this has become a thing of the past. Today's new homes are put together with power staplers and mucilage."

"I love older homes such as this one because they allow you to breathe. Most new homes today try to get everything they can into a small suffocating space."

"You won't get mature landscaping like this in a new home. To put in this type of landscaping would cost over $10,000 for the trees alone."

"The character of this neighborhood has already been formed. You don't have to worry about a cracker-box home being built next to you on a lot the size of a postage stamp. Such a home could seriously reduce the value of your home."

"With an older home you don't have to worry about special assessments for sewer, water, curb, gutters, streets and sidewalks. Everything here is not only in place, it is all paid for."

WARNING—Don't downgrade newer homes unless you know the buyers will be unable to buy one, or you feel strongly that the older home best meets the buyers' needs.

"I Don't Like the Location."

You can cure many things about a house, but you are stuck with its location. If you feel the location meets the buyers' needs, point out the positive features. Pointing out people who live in an area to whom your buyers can relate will often dispel a misconception that the location isn't desirable. Your references to neighbors should never be racially oriented.

Don't regard any location as bad. A location less desirable because of its features will be compensated by a lower price. Some buyers simply can't afford the areas and homes they would like. If this is the case, present the property as a stepping stone toward the home the buyers want.

"Look at this home as an investment in your future. Not only will it provide you with a place to live, it will give you a chance to build the equity needed to trade up to a home in the Lake Aire district. If you studied owners of homes in Lake Aire, you would find very

few owners who purchased those homes before owning houses elsewhere. Most have owned two, three or even more homes, moving up as they were able to afford better housing. The equity that inflation, as well as their monthly payments, gave them allowed them to buy their fine homes in the same manner that this home will be your first step toward the home you really want to own."

The following approach often works well with blue-collar buyers:

"This home on the West Side would cost you at least $30,000 more. That's an additional payment of over $400 a month. That's enough to pay for a Cadillac, a camper or a lot of other things that make life a lot more fun."

Generally, the more highly educated the buyers, the more they are concerned with location. Educated buyers will often sacrifice more for good location.

POWER RESPONSES TO BUYER OBJECTIONS: THE FINANCES

The property may seem perfect, but financing and costs open up a whole new world of possible buyer objections, from an unwillingness to pay the list price to fear of taking on the responsibility of a mortgage. Applying Power Selling techniques helps you turn such objections around.

"The Price Is Too High."

When this objection is raised you are in the position for a quick closing. Your response should be:

"Why do you feel the price is too high?"

If the purchaser can justify a lower price, go for an offer at the lower price. Keep in mind you have a duty to the owners. Don't jump to write a low offer without attempting to improve it.

"I Could Buy the Same House on the East Side for $10,000 Less."

Even if you disagree with your prospective buyer's statement, don't argue. A better approach is to agree.

"I am sure you can find a home in other areas for less money—but is that what you really want? Homes in less desirable areas will not

have anywhere near the appreciation of homes in the really choice areas. In addition, owners find that area affects stability. In order to sell homes in less desirable areas, owners find they have to make price concessions. We really rate value by the quality of life a home offers. This includes not only the house itself but other factors such as neighborhood, neighbors and security. I don't think you are the kind of person who is willing to accept what is second-best for your family."

"It's More Than I Wanted To Spend."

Counter with a view of the house as an investment.

"Investment counselors recommend buying the most expensive home you can afford even if it hurts. These are the homes that get the greatest appreciation. Besides increasing in value, inflation will actually reduce your payments. Payments which may now seem to be a heavy burden are, in a few years, likely to seem modest. A few years ago most people complained about crossing the $500 barrier; today a great many people would love to have a payment that low. With inflation you can't afford not to afford this home. With just ten percent annual inflation in real estate values, this home will be worth 50 percent more than it is worth today in a little over four years."

Keep in mind that what customers want to spend and what they can spend are not the same. You will be helping buyers if you can convince them that they can and should afford the home you are presenting. I have a friend who saves listings for many years. He shows a prospective buyer a listing from five or ten years previous and says:

"Wouldn't you like to be able to buy a home like this today at these prices?"

When he gets an agreement he continues:

"Five years from now I probably will be sitting at this desk talking to another couple seated where you are and I will pull out the listing on this house. I will ask them if they wouldn't like to buy this home today at the price on this old listing? Of course they would, because there are three things of which we can be certain—death, taxes and rising real estate prices."

If the price of a home is $10,000 more than a buyer wants to pay, you could say:

"You will probably live in this house for thirty years. That's 360 months. If we divide $10,000 by 360, it comes to less than $30 a month in costs. Isn't having a home like this worth that small difference?"

Actual stories of people you know who didn't buy when they had the chance and are now sorry can help make your point. With one recalcitrant buyer, I followed up a "horror story" with:

> "You may feel I am pushing you and you are right, I am. I never want you to say, 'I wish Bill Pivar had pushed me a little harder to buy when I could have afforded that house.' Believe me, I am pushing as hard as I can."

Some buyers act like Jesse James without the mask. They don't want to pay a fair price, they just want to steal a property. This approach may work on such buyers:

> "If you look long enough and continue to try, you will eventually be able to buy a home below its market value. You might save as much as ten percent. Any greater reduction could not realistically be expected. While a ten percent reduction would be a real bargain, it's going to take a long time to find such a bargain. Before you get your bargain, prices are likely to increase by 15 percent. That won't be much of a bargain for you. Actually, bargains are possible today, but price is not the only bargain. A below-market interest rate with owner financing can be equivalent in savings to a substantial price reduction."

Keep in mind that owners will generally be more receptive to better terms for the buyers than a reduction in price even when the net effect is the same. Through terms it is often possible to satisfy your Jesse James buyer.

When you have a prospective buyer who thinks prices will come down if he or she waits, ask the buyer:

> "How would you feel today if you had delayed buying ten years ago because you expected prices to come down? No more land is being made, so we can't expect an increase in supply to reduce prices. Most of the cost of a new home is really wages. Do you expect the unions to significantly reduce their wages in the future?"

When a prospective buyer objects to the price on a new home, an excellent approach is:

> "The builder hasn't raised [his/her] prices yet."

A statement such as this lessens the likelihood of a prospective buyer making a low offer. It can also help spur an offer, as it indicates an urgency to buy now.

"The Taxes Are Too High!"

"Taxes reflect the value. The taxes on this home are higher than on some of the homes you have seen in the same price range because the tax assessor believes this home is worth more than those other homes. I agree with the tax assessor in that I believe the house should justify a much higher selling price than is being asked. If the taxes were too low, you should really worry, as this would indicate the assessor didn't think much of the house."

This Power approach turns taxes that appear high into a positive feature.

For prospective buyers in higher tax brackets, you can also point out:

"Since property taxes are a deductible expense for federal income tax, Uncle Sam really will be paying a large part of the property tax bill for you."

Ownership Fee

A prospective buyer might object to a condominium owner fee or a fee to maintain a common recreational area. Point out:

"Maintenance fees are based on ownership. You actually own a percentage of all of these recreational facilities and the fees are paid by all of the owners. The fees are far less than you would have to pay as an individual owner for the amenities gained. In addition, you can expect the value of common areas to increase as well as the value of your home. This will be reflected in what you will receive on resale."

"I Can't Make That Large a Down Payment."

Many people don't really understand what they have in assets. For example, insurance policy loans have provided down payments for thousands of buyers. Besides borrowing a down payment using the buyers' collateral for a loan, it is possible to borrow the credit of another for a down payment. A relative cosigning on a loan is often the answer to obtaining the down payment.

Buyers who have other property can create their own down payment by giving a second mortgage on their property as a down payment for the new purchase.

Down payments don't have to be in money; I have had deals involving cars and even an outboard motor. Find out what barter property your prospective buyer has to offer. Today many buyers are using diamonds and other precious jewels as down payments on property.

For a discussion of ways to arrange purchases using little or no money, read my *Get Rich on Other People's Money* (Arco, 1981).

"The Interest Is Too High."

There are a number of responses to objections about high-interest loans:

> *"What interest rate are you currently getting on your savings?"*

If the answer is eight percent, continue with:

> *"The assumable loan is at 11 percent interest, which means the net cost to you is only three percent more than you are receiving on your savings."*

As an alternative, you can state:

> *"No one likes to pay high interest, but as long as we have inflation, we have to live with it. There is one bright spot and that is that Uncle Sam ends up paying a large part of it. Interest is a deductible expense for income tax purposes. If your adjusted gross income for you and your spouse is over $40,000, the chances are your top dollar in earnings is taxed at 33 1/3 percent (state and federal). In that case, 15 percent interest really only amounts to ten percent because Uncle Sam pays the five percent for you.*

Carry the tax table sheets for federal taxes with you to show the actual rates. If the prospects are likely to be in the top tax brackets, assume they are. Even if you are wrong, they will be flattered.

> *"Since you are probably in the 33 1/3 percent tax bracket for combined state and federal taxes, [Mr./Mrs.] Stockman, your actual cost for 12 percent interest is only eight percent. Don't you believe we can expect at least eight percent inflation in real estate values? Eight percent inflation would effectively cancel out all interest cost. Does zero interest appeal to you, [Mr./Mrs.] Stockman?"*

A similar approach:

> *"If I could get you eight percent financing, would you be interested in buying this home?"*

You then show the buyers that in the 33 1/3 percent combined federal and state tax brackets the 12 percent interest really costs them only eight percent. The interest deduction is one of the few tax advantages left for taxpayers. Be sure your buyers fully understand the tax advantage.

As an alternative approach, consider:

"Yes, I agree with you, interest rates are too high and they are likely to stay high. The reason they are high is because of inflation. Prices are high, too, but they will continue to rise, don't you agree? That is why a purchase now is in your best interest."

"I'll Wait Until Interest Rates Go Down."

"How far do you expect them to go down? I wouldn't expect more than two points if they go down at all, but, let us instead say four points. For a $100,000 loan, that amounts to $4,000 per year. Now how long would you expect it to be before rates drop? Let us say three years. Four thousand dollars times three years equals $12,000 paid in higher interest. Now, that is a worst-case scenario. But, consider what happens as interest rates fall. The number of buyers increase and we have demand-pull inflation, it never fails. In this case, a four percent drop in rates would mean a higher sales price, higher by far than the $12,000 paid in increased interest. Few buyers are sophisticated enough to realize that the best purchase opportunities are when interest rates are high and most buyers have left the market. Don't you want to take advantage of this buyer's market?"

Another Power response is:

"Interest rates are too high. I fully agree with you; however, because interest rates are so high you have a rare opportunity. Sellers know that high interest rates deter buyers. When there is high interest such as this there is a buyer's market with many sellers and few buyers. In order to sell, sellers know they must reduce prices. They know that former top market prices are not possible today.

"You have indicated that you are willing to pay $100,000 for a home. Assume you were to pay $20,000 down. That would mean $80,000 financed. At the current 11 percent interest the payment would be $761 per month for a 30-year loan. You would pay 11 percent if you could get a 11 percent loan, wouldn't you?" [Quote a rate two percent less than current rates so it will seem a bargain.]

"Let us assume instead you had to pay 13 percent interest, but you could get the same home for $90,000 rather than $100,000. Assuming $20,000 down, your payments on the $70,000 loan at 13 percent would be almost identical to the payments on an $80,000 loan at 11 percent. What I am saying is that because of the market, lower prices are possible that more than make up for the interest differential. To make higher interest even more attractive to you, remember that you can refinance at a lower rate when interest declines—which would mean a significantly lower monthly payment.

"Do you know what is going to happen when interest rates decline? There will be a lot more buyers around and, when buyers outnumber sellers, prices increase rapidly. There is no better time for a bargain than now, when interest rates are high."

"The Mortgage Payments Are More Than My Rent."

"Certainly the monthly payments are greater than rent, but your payments stop when the property is paid for. Rent goes on forever."

"When you buy, you know what your payments will be in five years. What will your rent be five years from today?"

"How much rent are you now paying, [Mr./Mrs.] Jones?"

"Let's assume for a moment that you live another forty years. That would mean 480 more monthly rental checks. Assume also that you have the nicest landlord in the world and for the next forty years your rent doesn't go up one dime. Let's see, that's $600 times 480, or $288,000, over 1/4 million dollars. That's a lot of money, but it would be a great deal more if your landlord raises the rent as landlords generally do. Tell me, [Mr./Mrs.] Jones, what will those 480 rent receipts do for your family?"

Here is a different approach to the same objection:

"While the rent payment would be less than your payments as a purchaser, it is actually cheaper to buy than to rent. Uncle Sam helps make the mortgage payments. Most of your payments will be taxes and interest, both of which are deductible expenses for federal and state income tax. If you are in the 33 1/3 percent tax bracket for the top dollar of your income (combined state and federal taxes), then a $900 house payment actually costs you only $600 because the government gives you $300 back in tax savings. The government encourages home ownership through its taxes. By not owning a home, you are failing to take advantage of a benefit offered you. Don't you deserve a tax benefit?"

For additional persuasive reasoning, see *Special Cases—The Renter* in Chapter Seven.

"I'll Get Stuck with All the Maintenance Costs."

A strong response would be:

"Renters pay for the maintenance, too. When you rent, you not only pay for the space the same as you do when you are buying, but you also reimburse the landlord for maintenance expense and a profit on top of that."

"I'd Better Rent for a While."

An interesting response to this statement would be:

> *"Do you agree that it would re reasonable to expect a ten percent rent increase each year? If you are currently paying $600 a month rent and if that rent were to increase ten percent each year, in only five years your monthly rental would be over $960, and in ten years it would mean a rent per month of over $1,550. We don't know how much your rent will increase in the future, but we can be sure it's going up. My ten percent per year could well be a serious underestimation of future inflation. By buying now, you will not only gain equity by inflation, but you will protect yourself against exorbitant future rents."*

As huge as those figures are, they are factual. Letting prospective buyers continue to rent is a disservice to them.

Similar statements can be adapted to meet any situation.

> *"Renting simply delays a decision. In the meantime, not only are prices rising, but the quality of your life will suffer."*

> *"Once you rent, it's easy to remain a renter. If you went through any apartment building, you would find that most of the tenants today wish they had purchased a home when they first had an opportunity to do so."*

> *"Renters don't get involved in the community. Renting does not give you a sense of belonging, a sense of having roots. Do you want to be a nomad, living at the mercy of some landlord's whims?"*

"The Financing Is Too Complicated."

Financing arrangements are a mystery to many buyers, and people fear what they don't understand. While prospects might not voice their concerns, the concern will be there, and should be overcome.

During the qualifying process you obtained detailed information on your prospective buyers' financial abilities. Now show your prospects how the proposed down payment and monthly payments fit their abilities. Don't use terms like *wraparound* or *carryback seconds*. Use simple language so your prospects fully understand what you are proposing. If there are balloon payments, prepayment penalties and so on, make sure they are fully explained. You should also assure your prospects that you will be there to help them with financial arrangements.

"I'm Worried About My Job [or the Economy]."

Try this reply:

> *"We are all concerned about _____. It's only natural. However, we can't live our lives in fear of what might happen. If we allowed our decisions to be governed by possible calamities, the only real estate any of us would ever buy is a grave-site."*

"If Anything Should Happen to Me, My Family Couldn't Make the Payments."

Consider using the following response:

> *"It's wise to be concerned about your family. That's why I was going to suggest a mortgage insurance policy. For just a few dollars you can provide complete protection for your family. In the event of your untimely death or even disability, your mortgage will be paid off by the insurance company. Not only does this remove the burden of payments from your family, it also provides them a home, a place to live that is fully paid for."*

"I Want To Sell My Present Home First."

If the prospects are financially able to buy without selling, I suggest:

> *"If you wait to buy until your home is sold, you will be under pressure to buy quickly. You could end up with a home you are not really satisfied with. Also, when you must buy, you are not in as strong a bargaining position as you are now. When an owner knows you must buy, concessions as to price and terms are not likely. But when you don't have to buy, you are the one negotiating from the position of strength."*

In some cases it might be proper to suggest that prospects refinance their present property and use the cash to purchase their new property. Having obtained cash through refinancing, the owner will be able to finance the sale of their old home with a low down payment. This could make a property more salable.

If buyers cannot possibly complete a purchase until they have sold presently owned property, consider an offer on the new property contingent upon the sale of the present property. When you present this sort of contingency offer, show the owners the listing on the offeror's property. If the owners believe that the offeror's property is more salable than their property, the offer stands a good chance of acceptance.

When the seller has a number of properties, as a developer might, there is a better chance of an offer such as this being accepted. The developer with many properties will often be willing to tie up a single one with a contingent offer.

POWER RESPONSES TO BUYER OBJECTIONS: THE PERSONAL ISSUES

At times objections arise not from the property or the money, but from the prospects' own emotional responses to the idea of buying a house and to each other's fears and needs. Knowing what to look for and how to respond will enable you to overcome these objections and move the process along toward a closing.

"We Want To Think it Over."

This is one of the most common objections you will encounter. It might be just an excuse or another attempt to slow down a transaction which the prospective buyers feel is developing too quickly. If you let your prospects leave, they will come up with reasons not to buy the property. Big decisions can be scary, so buyers often reach for reasons to avoid making one while claiming that they really want to buy. You must get the prospective purchasers to consider the purchase now. This is one excellent approach:

> "Whenever I can't make up my mind, I try to lay out the pros and cons on paper. I find that putting things down on paper makes my decision quite clear. I will show you what I mean."

Then lay out a legal-size sheet of paper as shown on next page.

Give the sheet and a pen to the prospective buyers and say, "Let's list the reasons to buy." Prompt the prospects with plus features such as location, size, floor plan, condition, transportation, schools, financing, built-ins, fireplace, automatic sprinkler system and other specifics. Naturally you include the features that most interest your buyers.

Now ask your prospective buyers to list reasons not to buy this home. Don't prompt the clients on the negative side. When they appear finished, ask if there are any other negative features they can think of. Often this exercise reveals objections you were not previously aware of. This helps you because until you know of an objection, you can't overcome it.

Reasons to buy	Reasons not to buy

When your prospects are finished, you should have a sheet with many reasons to buy and only a few not to buy. Because the clients did the writing, this fact will be very persuasive.

Now ask your clients to numerically rate their minus factors from most to least important. This will give you a better understanding of what is blocking the sale. If you can overcome the most negative factors, you should be ready to try for a closing.

If there are negative features you cannot overcome but you still feel the property is right for the prospects, point out the long list of plus features compared with the few minus ones. Observe that the property appears to meet their needs quite well.

This simple exercise not only gives you another opportunity to review the buyers' needs, but provides a further chance to summarize the benefits and try for a closing.

This plus-minus exercise might show you that you had not been communicating effectively with your prospects. In that case, consider making an appointment to show more suitable property.

A similar approach to thinking it over can be verbal.

"Certainly careful thought is required. A home is a big decision and you want to weigh all of the factors. Now, the location is within three blocks of your train station and it is within the Henry School District as you desired. The neighbors are primarily professional people and their homes are well kept. As for neighborhood, we couldn't ask for anything better, don't you agree?"

Now continue your summation and go to a closing.

The following response to "I want to think it over" is very effective when your prospects have been looking for a home for some time:

"[Mr./Mrs.] Schmidt, how long have you been looking for a home? I would hate to see you lose this home because of a delay. It is likely that it could take you another five months to find another home that would meet your needs. Even then it's unlikely it would be as nice as this one. With our inflation rate, five months from now you could well end up paying several thousand dollars more.

"While this home may well be available tomorrow, it might not be. Because [price recently reduced, recently placed on the market, and so on], this home has been subject to unusual interest. We have over two hundred salespeople in our multiple-listing service. If we assume each is working with ten prospective buyers in this general price range, it means you are conceivably competing against 2,000 other buyers for this home. Do you want to risk losing this house?"

This approach could probably be used as a lead into the plus-minus evaluation.

Another way to encourage a positive decision would be:

"You know, [Mr./Mrs.] Jones, poor listings seem to stay available forever, but good listings such as this sell fast. You obviously like this home, don't you? Well, others are going to feel the same way. It is an exceptional home because [mention features your prospects like]. I have had too many cases of, 'I wish I had listened to you' when just several hours' delay resulted in someone else getting their home. Let us go over the pros and cons of this house one more time."

Some salespeople will respond to "I want to think it over" by commenting:

"Let me help you. Let's see first what we don't have to think over. Location, that's no problem because you like the area. Size, it's what you said you wanted. In fact it has an additional den. Price, it is within the price range you indicated to me. Is there anything I've left out?"

This approach is really a summary of the plus features and the attempt to get a definite objection.

This is another very effective way to treat the "I want to think it over" objection:

> "I can understand that very well. We have looked at a number of properties these last few days and it becomes difficult to separate features of one property from features of another. Let's go back and look through the house again. It will help you in your decision."

Your prospects are temporarily relieved of making a decision and they will welcome that respite. Another visit will tend to dispel any feeling that they are being rushed into anything. If they are at all interested, they will not object to another visit. This will give you an opportunity to reinforce the positive features of the property as well as another chance at a closing. Should your clients again raise a delaying tactic, try one of the other approaches.

If your prospective buyers are presently renters, the following approach can be very effective:

> "[Mr./Mrs.] Brown, the United States has the highest ratio of homeowners in the world. More than 50 percent of American families, including my own, own their homes. I am sure everyone of us felt trepidations before we purchased our homes, but I don't know anyone who was ever sorry they became a homeowner. We overcame our natural fears; I believe you can also. Do you want to own your own home?"

When your buyers still want to "sleep on it" a final approach should be:

> "If the price were more attractive, would you decide today?"

This response will likely result in a positive answer and now it is simply a matter of deciding on a price for the offer to purchase.

The Family Feud

More than once I have found myself in the middle of a war zone between spouses looking at a house. If you get into such a situation, each spouse might ask you to take sides. Don't do it. Be calm and suggest you all go for coffee. This break is likely to defuse the situation. It is fairly common for one spouse to like a house because it is lower priced and dislike another house because it has a higher price. Arguments between spouses generally are based more on price than home features, al-

144 POWER REAL ESTATE SELLING

though the features might be stressed in the argument. Try to use a plus-and-minus approach as previously described to defuse the tension. Keep in mind that one spouse wants the more expensive home and the other spouse really has to be convinced to spend the money. While it is possible to do so, it is very unlikely that you will be able to convince one spouse to accept less than he or she wants if it is within their financial capacity.

If the parties persist in snipping at each other, yelling, crying or even refusing to talk, you are not likely to get an offer signed by both spouses. Make another appointment and hope they work out their difficulties. Of course, if one says, "You don't want to buy me a new house," and the other says, "Yes, I do!", allow him or her to prove it.

"My Spouse Wants It; I Don't."

You might run into situations where one spouse alone does the house-hunting and the other spouse then raises reasons why it is not a good choice. This usually indicates a spouse who does not really want to buy, but hasn't told his or her spouse this. You need a very forceful approach here. Don't allow the staller to think it over or he or she will come up with additional reasons not to buy. The spouse who's ready to buy will be on your side, but the staller will take any escape route offered. This is one of the times when you must be unrelenting.

When one spouse has selected a house without the assistance of the other, the staller will find it harder to object to the purchase if you say:

> *"[Mr./Mrs.] Jones, you should be proud of your [husband/wife]. We have worked for days tramping through homes and discussing your needs. [Mr./Mrs.] Jones deserves an Olympic medal in house-hunting. It took a lot of effort, but we have been successful. This is the house [he/she] wants for the family."*

This Power approach works when the staller resists after seeing the house:

> *"[Mr./Mrs.] Jones indicated when we started our house-hunting that you insisted on limiting your initial investment to $10,000 and your monthly payments to $700. [He/She] also said you need three bedrooms, two baths, a two-car garage with room for a workbench, a full basement, and you wanted it on the South Side. That describes this house to a T. Was [Mr./Mrs.] Jones correct as to your requirements? Your basic needs are still the same, are they not? Am I correct that this house meets those needs?"*

The answer will undoubtedly be yes.

Now use one of the closings from Chapter Seven. If one doesn't work, switch to another. Keep in mind that the reason the staller is hesitating is probably a reluctance to spend the money. Emphasize the tax benefits of the purchase as well as the profit possibilities offered by appreciation.

"We Feel Committed to Another Agent."

Clients sometimes hesitate because they feel obligated to another agent. Keep in mind that if they were as loyal as they say, they never would have contacted you in the first place. Never knock the other agent. Your response might be:

> *"In buying a home you are making the biggest investment of your lives. You will live with your purchase for many years. Therefore, you want to be as objective as possible. If_____ has shown you a property that meets your needs better than this house, I would strongly advise that you buy it. [The other salesperson obviously has not or they wouldn't be looking now.] But from what you have told me, I don't believe there is a home on the market today that meets your needs better than this house. A home is too great an investment to make based on factors other than the home itself. Don't you agree?"*

"I Don't Understand This Agreement."

The standard clauses in the average purchase agreement are confusing and frightening to prospective buyers. The forms look like a product of a committee of 20 Philadelphia lawyers. A quick look at the endless boilerplate makes it easy to understand why many buyers want a lawyer before they sign anything.

This is one objection you can head off before it starts. Some offices are now using standard agreements written in English by humans. Follow their lead and your buyers will find such forms much less threatening.

Whatever form you use, you can defuse the tension by keeping an eye on the paragraphs that deal with default. These are the parts that detail what happens if a party refuses to fulfill the agreement, and they are the parts that cause the most confusion and suspicion. Prepare a simple explanation of each of these paragraphs so you can interpret it to a buyer in simple terms. Make certain your buyers fully understand any contract that they sign.

WARNING—In some states your explanation of contract terms would be regarded as the unauthorized practice of law. If such is the case in your state, have your office's attorney prepare a brief written explanation of these paragraphs.

"I Don't Have My Checkbook."

A small deposit increases the chance a buyer will back out of an agreement. If purchasers claim all they can make is a small deposit because of some reason such as forgetting their checkbook, accept the low deposit. However, provide in the offer for the deposit to be increased substantially within a set number of days after acceptance.

If a buyer claims to have no check or money you can accept a promissory note (carry note forms in your briefcase). The note should provide for cash redemption within a stated period of time, such as ten days, unless the offer is refused. You must, of course, tell the seller the form of the deposit. While promissory notes are better than nothing, a higher percentage of buyers using them default than those using cash.

POWER RESPONSES TO BUYER OBJECTIONS: THE ADVISORS

Still another kind of objection you'll encounter arises when prospects want to bring other people into the decision. Sometimes this is a good idea; at other times it is an excuse to avoid the decision entirely. Here are some ways to know which is which, and how to handle each one in a way that increases the prospects for a sale.

"I Think I'll Talk It Over with My Cousin [Brother/Friend/etc.]."

> "Has your _____ been successful lately investing in real estate? I [or my firm] have made many investors financially independent because of their purchases. I would be happy to arrange for you to talk to several of them. Money is made in real estate investments by people who have the courage of their convictions. If your _____ lacks the courage to invest, then how can [he/she] possibly recommend that you invest? To do so would be to admit [his/her] shortcomings. I have nothing against getting expert advice, but get the advice from real experts, successful real estate investors."

Many salespeople like to use the following statement:

*"If your _____ tells you not to buy and you follow
their advice and don't buy, will your _____
make up the loss you suffer because you end up paying thousands
more a year from now? Of course [he/she] won't. It's your money.
Don't you think it should be your decision?"*

"I'd Like To Discuss It with My Accountant."

While the objection could be an excuse, it is a reasonable request and
should be treated as such.

*"That's very wise. I like working with people who make decisions
in a professional manner. I will prepare an investment package on
the property and deliver it to your accountant. Who is your accountant?"*

A better approach would be:

*"Let's call your accountant now. Perhaps we can arrange to discuss
the property over lunch."*

Don't try to avoid an accountant. If you have done your preparation well, an accountant can be a strong ally in convincing prospects to
buy homes as well as income property.

"I Want To Check with my Attorney First."

Most real estate professionals shudder when a buyer mentions an attorney. Attorneys tend to ruin deals. Very few attorneys are really astute in
real estate matters, and even those few who are can cause you trouble.
The problems arise less in legal areas than in other advice. Many attorneys just can't help giving their advice beyond legal questions. I have
heard attorneys advise clients "Don't offer more than $_____
and tell them to take it or leave it!" Others will suggest the clients wait,
because it is a poor time to buy. Although neither appraisal or economics are within an attorney's usual area of expertise, this doesn't stop
many lawyers from throwing in opinions based upon little more than
hunches. Sales often are lost when clients go to the attorneys by themselves. If you are there with them, an attorney is much more likely to
stick to the area of "legal sufficiency."

You want the attorney to review the contract regarding legal matters. The attorney will ascertain if statutory requirements are met, if his
or her client is waiving any rights, that the contract clearly and completely sets forth the agreement and that the agreement contains

nothing to the client's detriment that the client is not fully apprised of. Attorneys often will want to make additions, modifications and deletions to the agreement.

When prospective buyers say they want to check with an attorney, ask who their attorney is. You can then call the attorney and, after introducing yourself, say:

> *"Mr. and Mrs. Jerry Plainfield are in my office. We would like to set up an appointment so you can go over a purchase contract with us as to legal sufficiency."*

Be sure to get yourself in on the appointment. You might ask if the attorney has a few moments to spare within the next hour.

If a prospective buyer wishes to consult with an attorney but does not have a local attorney, it would be proper for you to recommend several attorneys who you know to be knowledgeable in real estate. Do not, however, recommend your own or your firm's attorney as this could appear to be a conflict of interest.

If you are unable to get in contact with the buyers' attorney or if the attorney can't see you for several days, complete the offer with the following contingency: "This offer is subject to the approval of _____ within _____ days of this offer." Taking this offer with the contingency will keep your buyers off the market until the approval is obtained; it could also get the buyers to begin thinking of the property as their own, if the offer is accepted. I once used such a clause, and the attorney advised my prospects not to buy. They were really dejected, so I suggested they see another attorney. This one gave them the green light and they became happy buyers.

Another approach is to ask the attorney on the phone if he or she is familiar with the standard purchase agreement used in the area. Ask if it would be all right to go over the additions to the form with him or her with the clients on an extension phone. This is the best way to go if the attorney is willing.

Never argue with the buyers' attorney. Go along with any changes he or she suggests, even though you think they are unnecessary. While you may actually know more about the law as it relates to real estate than the attorney, the buyers regard their attorney as an expert. Don't embarrass the attorney in front of his or her clients. If the attorney has made a serious error, contact the attorney privately to discuss the problem.

"I Would Like To Talk This Over with My Banker."

> *"Your banker will tell you it isn't a good time to buy real estate. No banker in his or her right mind would advise you to do anything except to keep your funds liquid, meaning in his or her bank at 5 1/4 percent interest. Is that the kind of advice you want?"*

SHAM OBJECTIONS

Some objections are not really objections at all. Recently, after deciding I was going to buy a building, I made a fuss over several minor cracks in the foundation, talking about possible structural damage and estimating the cost to correct the problem. My objection was really just a bargaining tool to make the owner more receptive to my offer, similar to a person who takes an item of clothing to a store manager, pointing out a spot or flaw in order to obtain a discount.

Other buyers are just like me. I am, however, a poor actor and an experienced seller would have spotted my objections as a sham. He or she might even have been moved to paraphrase Shakespeare: "Methinks he doth protest too much." If I considered it a major problem, I wouldn't have repeated myself. I was obviously trying to convince someone else. Too many objections mean no *real* objection. My other mistake was that I was in no hurry to leave. These are two indicators of a sham objection. A third is pointing out multiple minor defects.

When you spot sham objections, don't bother trying to overcome them. If the prospects want to buy, no selling is necessary. You can save a great deal of time by getting to the bottom line and asking the buyer, "How much do you want to offer?" Try to get the prospective buyers to raise their offering price as much as possible, but keep in mind that buyers who use sham objections seldom pay list price.

FROM OBJECTION TO CLOSING

Your prospects have brought up a variety of objections, and you've shown them that their problems can be solved if they decide to buy this property. You have arrived at the crisis point in the sales process. The next chapter shows you what the closing is, why you must learn to move your prospects to the closing stage and how to use Power Selling techniques to turn the prospects' interest into a signed agreement to buy.

7. Power Closing

You might be the most knowledgeable real estate expert in the world, but if you can't or won't close, you are really a clerk, not a salesperson. A clerk shows properties and takes orders. A salesperson convinces prospects to buy. People like to buy real estate from salespeople, not clerks. They want to be convinced. The close is simply the end product of all your efforts. It should come naturally from all that has preceded it. Without a close, you have wasted all your efforts. At times it almost seems that some salespeople are afraid of success. They do all of their homework then fail to present a closing.

You must realize that while buyers want to be convinced to buy, they generally have a natural fear of change. They need to be assured that purchasing the property is the right thing to do. A home purchase is the largest investment people ever make, an investment they will be paying off for many years. Because of this natural apprehension, prospective buyers will often try to take the easiest course: to refrain from making a decision. This natural reticence must be overcome with positive motivation. You must make it easy for buyers to say yes.

People go shopping to fulfill a psychological need. In home buying, basic shelter as well as psychological needs are fulfilled by a purchase. You can only help fulfill those needs by closing the sale.

Asking people to buy is not pressure when a home will fulfill their needs and provide them with a better life. Failure to ask them to buy, on the other hand, does them a disservice and breaches your agency agreement with your owner.

Prospective buyers who have previously purchased real estate generally will be more receptive to a closing because they feel less apprehension. If they have had previous real estate problems, however, the closing may prove even more difficult.

Don't get paranoid if prospects seem to distrust you. People are apprehensive about salespeople in general—it isn't just you. People are afraid they will. be sold something they don't need, don't want or should not buy. You can lessen this natural apprehension by clearly responding to the buyers' needs. If you worry about the buyers' needs, your own needs will be taken care of.

Real estate is a strange business: Although we legally represent the owners, we counsel and often become close friends with our buyers. Our first obligation is to make the best deal possible for our owners, yet we will not succeed unless the sale also honestly meets the buyers' needs.

HELP THE BUYER: CLOSE!

You are not doing buyers a favor by failing to press for a closing. Many people have considered buying real estate for years and have watched while prices rose ever higher. They now say, "I could have _____" or "I should have _____." The likely reason they didn't buy is that no one asked them to. Salespeople showed them properties but didn't attempt to sell them any. Many painters paint good pictures but don't know when to stop. Selling is very similar and many salespeople keep talking or painting when they should be packing up their easel. In selling you pack up the easel with a closing.

Many salespeople act as if asking for money is dirty. There is nothing wrong with asking a person to put up money to buy a property. If anything, it is wrong to show prospective buyers a property that meets their needs and then fail to vigorously attempt a sale.

People have told me how they wish now that I had been more persuasive and sold them a property I showed them years ago. I failed; I should have worked harder. I did a disservice to the prospective buyers when I failed to use every legal and ethical means at my disposal to convince them to buy. If you want to be well liked then go for the closing. After people buy they are generally happy about their purchase and have a positive attitude about the person who sold them their home. Most home purchasers are improving the quality of their lives. By selling them homes you are making them happy.

The selling effort is like a car tire: too little pressure and it goes flat. When I tell people that, some point out that too much pressure is a blowout. The fact is, asking people to put out money to obtain their needs isn't excessive pressure, and doesn't turn people off. What turns people off is pressure to buy something they don't want. They don't want it because either:

1. The item doesn't meet their needs, or
2. You have failed to sell them on its benefits.

When you attempt to force people to buy a property not suited to their needs, that is abusive pressure and cannot be tolerated. But the use of strong persuasion to convince prospects to buy a property that meets their needs is not abusive pressure; it is Power Selling.

If you insist on waiting until your customers tell you they want to buy, you will need a spouse with a high-paying job; you are not going to contribute much to the household budget. It has been said, tongue in cheek, that without the first real estate salesperson we would still be living in caves. There is a strong element of truth beneath the humor. People want improvements in their lives but resist because not to change is easier. The easiest decision is no decision. Salespeople, by reinforcing and actually creating wants, have helped to give us our present standard of living. The best thing you can do for people is to sell them properties that meet their needs and satisfy their wants.

Take the attitude that people love to buy. Help them do what they love.

THE PLANNED CLOSING

Closings work best if they are planned in advance to suit each prospect and situation. Look over the possible types of closing and choose the most appropriate one, plus several backups. Being prepared will help you keep a calm appearance so you soothe your buyers' anxiety instead of increasing it. A calm appearance gives support to your buyers. Follow these four steps to a closing:

1. Summarize the benefits the property offers the buyers.
2. Show how the property meets the buyers' needs.
3. Go over any additional plus factors of the property which distinguish it from other available property.
4. Close.

WHAT, WHEN AND WHERE

When a prospective buyer responds positively to a home, a good approach is to encourage him or her to verbalize this approval. This can be done with:

> *"What features of this home do you like the best, [Mr./Mrs.] Smith?"*

By verbalizing their approval prospects take on a mental attitude receptive to closing.

When you're not certain about the buyers' interests, ask questions. If you are not certain about their answers, rephrase them. You want to know buyers' interest in a home and how they relate it to other homes you have shown. Don't assume a buyer likes a particular home best—ask!

After a showing, ask questions such as:

> *"How do you like this home?"*

> *"How does this home compare to _____?"*

> *"Of the four homes you have seen today, which best meets your needs without regard to price?"*

By selling the wrong house you could actually be talking the buyers out of a closing situation and placing them into a no-sale mode.

You have probably heard that buyers must be ready for closing. This is, of course, true. They can't be allowed to feel they are being rushed. Buyers will be prepared for closing when you have pointed out how the property meets their needs, as well as specific advantages of the particular property. All the prospective buyers' questions must have been answered. Your questioning should have evoked positive responses so that the closing seems natural. By your questioning, ascertain that both spouses would like to own the property and that neither has any significant objections that have not been overcome.

If your prospective buyers are responding positively, it is not necessary to complete a preplanned presentation. Close now. The time to close is when the buyers are ready. If you continue a presentation too long, you could strike a negative chord and lose your opportunity. Don't worry about closing prematurely. It is far worse not to try than to attempt a premature closing.

If you fail at a closing attempt, you can try again later. Many salespeople have tried to close a half dozen or more times before succeeding. Closing is not a one-shot, take-it-or-leave-it proposition. You can (and should) try, try again.

Closing Signals

You are not totally on you own, though, in deciding when to try a closing. Your prospects will often give indications they are about ready for your closing presentation. Here are some signals to watch for:

"What Do You Think?" When prospective buyers ask your opinion, they are usually seeking reinforcement of their own conclusions. Know their conclusions before you answer. Ask questions first and then provide reinforcement in an honest and positive fashion.

If prospects want to know which of two properties you feel would be better for them, ask questions such as:

"Which feature do you like best about the house?"

After you have heard the positive features of both houses, ask:

"Which of these two homes would you feel more comfortable in?"

The home the buyers choose is the one they want most. It's a signal for the closing.

"Can We See It Again?" When the prospective buyers want to see a particular property a second time or ask you just to drive by it again, you know they are interested. If prospects request a second showing, be ready with the offer to purchase you have prepared in advance.

Just Can't Leave. If prospective buyers seem to linger or spend an inordinate amount of time in a house, they are interested.

Excess Criticism. If prospective buyers are overly critical about features of a home, chances are it really means they are interested.

Whispers. If the couple whispers together, it is a positive sign. If they were uninterested they would not be whispering.

Measuring. If they want to measure anything or seem to be "stepping off" a room, they are interested in buying.

"What Stays?" If they ask if anything stays with the house, they are interested. Your response should be:

"Do you want it to stay?"

Before suggesting to buyers that an item the buyers like be included in the purchase, you have a duty to the sellers to obtain a reasonable compensation for it.

"If the refrigerator could be included in the sale, would you want it?"

"If it can be part of the purchase price, what do you feel should be a fair price for the refrigerator?"

Whatever the purchaser answers, write up an offer to purchase that includes the item. (See *Trial Closings* later in this chapter.)

"Don't Know." If prospective buyers say, "Well, we don't know," it's time to come on strong about the benefits a property offers. The buyers need to be sold.

Emotional Responses. Would-be buyers *look* at houses that make sense to them. They often *buy* houses that satisfy their emotional needs. Any indication of interest should be explored, even if the house doesn't meet any of the standards the prospects said they required.

A friend of mine discovered that truth while taking a couple to see a condominium. The husband was being transferred to the area and the couple said they wanted a deluxe two-bedroom condominium on a golf course. It had to be on one floor. They had sold a large home and didn't want to bother with home ownership any more, especially now that their children were all married. On the way back from the showing the wife spotted a "For Sale" sign in front of a large English Tudor home on a huge lot. She wanted to see it. The six-bedroom home was beautiful but not at all what the couple had thought they wanted. They became the owners of a fine English Tudor home.

Prior to Closing

Remember that you have a duty to fully disclose to your prospective buyers any detrimental facts you know prior to any offer. This duty has been extended in several states to include anything detrimental that a reasonably diligent inspection by an agent would reveal. Even if your state laws do not require such disclosures, you have a moral obligation to the prospective buyers to spend the time to give them the advantage of your expertise and to make a reasonable visual inspection. For your protection, known property defects should be set forth in writing. Many firms use forms for this purpose. In California the owner also signs an inspection form regarding known defects. If your state has any mandatory disclosures such as restrictive covenants and so on, you should, of course, fully comply with these disclosures.

Where To Close.   The place to close is wherever you happen to be when the prospects are ready to buy. If you are at the property and the owners are not there, that can be a great place to close.

If it's going to be a long drive back to your office, you can close in your car. This is another advantage of having a full-size sedan.

Many sales have been lost by salespeople who drove back to their offices to close. They missed the magic moment and their buyers, who were naturally apprehensive, developed reasons to delay making a decision. Buyers are often nervous and almost anything can make them want to think it over. If you are going to close in your office, make sure you will not be interrupted. Any interruptions can bring about an early departure by your prospects.

Many salespeople like to close at coffee shops, which are non-threatening, neutral environments. Don't ask if your prospects want a cup of coffee—just pull in and say, "Let's have a cup of coffee."

CLOSING FAST

Some salespeople don't even try closing on the first showing. They say most people view a property several times before buying, so it's best to wait until after the second or third showing. I think this is ridiculous. The reason most homes are not sold on the first showing is not that it takes two or three showings to convince buyers. It is because the salesperson is not really competent. He or she is waiting for the buyers to sell themselves and let the salesperson fill out the paperwork like an order-taker.

It is dangerous to be so low-pressured that you let the buyers go without an attempt at closing. Buyers can stray to another real estate office before you get the important signature on a purchase agreement.

EXCUSES NOT TO BUY

While you are trying to sell customers on how a house meets their needs, they might be trying to sell you on the idea that the property is not suitable and they should not buy it. Don't let your prospects use excuses to avoid a purchase. Excuses are not reasons: They are red herrings thrown out as defense mechanisms to avoid making a decision. If prospects raise many reasons not to buy, they are making excuses. By replacing these with an excuse to buy, you move another step toward the sale.

EXCUSES TO BUY

We all know someone who buys a new car for $5,000 plus his or her one-year-old car, and then says, "Well, it needed new tires and a tune-up. Besides, I need a reliable car and my old one had 20,000 miles on it, so I could expect future problems." The reasons given are weak, but they *are* reasons. Buyers are looking for an excuse to buy something they want. They need justification.

The same holds true for real estate. People often need excuses to buy when they are unable to logically justify it. This is especially true in the sale of second and luxury homes.

I know an investor who controls well over ten million dollars' worth of prime investment property. He lived for many years in a very nice tract home in the $100,000 range. He used to say it was foolish to spend a lot of money on a home. One day I received his invitation to a house-warming party at his new address. His new home must have cost over a half million dollars. He told me that today this kind of house isn't really a luxury. It is just part of a total investment package. I found out later that his broker had used the exact same language. The broker had discovered the button to push that would give him the excuse he wanted.

THE GOOD WORD: POSITIVE CLOSING VOCABULARY

Land salespeople have become experts in motivating buyers. While most of their tactics are deplorable, some of their ideas are both ethical and valuable.

Land salespeople have found that buyers hesitate to *buy* but jump to *invest*. Buying requires spending, but *investing* denotes putting the money to work. Land salespeople find thousands of buyers eager to "invest" their money in near-worthless lots.

Choose your words carefully. *Down payment* has the connotation of giving up something until it becomes an *initial investment*.

Instead of asking for an *earnest money deposit*, you can ask for a *percentage of the total investment* to accompany the agreement.

Don't ask prospective buyers to sign a *purchase contract*. People are leery about signing anything, especially a contract. Instead ask them to *okay their agreement*. *Agreement* avoids the negative connotations. Place check marks for their signatures, preferably with colored ink or marker so they see where they are to sign. *Okaying* sounds a lot less ominous than *signing*, even though the buyers really understand that they are to sign the agreement. And if it's *their* agreement, they understand that they have discussed and approved the provisions already.

There is nothing dishonest about this wording. Even the most naive buyers realize they are signing an offer to purchase, but the wording helps the buyers overcome some of their natural hesitancy.

Never use the term *commission* with buyers or sellers. The word has a negative connotation. A better word is *fee*, but still better, don't discuss fees at all. Buyers will get the idea you are more interested in yourself than in meeting their needs. If you are thinking about your commission, your mind is not on effectively closing the sale.

When you hand the purchase contract to the buyers, you must not appear nervous. Be natural, as if you expect them to sign it.

TRIAL CLOSINGS

After you overcome owners' objections, immediately try a trial closing. If they raise another objection, overcome it and try your closing again. Trial closings or indirect closings are attempts to get buyers to agree on something that implies they have agreed to buy.

"Does thirty days for closing meet your needs?"

"Is January 1 occupancy satisfactory with you?"

This could also be asked with a choice such as:

"Would a thirty-day closing be all right or would you prefer to set if for sixty days?"

Notice that you did not include the choice *not* to buy. Always phrase a question in such a way that no negative response is presented as a choice.

Some other trial closing statements:

"The normal investment made with the offer is between five percent and ten percent of the price, which would be $2,000 or $4,000. Which do you prefer?" [Buyers will usually indicate the lower figure.]

"Would you like to assume the existing nine percent loan or do you prefer to refinance?"

When you use a trial close, wait for the answer. Don't let the buyers get you to talk first. Often, when greeted with silence, agents continue with other reasons to buy and lose the closing opportunity. Don't ruin your moment of truth. If you are unsuccessful with a trial closing, continue with reasons to buy, ask more questions and try again. After every closing you must again wait for the buyer's response. If you are the first to talk you will have broken your chance to close and let the buyer off the hook. You must wait for the buyer's response even though the silence will seem deafening.

A variation on the trial closing is to get the buyers to agree on a number of small things, even on a color to repaint a wall.

I sold new homes for a builder before they were completed. I had tile samples, carpet samples and paint color charts. After showing the houses to prospective buyers and asking which house they preferred, I would sit down with them to explain financing, not asking whether they actually wished to purchase the home. I would bring out samples and get their choices from cabinet finishes to exterior paint. If they were unsure, I would write, "To be decided." I entered all this material on a buyer's specification sheet, which was part of our sales contract. By the time we finished with all the selections, it seemed the most natural thing in the world for the prospects to approve the sales agreement. If you get agreement on the small things, the big things follow.

A HANDBOOK OF CLOSINGS

Great salespeople perform like artists and their repertoire consists of, among other things, a collection of closings that apply to any situation and appeal to every personality. Knowing what to use, and when, comes with hard work and practice. Once again, exercising your imagination can train you to consistently apply the right closing at the right time. Study the closings that follow and think about the principles behind them. When they have become second nature, you will be ready to handle any closing situation a buyer can devise.

Yes, Yes, Yes

If you get a series of positive responses during your sales presentation, the purchase suggestion becomes the logical next agreement. Sales trainers for years have urged asking questions that will elicit a positive response:

"Am I correct that financial security is one of your concerns?"

You know the response will be yes.

A series of pertinent yes-oriented questions for a particular property leads to a natural sale. Here is a series used to sell Antelope Valley Land:

"Do you agree with Will Rogers that to make money in real estate you should find out where the people are going and buy land there first?"

"Do you agree that the areas of our country that can expect the greatest population growth are in the Sun Belt?"

"Do you agree that California can expect a goodly portion of this growth?"

"Do you agree that because of climate most of this growth will be in southern California?"

"Do you agree that the major growth will be radiating out from the Los Angeles area?"

"Do you agree that the Antelope Valley is the largest undeveloped land area within Los Angeles County?"

"Do you agree that the Antelope Valley is the natural expansion area for Los Angeles?"

"Would you like to own two and one-half acres—enough for ten city lots—in the path of the next major expansion?"

Such sales presentations work. By agreeing repeatedly, customers place themselves in a situation where the final agreement is the natural culmination of what they've agreed to already.

Whether or not you use a formal yes-yes-yes approach, phrase your questions in such a way that a positive reaction will be forthcoming when approaching a closing. You want saying yes to become a habit.

The Direct Approach

Some clients will agree with everything you say but balk at buying. Try filling out the purchase contract and handing it to your prospects with a pen. Make the prospective buyers come up with their objections. Unless they voice an objection, you cannot overcome it. Sometimes the best response is as simple as a straightforward question, "Is this the house for you?" If the response is positive, you have a sale. If negative, you have an opening to find out why and try to overcome the objections.

Some salespeople like this direct approach. Without actually asking the prospects to buy, its meaning is understood by all. Other variations of the direct approach might take forms like these:

"*Do you want to buy this property?*"

"*Are you ready to make an offer?*"

The problem with these questions is that they give the buyer an opportunity to say no, to find a direct escape.

Some salespeople prefer a more subtle approach.

"*This home would make your wife very happy, Mr. Smith. Don't you agree, Mrs. Smith?*"

If the answer is positive, continue with:

"*Well, let's buy it for her.*"

Here is the direct question put into a more tempting word picture:

"*Do you want to go to bed tonight knowing your house-hunting days are over?*"

If you fail to close, this final try pulls no punches:

"Why don't you want to buy this house?"

Here you are forcing the prospective buyers to come up with reasons. If they do and you can overcome them, try another closing procedure.

Many people don't like direct closings. They prefer more subtle approaches. Subtle is okay but don't be so subtle that the customers don't realize you want an offer.

When I went to college, a very quiet and fairly plain fellow lived in our dormitory. What made him stand out was that he always seemed to have dates with the better-looking girls on campus. When anyone asked him how he did it he would say, "I just ask a lot of girls." If you ask enough people to buy, you're going to make sales even though your sales approach isn't the greatest.

"Give Me Your Money."

One of my former students developed into a superstar as a salesperson. She didn't fit the superstar mold: She is very short and weighs well over 200 pounds. She dresses very plainly and wears no makeup. She never completed high school and has a fairly limited command of English. In class she always seemed lost and frequently asked questions that indicated she was having problems.

In her first year she became the most successful salesperson in a large franchise office, selling 27 nontract houses in a month. She became one of the prime testimonials for my classes in real estate sales.

I was in her office one day when she came in with a couple. When they were all seated, she said, "I'm going to sell you that house. The price is $47,500. Take out your checkbook."

To my amazement, the husband did. "Give me a check for $500," she demanded. "Make it out to our trust account." She never asked any questions. She simply asked for money. This is not what I'd taught her, but it worked. She was asking for money before she got an agreement on anything. She had not even begun to fill out an offer. Her broker said she qualified her prospects at length and managed in a few hours to build up an amazing rapport with her buyers.

I don't advise this give-me-your-money approach to anyone not wearing a mask, but it does work for this salesperson.

Assuming

In one direct approach you assume the prospects will buy. You use a purchase offer form to take down information. If prospects object to your filling out an offer form, downplay its significance.

"I'm filling this out for your benefit so you will have all of the facts before you in order to make a proper judgment."

When you are finished with the form, give a copy to the prospects, explaining what the agreement states. Ask:

"Is it satisfactory as is or are there any changes you would like to make?"

If they recommend changes, you have an offer and if they feel it is satisfactory, you have an offer. Go over the benefits briefly once again and hand over the pen.

When you get the pen in a person's hand with a document before him or her, to sign is a natural reaction. One owner told me in no uncertain terms that he would not accept an offer. I handed him a pen. He said, "What the hell," and signed.

In another type of assumption closing, you ask a question that offers choices, either of which is to buy. Examples are:

"The owner would like to give possession in 30 days. Is that satisfactory with you or do you want possession sooner?"

"Do you want to assume the first mortgage or do you prefer to obtain new financing?"

"As you know, the owners have offered their home at $97,500, which I believe is a very fair price. An offer at that price will assure you that the home is yours. Do you want to make your offer at $97,500 or do you have another figure in mind?"

If you get a positive reaction to any of the above questions, start writing the offer. These questions are simply trial closings.

"Let Me Write This Up."

A variation on the assume approach is to say:

"Let me write this up so you can consider this property."

or you could state:

"Why don't I write down exactly what we are talking about so we are on the same wave length—it will help you in making any decision."

Your prospects will love this, as you appear to be opening an escape route. They don't realize you will want them to consider it *now*.

You now go over the offer with the buyers as you did with the assume approach and go for the closing in the same manner.

While working a model home at a new development, I wrote up over fifty purchase contracts in one day and got my prospects to sign twenty-two of them. When you have several people waiting to get their information and others are buying, it can create an atmosphere where those waiting start to worry that you will run out of houses before you get to them. (In slow times it is hard to imagine such boom times.)

Mathematical Approach

This is another variation of the assume approach. To use it, you say:

> *"Let's check out the numbers on this home."*

Then start asking questions on specific initial investments. By using your amortization tables based on new loans, loans being assumed and owner carryback loans, you will arrive at a monthly payment figure. This naturally leads to practical questions:

> *"Do you want me to compute the figures based on [the list price]?"*
>
> *"The owners indicate they will carryback a loan for the balance. What interest rate would you like me to figure?"*

Write the figures down on a sheet of paper:

Initial Investment $_____
Monthly Investment $_____

If these figures come within the qualifying range, ask:

> *"When would you like possession?"*
>
> *"Do you want to take title in joint tenancy?"*

Then assume the purchase and start writing in the figures.

What If?

If prospective buyers come up with an objection not easily overcome, this approach sometimes gets things moving again:

> *"If the owners agreed to carry the financing themselves at _____, would you buy this home?"*
>
> *"If the owners agreed to give you sixty days to sell your present*

home _____, *would you buy this home?"*

"If the owners reduced the down payment to _____, would you buy this home?"

If the purchasers are upset over a repair needed or replacement required, you know they are interested. A direct approach would be:

"If the sellers were willing to make a price adjustment to [replace/ repair] _____, would you be interested in purchasing this home?"

If you get a positive response:

"What do you suppose it would cost for _____?"

Using the buyers' figures, start writing up the offer. If the buyers have no idea of the cost, either suggest an amount or provide in the offer that the seller will make the repair or replacement. This is one of the few instances when you should recommend a price adjustment. You should, of course, explain your actions and reasons to the owner.

If the buyers need appliances, you could say:

"If the owners would leave their washer, dryer and refrigerator, would you pay an additional $500?"

If the answer is positive, you have an offer; if the answer is negative, then ask:

"How much additional would you pay?"

If the answer is nothing, write up the offer at list price including the appliances.

This variation of the *if* approach is very effective:

"If you were to make an offer, would it be at the price of $____ or did you have another price in mind?"

If the buyers indicate a lower price, ask the basis of the price and try to get it increased. (Assume that they are offering to purchase at the price they state and start writing up the offer.)

When you cannot use the *if* approach because buyers are not communicating their objections, be direct:

"Is there any reason why you should not buy this property?"

"What, if anything, is the problem? Unless I know why this property is not suited to your needs I can't help you find the right home."

Once you have the objections, you can use the *if* approach.

"Subject to" Offers

A *subject to* offer is really an *if* offer. The buyer is requiring something to happen or to be done as a condition of making an offer. An *if* is a contingency. The more contingencies an offer contains, the less chance it has of acceptance; still, an offer with contingencies is better than no offer at all.

If you are writing an offer with a financing contingency, be specific about the amount of points, interest rate and loan amount. Try to set the maximum interest the buyer will be obligated to accept at least one-half percent above current rates (one percent is preferred) to cover interest fluctuations. Financing contingencies set too tightly allow escape hatches for minor fluctuations in interest rates.

You are unlikely to obtain an unqualified offer to purchase from one spouse without the other spouse's approval as well. In fact, few salespeople are able to sell a single spouse. It is actually easy if you suggest to the buying spouse that he or she tie up the property with a contingency offer until the other spouse can see it. The offer would be subject to the approval of the other spouse within a stated period of time, usually just a few days. This is one of the few times I advocate suggesting an escape clause. The reasoning is that no escape clause will likely mean no offer. When you have a deposit with the offer you have a psychological advantage when the other spouse sees the property. The home is sold unless there is disapproval. You have one spouse on your side, usually proud of his or her choice. At least two-thirds of your spouse-approval sales should close unless you did not properly qualify the prospects.

Low-price offers should not have contingencies. You want the offer to appear as attractive as possible. It is difficult to expect a seller to accept a significantly lower price as well as allow escape provisions in the offer.

After the offer with contingencies has been signed, ask your prospective buyers:

"How much do you want this home?"

You can expect a positive response. After all, they just signed an offer and gave you a check. Explain to the prospective buyers that contingencies reduce the chance of acceptance. Try to get the contingencies modified or removed. I have found it is usually much easier to clean up an offer after I have it signed than to press for a clean offer at the start.

"This Is What You Wanted."

In this approach you repeat each feature wanted by the prospects that the house has. The repetition you see in the following example tends to emphasize the suitability of the house.

> "[Mr./Mrs.] Jones, you wanted a home in the Hiawatha School District. This home is in the Hiawatha School District.
>
> "You wanted a three-bedroom home. This home has three bedrooms.
>
> "You wanted two baths. This home has two baths.
>
> "You wanted a family room. This home has a family room.
>
> "You wanted a large, fenced yard. This house has a large, fenced yard.
>
> "You wanted a double attached garage. This home has a double attached garage.
>
> "You wanted a home priced under $80,000. This home is priced under $80,000.
>
> "[Mr./Mrs.] Jones, we have found the home for you. Is April 1 occupancy satisfactory or do you prefer May 1?"

Keep a written record of buyer objections about particular homes. By reviewing the objections prior to showings you can use them for your this-is-what-you-wanted closings.

Summation Method

The summation closing is similar to the this-is-what-you-wanted closing. A typical summation closing would be:

> "Well, we did it. A three-bedroom, two-bath home under $100,000 with double garage, room to park your RV and a rear kitchen overlooking the large fenced yard—and it's in the Westview school district. Would March 1 occupancy be satisfactory or do you prefer April 1?"

Note that the closing flow is natural. The choice given is between occupancy dates, not whether or not to buy.

The Evaluation

Your prospects actually sell the property to themselves with this device. To set it up, say you wish to return to your office after the showings to discuss the homes the buyers have seen. Explain that only by fully understanding their reactions to homes can you really help them—that you want to know the negative features as well as the positive features of the homes you have shown.

Hand your prospects an evaluation sheet for each of the homes you visited. A Polaroid picture can be attached to each sheet to minimize confusion. You can fill in the top portions of the sheets in advance. The results could lead into an immediate offer; if not, they will help you to decide what other properties to show these prospects.

If prospective buyers indicate they would buy at a ridiculous price, find out the extent of their interest by asking questions. If they don't really like the house and would only buy it if they can steal it, don't try for an offer.

The beauty of using these evaluation sheets is that buyers frequently put themselves through the closing and feel no pressure from you. They believe they made up their minds on their own.

The only disadvantage of this method is that you may write up more marginal offers than with other closings. However, a marginal offer is better than no offer, and you can often negotiate an acceptable purchase on the counteroffer. Once you've received a first offer, later offers will come more easily.

A variation on this approach is to give forms to both husband and wife and tell them not to show them to each other. Tell them you will compare them after they are finished. By comparing the evaluations, you actually perform a tremendous service for your buyers. Frequently, husbands and wives fail to really communicate. They are swayed by their own sometimes mistaken idea of how the other one feels.

When both spouses are positive about the same property, you are ready for a closing. That each spouse has similar positive feelings about a property tends to reinforce both of their opinions.

Some salespeople give their prospects clipboards and pens and ask them to evaluate each house as they visit it. This can be very effective because details will be filled out while each house is fresh in their minds. This is an excellent approach when a great many homes are likely to be viewed.

Evaluations in which several prospective buyers say a listing is overpriced can be presented to the owners for an adjustment to a more realistic level.

Evaluator _____

Address _____

Description (fill in from listing)_____

_____

_____

Price _____

Features I liked _____

_____

_____

Features I didn't like _____

_____

_____

I consider the price fair   Yes ☐   No ☐

☐ I would consider buying this home if the price were reduced to
   $ _____

☐ I would consider buying this home if the home had _____

_____

_____

☐ I would consider buying this home if the owner would include _____

_____

_____

☐ I would consider buying this home only if _____

_____

_____

☐ I would not consider buying this home under any circumstances.

"How Long Will You Look?"

This approach should be used if the prospective buyers have been looking for a long time. It is a simple and forthright statement of fact followed by a question designed to lead to an offer.

> *"[Mr./Mrs.] Riley, you have been looking for a home for over __ months. We have finally found a home that meets your needs. If you don't act now it could take another __ months or even longer to find another home you like as well as this one, and by then it could conceivably cost you thousands of dollars more. Are you willing to spend the next _____ months looking for your next home?"*

Competition

People don't like to lose things even when they haven't made up their minds whether they want them. A person looking at an item at a sale will suddenly decide to buy it if someone else wants it. The same holds true in real estate. People don't like to lose a property even though the property was never theirs to lose. You can use this human competitive urge to your benefit by using it to resolve indecision into an offer.

If an offer comes in on a property and you have interested prospects, tell them the situation.

> *"An offer has come in on the home on _____ Street that you wanted. I don't know the amount of the offer but chances are it isn't for the full price. You still have a chance if you get over to my office right away so we can have your offer submitted with the other offer."*

If someone else has a showing appointment on a home your buyers are interested in, this call may spark a decision:

> *"_____, who works in my office, has some prospects very interested in the house you want on _____ Street. They made an appointment to see the house a second time this afternoon at 3 P.M. I would hate to see you lose this house. I think it's perfect for you. Can you get over to my office in the next hour?"*

You are expressing urgency, but not asking your prospects to buy; that is assumed.

You will have plenty of actual situations that call for the competition technique without manufacturing them yourself. Be absolutely honest in your presentations.

Photo Finish

If during a showing you feel the home fits your prospects' needs and you are receiving a positive response, pause outside the home. Your closing would be:

> *"I think this is the home for you. I have a foolproof way to find out if I am right."*

Take a color Polaroid photo of your clients in front of the house. Hand the photo to your clients, saying:

> *"Yes, I think this is your home, don't you agree?"*

After closing, I have found that my buyers showed that photo to all of their friends: "See us and our new house?" Using the Polaroid is a super closing.

A variation of this closing is to take photographs of your prospects in front of several homes. When you can sit down, spread the photos in front of the clients and ask:

> *"Now, which is the house for you?"*

If you are certain which house the clients are most interested in, consider:

> *"Pictures don't lie; it's obvious this is going to be your new home."*

The Reversal

While working for the federal government I had an extremely argumentative supervisor. If I said something was black, he would set out to prove it was white. I quickly discovered that if I wanted something, I had better argue for the opposite option. I would mention the supporting reasons for the preferred course of action but treat them as insignificant. My supervisor would seize on my reasons for supporting the course of action I didn't want and slash my arguments to shreds. He would then reinforce the reasons I gave for the other course of action and direct me to go ahead with it.

There are not many buyers that ornery, but I did run into one. The wife was very receptive to my presentations, but the husband disagreed with everything I said. I had showed them several homes that she loved, but he was impossible. Finally I told him, "I really don't think this next home is right for you. For one thing it's too big. You really don't need a fourth bedroom."

My buyer immediately took the position that he could use the extra space. I pointed out that the yard was too big and would take too much work, and he told me it would make a great garden. My closing was, "I don't think you want to buy this house." He, of course, was true to form and a sale was made. His wife later told me she was happy and knew what I had done. It seems the children had been using the same tactics on their father for years.

"You Can't Afford It."

This approach is similar to the reversal technique. I have used it successfully, but it should be saved as a last resort. When you are about to give up on a prospect, it is well worth a try. The approach has been successfully worked by used car salespeople for years. The you-can't-afford-it approach consists simply of telling your clients that you feel a property is too expensive for them.

> *"This property is probably a little too expensive for you. Perhaps we should try to find you more modest housing."*

> *"I think we'd better look for something less expensive for you because the monthly payments on this home will be beyond your means."*

If the prospective buyers have previously objected to upkeep costs, you could state:

> *"This home is for a buyer who doesn't have to worry about maintenance costs. I think we'd better look for something a little more modest."*

What you are doing is challenging the buyers. To some it's like waving a red flag in front of a bull. The approach works well on newly wealthy people and people who need to prove themselves because of insecurities. The typical target for this approach wears heavy gold jewelry and drives an expensive automobile. It should only be used when you are absolutely certain the prospective buyer *can* afford the home.

The buyers will be happy with their purchase and will tell their friends how they showed that salesperson what they could afford.

This approach can be so effective that it should be outlawed. It isn't really fair to have someone buy a home to prove themselves. I have never used the approach on anyone I liked.

Plus and Minus

If prospective buyers indicate they are interested in a home you showed them but are also interested in a home shown by another agent, offer to help them make up their minds. Prepare two sheets like this one:

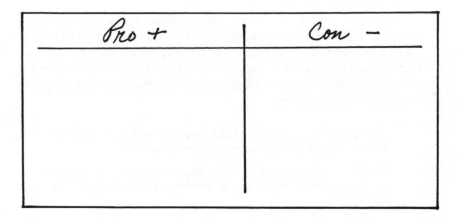

Use one sheet for the home you want to sell and the other sheet for the other property.

Ask your prospects to put down the plus and minus features of both properties. Make suggestions on the plus features of the home you showed. If you know the other property, you could mention negative features. When you are finished, your property should look the more desirable of the two. Now go for a closing. Keep in mind that the buyers are not sold on the other property. If they were, they wouldn't be with you.

The plus-and-minus approach is often used when buyers are unsure about two choices a broker has offered them. I recommend strongly against such use. The prospects most likely will not see a clear winner and will want to think it over some more.

Your Choice

Whenever your prospects are undecided, find out which property they like best.

> *"If the properties were priced the same, which one would you prefer?"*

The home they want will almost surely be the one that is priced higher. Instead of trying for a lower offer, a better approach is to go for a full-price offer.

> *"A home that gives you greater enjoyment is well worth the slight difference in price. You are going to get years of living enjoyment. Isn't that worth a few dollars difference? This is the home you really want, so let's buy it."*

Start writing up the offer.

Keep in mind that the price initially paid becomes less important as the years pass. It is the enjoyment buyers obtain from a home that is of greatest importance. You are helping the buyers if you put them in a home that will provide greater enjoyment, even though at a higher price, providing they can afford the home. Don't, however, attempt to put buyers into purchase situations they cannot afford. You are likely to waste your time because the sale won't be completed. Either the buyers will find a way to back out of the sale or financing will be unavailable because of the purchasers' limited repayment abilities.

SPECIAL CASES

The closes you've studied so far can be varied to fit almost any closing situation. This section gives examples of special situations and tips on how to handle them. Always keep in mind that prospective buyers won't buy unless you ask them to. Whatever closing or closings you use, use them. Don't assume, based upon your own feeling, that a client is not interested. Don't even base this on what the prospect has told you. Always attempt at least one closing.

The Clincher

Your prospects are sitting in your office with an offer in front of them and pens in their hands. But nothing is getting signed. If they are reading the offer, remain silent; but if they are not reading the offer this is the time for the clincher. Often the clincher—the final motivating spark—can be as simple as a reassurance of value.

> *"If the owners accept your offer, you will have made a really great purchase."*

> *"I envy you, and I am sure your friends will feel the same way when they see your lovely new home."*

The clincher might be the simple assurance that you will take care of the financing or other matters of concern to the buyers.

Sometimes real estate salespeople hold back a bit of good news to use as a clincher.

> *"Oh, I forgot to tell you, the seller is leaving all the lawn and garden tools including the new Rototiller that converts into a snow plow."*

Don't forget about the power of family affection when you look for the clincher that will help your client make the decision he or she is trying to justify. Love for spouse and children is often the primary motivation for a purchase, and your prospect needs you to assure him or her that this is the best way to express it.

> *"It would be great if you could get your children into the new Northside School by September."*

> *"Next to your children, this is the finest gift you could ever give your [wife/husband]."*

> *"Won't you feel more secure knowing your family has a fine home in a neighborhood like this?"*

> *"A home is much more than a structure. It's family security; it provides for family strength and continuity. A home is an expression of your love for your family."*

The following push works well with many hesitant buyers:

> *"[Mr./Mrs.] Jones, no one ever won a race by not entering it. If you want a home you must make an offer. Now, this home is within your financial ability and this home best meets your needs. If your offer is accepted you will have made an outstanding purchase. The worst thing that can happen is for the seller to say no, in which case any deposit will be immediately refunded to you in full. What do you have to lose?"*

Have your clinchers ready by thinking of reasons to buy and saving them up for this occasion. The clincher is the last push and can make the difference between success and failure.

The Hesitant Husband

In my experience, usually the wife is more interested in buying than the husband. It is usually the husband who comes up with the excuses not to buy. A real estate salesperson recently told me about an effective but simple signing technique. She gives copies of the offer to both husband and wife. The copies have a check mark in red where they are to be approved. She then hands the pen to the wife, not the husband. The wife signs and the husband goes along without objection.

"Help Me."

When you have failed to close and the customer is about to depart, this last-chance strategy has been known to turn things around:

> "I hate to ask, but [name], I wonder if you could take a minute to help me. I know I am not the most glib salesperson in the world, but I really felt that I would sell you [property] because it seemed to me that it really is right for you. Obviously, I was mistaken. Either the property doesn't really suit you, or I have a problem with my sales approach. If my sales approach is not satisfactory, what could I do to improve it? If the property is wrong for you, what specifically is the problem so I can find a property that better meets your needs? Perhaps it's a combination of both. Anyway, I would really like you to be honest with me. Don't worry about hurting my feelings."

People have a hard time resisting a call for help. If they reveal a problem with the property, you have another opportunity to overcome it and close. Normally, they will not say it is your fault, but if they do, be positive, not defensive, about the criticism. Thank them and then go into another closing.

The Unpriced Sale

This technique is excellent when buyers are overly concerned with list prices, or when the property you are showing is overpriced.

Don't mention the price. Tell the prospective buyers:

> "Price isn't really important because you are going to determine the price, and I am willing to bet you won't pay one dime more than the property is worth."

If the prospects agree that they like the house, tell them you will write up an unpriced agreement and they are to fill in the total investment. As you hand your prospects the agreement, tell them the list price. Inform the prospects that the more realistic their price, the greater the chance it will be accepted. If the price they give is unrealistically low, suggest the offer be increased to a more reasonable amount.

The Renter

I once worked with a salesperson who used this true story whenever he was closing prospects who were renters:

> *"My father rented for over forty years. He was an organized man and kept every rent receipt. [The salesman then took out the rent receipts bundled together in piles with rubber bands.] There are over 490 rent receipts here and that represents over forty years of my father's life. About 25 percent of his wages went to rent, so there really are ten years of hard work tied into these piles. You know what they are worth today—nothing. I decided I was not going to give ten years of my life to any landlord. Are you willing to give your landlord ten years?"*

He then handed the prospective buyers a pen and the purchase agreement.

Hard, Hard Sell

When I first started selling real estate, I sat at open houses every Sunday. A couple came in on my second open house and made a very low offer, which was refused.

My broker told me that this couple had made many offers over the years. This was the fourth with our firm. All offers were refused. They were renters and wanted a house but didn't want to buy it. They wanted to steal it.

Several years later they were interested in a house I had listed. I showed the house and the husband made a ridiculous offer he wanted me to write up. I had already decided how I would handle them. I said:

> *"You apparently have time to waste so you want to waste my time and the owner's time as well. While you have been going around making ridiculous offers, prices have gone higher and higher. You have two choices. One is to make a reasonable offer. The other is to decide you will spend the rest of your life in the apartment. Do you like this house?"*

His answer was yes.

"Well, dammit, I am going to write a reasonable offer and you are going to sign it, and I don't want to hear one more word out of you!"

The offer was signed and accepted. The buyers later had me over for a social gathering.

Note—Although you must present every offer received, this does not preclude you from trying to improve the offer.

This was an extreme solution to an extreme situation. Incidentally, my idea for the closing wasn't original. I had seen a variation of this approach used in an antique shop when a buyer made an extremely low offer for a vase. The owner said:

"Either talk sense or get the hell out of my shop. Now do you like the vase?"

The answer was yes.

"Then you will pay $_____[the shop owner named a price], which is a fair price."

The shop owner immediately started wrapping up the vase and the sale was made.

The Low Offer

If buyers suggest an offer at an unrealistic price, another approach is to start writing up the offer. Ask for correct spellings of the names if you are unsure. Put in everything but the price.

Seeing you write up an offer with their names on it often gets buyers to imagine themselves as owners. Chances are good they will think they can steal the property and you will be their accomplice.

Now ask the buyers:

"Do you like this house? How serious are you about this offer?"

The buyers will say they are serious. You then state:

"If you were the sellers, I wonder if you would accept an offer for $_____? I don't think so."

If you have comparables, use them. Use the information you would use to get a seller to accept a reasonable offer. You represent the owners, so you must try for the best offer possible. Point out that an offer such as this has little chance of acceptance, but worse yet it could alienate the owners so that they refuse to come up with a counteroffer. Explain that although low offers might be accepted, this offer is just too low.

Point out to the buyers that if a better offer comes in during the negotiation process, it is likely to be accepted without any further negotiations with them. Continue with:

"How badly do you want this property?

"You said you were serious buyers. I would like to suggest that you make your offer more realistic so that I can come to you and say, 'You have bought yourself a house.' What should I fill in here?"

If the buyers indicate they don't wish to raise it, then try:

"Raise the offer by five percent and I will do all I can to get the offer accepted. Five percent comes to just $_____."

Fill in the numbers without asking and hand the offer and a pen to the buyers. The worst that will happen is that you will have to rewrite the offer. You can usually get the buyers to raise it at least five percent.

If a customer asks if an owner will accept less than the list price, I suggest:

"If you like it, buy it. Is it worth it to you to risk losing a home that you like for only _____ percent off the price?"

If buyers suggest a price such as $89,900, suggest they round it off to $90,000. Explain that the additional $100 will have a great deal of psychological benefit in getting the offer accepted. To the sellers, $89,900 is an offer in the $80,000 range, while $90,000 seems a great deal more and is more likely to be accepted.

Even when the offering price is reasonable, if it is below list price you have a duty to try to make the offer the best possible offer you can get. One way to do this would be to state:

"[Mr./Mrs.] Jones, how did you arrive at the price of $____?"

Most likely your buyer will not have strong support for the offer; if so, continue with:

"[Mr./Mrs.] Jones, don't you think the home is well worth $_____?"

If the buyer agrees with you, state:

"Let's not take a chance of losing your home for a few dollars. Let's write it up at full price."

If the buyer does not immediately object, write the full price on the offer.

Whenever purchasers wish to offer less than list price, explain to them:

> *"With an offer below an owner's price, your chances of having it accepted will be increased significantly by a larger-than-normal deposit. An owner has a hard time turning down a below-market offer when the buyers have shown sincerity by making a substantial deposit. Remember, your check is held uncashed until your offer is accepted. How much of a deposit could you make?"*

Keep in mind it is easier to overcome problems of getting offers accepted in the initial drafting than while working with counteroffers. Strive to make the offer you get the best offer obtainable at the time.

Don't rush to get a low offer accepted. Instead, work to get the offer up into the region of reasonableness. Let the buyers know that an offer that low may anger the seller and you will end up with a complete rejection, not a counteroffer. Let the buyers know their best interest would be served by putting their best offer forward—not by holding back. As an example, if purchasers wished to offer $87,000 on a home listed at $100,000, a good approach would be:

> *"If the owner countered with $90,000, which is only about three percent more, you wouldn't want to lose your house for only three percent, am I right?*
>
> *"If you would accept a $90,000 counteroffer, let's offer $90,000 now and try to buy the home without a counteroffer. Let's avoid the risk of another buyer coming in with a higher offer."* [Now write $90,000 on the offer and give it to the buyers to sign.]

When you have received a very low offer, one technique is to call your office in the buyers' presence and say you have taken an offer:

> *"No, don't show it as sold, the offer is quite low."*

This gives you another opportunity to try to raise the offer. It also forewarns the buyers that they shouldn't be surprised if their offer is not accepted.

Even though an initial offer has little chance of success, it serves the purpose of starting the negotiation process. Prospective buyers who originally would not raise their offers will often respond favorably to a realistic counteroffer.

After you take a low offer, prepare the buyers for a counteroffer. Mention that if the offer is accepted as is, they will have stolen the property.

More Information

If you are unable to close on a property in which it is obvious your prospective buyers are seriously interested, suggest that you get them more information on the exact loan balance, tax bills, utility bills or other details. This is really an excuse to set up another meeting to again try to close.

DON'T PROVIDE AN ESCAPE HATCH

Never give prospective buyers an easy way out; I have seen many salespeople do just that. Asking prospective buyers, "Would you like to think it over?" is almost as bad as suggesting the buyers wait until prices fall, interest rates drop or hell freezes over. Buyers don't need your help to look for excuses. They will find enough on their own.

VOICE AND EYE CONTACT

While not a closing technique in itself, the way you use your voice can influence the success of your efforts to close. If you are an extrovert, you probably speak at fairly high volume. If you usually speak out loudly and clearly, you can provide special emphasis by lowering your volume and pitch. This gives the impression of confidentiality. You can use this low level to suggest offer or counteroffer terms.

While eye contact is always important in sales, it is especially important now. If you have difficulty looking people in the eye, focus your eyes on the bridge of your client's nose. You will give the impression you are looking right at the person. People often distrust people who look away from them when they talk.

SOOTHING BUYERS' REMORSE

After you have an offer, explain that buyers usually worry whether they have done the right thing. At times they get so nervous they can't eat or sleep. This is normal for all buyers. If buyers can't overcome their fears, they may remain renters for the rest of their lives. By explaining buyers' remorse in advance, you help your clients to deal with their feelings and realize they are not unusual.

Put a copy of the offer in an envelope and hand it to the buyers. Be certain to reassure the buyers that they have made a wise choice and that the home is an exceptional value even at a higher price.

8. Offer/Counteroffer

Your closing presentation is a success: You have an offer. You are now ready for the final step that, if it works, rewards all the effort you've expended thus far. This chapter shows you how to close the sellers—how to get the offer accepted. It takes you through the best ways to present the offer and handle counteroffers under various conditions and requirements.

When you have an offer for property listed by another broker, have the listing agent set up an appointment with the owners as soon as possible. Keep in mind that your buyers can withdraw an offer at any time prior to its acceptance. Many good offers also are lost because a competing offer comes in while the agent's presentation is delayed.

Under no circumstances should you give the listing broker the details of the offer. The listing broker can then honestly say he or she does not know when the owners ask, "How much?"

Another reason for not giving advance information to the listing broker is that the broker's salespeople could use your offer to obtain offers of their own, leaving you with nothing. A real estate salesperson once called me about a commercial building I was considering purchasing. The salesperson told me that another office had just taken an offer $20,000 below the list price. He suggested I make an offer $500 higher so that if the seller accepted that large a reduction, I would get the benefit of it, and of course he would get the sales commission. Unfortunately, this has become common, so I recommend withholding the details of an offer even from salespeople in your own office.

SETTING THE APPOINTMENT

There is more to presenting an offer than just giving the price. Avoid phone presentations. An owner can say no over the phone, but not yes. Yes requires a signature. With a phone presentation you have everything to lose and absolutely nothing to gain.

The listing salesperson should inform the owners that all offers will be presented in person because it would not be fair to give information over the phone without the buyers having the complete offer. Some owners will still try to obtain information prior to the presentation.

If your offer is for one of your own office listings, have someone else call your owners while you go out for coffee. It could be another salesperson, your office secretary, your broker or even your spouse. The person calling should make an appointment to present the offer and should know no details of the offer, so subterfuge does not have to be used:

> *"[Mr./Mrs.] Klyde, this is Mabel Beers, the office manager at Fast Sell Realty. I have some good news for you. Mrs. Schmidt just called in. She has found a buyer for your home. Would you and [Mr./Mrs.] Klyde be home at 7 P.M. so Mrs. Schmidt can deliver an offer to you?"*

If the owners call you prior to your appointment, you can bet they want to find out details of the offer. An excellent approach would be:

> *"Are you both at home now?"*

If they are:

> *"I will be right over."*

This approach is much better than trying to avoid giving out information over the telephone.

If you can't evade either giving the owners information over the phone or coming up with a good excuse, try:

> *"It's not really fair to the buyers to discuss their offer on the phone. I think the offer deserves careful consideration and I will have to explain several of its provisions. I will tell you one thing; you will want to see this offer."*

The last sentence is upbeat. It creates a positive image of the offer without really saying anything. Another possibility:

> *"I promised the buyers that I would present the offer in person. I am not going to hide anything from you and I would like to honor my promise."*

Both of the above are far superior to the approach that has been taught in books and seminars for years: "Office policy dictates that we not discuss the offer prior to presentation."

If the owners ask if you have an offer, be absolutely honest. Tell them:

> *"Yes, I am very pleased to tell you I have been working with the couple who viewed your home this morning, and I have just received an offer."*

You must not, however, give any details of an offer over the phone unless it is exactly in accordance with the listing.

One broker I know doesn't tell owners she has an offer. Instead, she says:

> *"I have someone interested in your property. I would like to stop by your home tonight at seven to discuss the property with you and [Mr./Mrs.] Brown. Would both of you be available at that time?"*

The statement is quite true, and discourages the owners from imagining the terms of the offer before it has been presented.

If owners know the offer is coming, the broker told me, some of them decide in advance to reject less than full price without considering any other benefits. In one case the broker met with verbal attacks when she arrived to present an offer to the sellers. They said they would not accept any offer. They wanted full price. When they calmed down, the broker explained that she had a full-price offer.

Another agent I know likes to arrive with an offer after giving only about five minutes notice. He calls the sellers and asks if he can come right over because it is very important. He thinks this reduces the tendency of some sellers to put up emotional armor against offers on their homes.

Out-of-Town Owners

You will at times have to deal with out-of-town owners. Many offices handle these offers by telephone, giving all the details. With multiple owners, a conference call can be arranged. To get immediate acceptance, you could have the owners send a telegram to you accepting all of the provisions of the offer. Compose the telegram in advance and dictate it to the owners. A counteroffer could also be taken in this manner. While I have seen many offers accepted this way, the failings of phone and mail negotiations usually outweigh their benefits.

One broker I know specializes in the sale of ranches. Ranch owners often are not only absentee owners but may reside in other countries. This broker calls his owners and tells them:

> *"I've sold your ranch. I'm coming with the paperwork. Pick me up at the airport at 9 P.M. I will be on _____, flight number _____."*

He tells me his percentage of rejected offers for out-of-town owners has decreased 50 percent since he began making personal presentations on all offers. Even when an offer is rejected, he usually is able to get an attractive counteroffer that would be difficult to negotiate by telephone.

I agree with him. It's poor economics to try to save a few hundred dollars in plane fare when an accepted offer could mean thousands in commissions. Having sellers pick you up at the airport creates an atmosphere of urgency and importance around your offer. You wouldn't fly in to present it unless you believed the offer was very exciting.

All Together Now

Present your offer as soon as you can get the husband and wife or other owners together. When an offer is presented to the owners separately, they have time to listen to others who don't really comprehend the offer or the complete situation. Owners will also get together on the phone before you have talked to all of them and make decisions before the offer is fully presented. Separately presenting an offer for less than full price and terms will make acceptance or a counteroffer almost impossible to get.

If owners have small children, make the presentation after bedtime or they will surely find ways to divert the owners' attention away from the offer.

THE POWER OF PREPARATION

Be as prepared to present an offer as you were to obtain the listing. Working to prepare yourself for the offer presentation will greatly help your chances of completing the sale. If the property is listed with your office, check with the listing salesperson. Find out the sellers' motivation, how long they have owned the property, how they purchased it, how long it has been on the market, what activity the property has had and whether there have been any previous offers. Use these facts to prepare your presentation and answer seller objections. Normally the listing salesperson will be very cooperative because he or she wants a successful sale and a commission.

Use a little role-playing and place yourself in the owners' position. Ask yourself what you would object to, and why. Plan how you can best overcome these objections. Normally, an offer's problem areas are price or financing or both. Decide how you are going to help the owners overcome these problem areas and convince them to accept the offer, if it is fair, or get the owners to make a counteroffer that has a reasonable chance of being accepted.

Write down key words for the various points you intend to make. After a while you will be able to make smooth presentations with just a few words to guide you. If your offer requires some seller financing, such as the seller carrying a second mortgage, be prepared to tell the sellers all about the buyers: where the buyers work, how long they have worked there, how long they have lived in the area and other details that will make them real people in the sellers' eyes. Obtain the buyers' permission to run a credit check on them. This credit information not only protects the sellers, but shows them you are interested in their best interests.

Just as you use comparables to obtain a listing, comparables can be used to get an offer accepted. To be meaningful, your comparables must be recent and accurate. Find out the actual sale price, as well as the terms and original list price.

The Proceeds

Before you present any offer, prepare a realistic estimate of what the sellers will actually realize from the sale. It is better to be conservative than to overestimate what the seller will receive. Sellers who are surprised at the last minute by having to pay points or by otherwise receiving less than they anticipated will be bitter sellers, or they will back off from the sale entirely.

Who Presents the Offer?

If your offer is on the listing of another broker, that broker is entitled to present the offer, but you, of course, have the right to be there. If you feel you are more capable of making the presentation than the listing salesperson or broker, don't hesitate to ask if you can make the presentation at least up to the point of handing the sellers your offer. Listing brokers and salespeople will often agree to your making the presentation. There would be fewer problems if everyone really understood the offer presentation process and was prepared for it, but some inexperienced salespeople come to the owners with no idea of what they will say.

Meet with the listing broker or salesperson at your office if possible. This will give you a slight psychological advantage. Go over the offer and your preparation material. When the other party sees your preparation, he or she might be more willing to let you make the presentation.

SETTING THE MOOD

When I present an offer I like to be as physically close to the owners as possible. Across a living room is too distant. I usually suggest offers be discussed over a kitchen table. You can take charge right from the beginning by suggesting seating arrangements to "better review the offer."

A compliment is an excellent icebreaker, such as the wonderful job they have done on the lawn. Mention a feature that played a big part in the sale, such as the basement darkroom. If you can't think of a house compliment, compliment the owners' dog, cat, canary or even appearance. If the owners are retiring and moving to Florida, tell them, "You're going to have a long wait until you're eligible for Social Security." They may assure you they are eligible already and you can be amazed. This usually puts owners in a receptive mood.

If the owners will be buying another property after the sale, ask them if they have found what they are after. Discuss the type of housing and the area they are interested in. A short discussion often reinforces their desires and puts them in a selling frame of mind.

Some years ago I arrived at the appointed time to present my offer and the entire family was glued to the television set. They wanted me to present the offer during commercial breaks in "Have Gun, Will Travel." I asked if we could go into the kitchen to discuss the offer because I felt I needed their undivided attention. The wife told me their favorite shows were on that night and she wanted to watch. After finding out when her shows would be over, I returned at 10 P.M. to get the offer accepted. I was not about to compete with a television set.

If the owners have friends, relatives or neighbors present, suggest you go into a separate room so as not to disturb the others. If you find you are playing to an audience, you may have to convince the crowd. The owners, too, may play to their spectators. It's hard enough to deal with a husband and wife in the emotionally charged sale atmosphere without having the owners performing for their friends.

If one spouse is not ready, wait. If either is interrupted and must leave, wait or ask when you should return. Don't accept, "Whatever [he/she] says is all right with me." It won't be.

ANATOMY OF AN OFFER PRESENTATION

Your offer presentation should be broken down into three parts: the background, the buyers and the offer.

The Background

In the background portion of the presentation, review the history of the sales effort:

> "It has been 87 days since you listed your property with Statewide Realty. A previous 90-day listing with Kyle Realty expired without an offer. This is the first offer received on your property in 177 days of effort—almost half a year. As you know, both Kyle Realty and Statewide Realty advertised your home and both made your house available to our multiple-listing service. The records of Statewide Realty indicate your home was shown 28 times. I don't know how many times Kyle Realty showed your home. In addition, Statewide Realty had three open houses and Kyle Realty had at least one open house.

> "One problem we have had in locating a buyer is that your home has only two bedrooms. The den off the living room is really not suited for use as a bedroom. This area is mostly a family area with the average age of new buyers in their thirties. Most of these buyers want three bedrooms."

You have reviewed how long it took to get the offer, the effort that was expended, as well as problems with the house. It is important that any negative features raised by prospects be mentioned if the offer is for less than the list price and terms. These will be recognized by the owners and will help make them more receptive.

The Buyers

You want the sellers to like the buyers and be glad they will be living in their house. This is very important when the offer is for less than the sellers had hoped for. The next part of your presentation might go something like this:

> *"The buyers are the Smiths, the young couple I had over Thursday afternoon. Ted Smith is a maintenance supervisor with Golden Electronics, while Alice Smith is an associate editor with Lewis Publications. They have a daughter, eight years old, who goes to Kilbourn School.*
>
> *"The Smiths looked at a great many homes, but it finally boiled down to your home and a three-bedroom home at 1811 Elmside Way."*

Be honest in the presentation. Normally, buyers are considering several homes. By mentioning a feature of the other home that this home lacks—three bedrooms—you are again reminding the owners that their house has a problem. Continue with the story of how you tried to show the buyers that the benefits of this home outweighed the problems.

> *"I realized how long your have been trying to sell your home so I really worked to convince the Smiths that your house better meets their needs. I emphasized that your home is within walking distance of Kilbourn School. The other home would have required little Cindy to take the school bus.*
>
> *"Although Mr. and Mrs. Smith wanted a three-bedroom home because it would make eventual resale much easier, I pointed out that they should be interested in living enjoyment, not resale, and your home came closest to meeting their housing priorities."*

Make sure the owners appreciate what you have done for them. The offer you are presenting is the result of your efforts to do your best on their behalf.

The Offer

Throughout your presentation, consider the motivations of the owners. Point out specific benefits to them. Before you give the owners the offer to read, get agreement on all the minor points first.

> *"The Smiths would like possession by September 1 so that Cindy doesn't have to change schools. Is that convenient for you?*

"The offer calls for you to leave your fireplace screen and tools. Although not shown in the listing, I believe you intended to do this. They appear custom-made for the house. Is that satisfactory?"

If the offer has other positive features, point them out. Let the sellers know if the buyers have no contingencies, are unlikely to have credit problems or are willing to go along with special possession or closing requirements.

If an owner will receive profit from this sale and is either over 55 or will purchase another home within two years that costs the same or more than this sale price, explain that this profit can either escape taxation entirely, or that the taxes can be deferred.

Then present the earnest money:

"The Smiths have given me their check for $5,000 as earnest money with their offer to show their sincerity."

Lay the deposit down on the table in front of the owners or attach it with a paper clip to the offer.

After you have covered the matter of the earnest money deposit, hand the owners the offer and let them read it. Watch their faces as they read. Some brokers like to give the price verbally to the owners. Others will not hand over the offer until they feel the buyers are ready to sign it. In any event, always provide a pen with the offer.

POWER STRATEGIES I: THE UNDER-LIST OFFER

This approach prepares the owners for a very low offer:

"The Smiths are going to buy. If not your house, another. I worked hard with them to obtain this offer. It's not what I had hoped for, but during the 177 days your home has been on the market, it is the only offer we have received and we have 37 salespeople in our office and over 2,000 salespeople in our multiple-listing service.

"This offer takes the Smiths off the market. They are your buyers now, if you want them. By accepting their offer, you will form a binding contract. If the offer is not acceptable to you, you could make a counteroffer, and perhaps we can use that to negotiate an agreement. But I must caution you that a counteroffer legally frees the buyers to buy any other property, while your approval of the offer binds them."

Now give the owners the offer and, of course, a pen.

When owners are adamant about one element of the offer, change the subject, discuss other points to relieve the tension, then return to the problem areas. Often after a diversion the owners feel more receptive.

Remain calm and use a low, calm voice when an owner becomes agitated. The calm approach is generally more effective than a strongly emotional one.

Let the owners read the contract over without interruptions. If they have any questions, answer them honestly and completely.

Justifying the Offer

Provide some background for the low offer.

> "The Smiths wanted to pay $68,000, but I told them this was not a reasonable offer. I pressed for a full-price $78,000 offer. I spent over an hour on the price. I feel their $72,000 offer was the best offer obtainable. This is the list price for the three-bedroom house on Elmside Way.

> "The Smiths did not feel they could go any higher. They feel a higher monthly payment would stretch their finances too thin for comfort."

The owners must not feel that the buyers are being arbitrary, or they will tend to respond in kind. Your statement reinforces that buyers can choose from many sellers and reminds the owners you are on their side and really working on their behalf.

When you feel an offer is in the ballpark as presented, press for an unqualified acceptance. To do otherwise would not be in your owners' best interests. Don't worry that the offer is for less than the list price. Owners don't determine value with list prices; buyers determine value with offers. If the offer is within the range of actual sale prices for comparable properties with similar terms, then it is a good offer.

Explaining Real Prices

If a sale is without lender points to be paid by the seller, you should explain how much they would have had to pay had the offer been subject to a new VA loan. You could show that what they are receiving is equivalent to an offer for thousands more with a VA loan. Owners will often compare ads for homes with VA financing but not realize what it could mean to an owner in terms of costs.

Owners also will compare builders' prices. They don't understand that when builders offer below-market interest rates they are actually buying down the interest rate by paying the lender. This means their true sales price is much less than ads quote.

Explaining buyer points for loans can be very effective in persuading an owner to accept an offer. The fact that the buyer must pay $5,000 in lender points makes a $145,000 sale price actually $150,000.

> "The buyers are actually paying $150,000 for your home. They are paying you $145,000 and $5,000 to the lender for the loan. This is no different from paying you the $150,000 and having you pay the $5,000 in points. In fact, in a number of loan situations it is the seller who pays the points. So you see, the buyers are buying a $150,000 home and paying $150,000 for it."

Be Surprised

If the owners indicate they will not accept what you consider to be a good offer, act surprised. It will throw the owners a little off balance. You could say:

> "Perhaps you don't fully understand this offer."

Go over the minor points first and then the price. Ask the owners what in particular they object to.

Showing the Sellers

If owners are unrealistic in their price demands, you might get them to consider a reasonable offer by actually showing them other listed properties of a comparable nature as well as properties that recently sold. As you drive by each property, show your owners the multiple-listing data or the sales data from your listing service.

You will probably need a special appointment for an owner-showing trip. Plan the trip carefully to find realistic comparables. Figures and photographs are not as impressive as actually seeing the homes.

Ridiculous?

If the owners indicate the offer is ridiculous, this approach can be effective:

> "Money to me is not ridiculous. I have a check in my hand for $5,000. That's not ridiculous, it's real. It's enough for me to want to closely evaluate this offer. Let's put the price aside for just a few minutes and consider the rest of the offer first."

Try to get agreement on everything but the price. Go through the entire offer. When you return to the price, the owners are likely to be in a more receptive mood.

Don't jump to write up a counteroffer. Anyone can do that and many do, which explains why success eludes so many salespeople. Work for acceptance of reasonable offers.

If the owners act insulted by the offer, let them vent their hostility. I have often started a presentation in a hostile environment and ended with an acceptance. Being hostile is often a defense shield that can be penetrated by facts and logic.

On the other hand, if an offer is really ridiculous, recommend not that it be rejected, but that a reasonable counteroffer be made.

Watch for clues to the sellers' reactions in their body language. Whispering to each other is a good sign. If their reactions were negative, they probably wouldn't be whispering; they would come across loud and clear. If an owner folds his or her arms, it is usually a sign of resistance to the offer.

Don't act as if the offer were something to be ashamed of. You have a substantial deposit showing that the buyers are serious. Treat every offer as a serious one.

If another agent is presenting a completely unrealistic offer to your owners, don't let that agent browbeat them. It is unethical to push owners to accept an offer that clearly is not in their best interests. However, few offers are so low that you would recommend rejection.

"A Friend Said..."

Owners might say a friend, relative, another broker, banker, cousin and so on told them not to accept less than a set amount (usually the list price). This is a good response to this type of owners' defense:

> "I deal in real estate professionally. I feel I know the market and feel strongly that the offer before us is reasonable and should be accepted. However, let us assume for a moment that you do not accept the offer and we lose the seller. Assume that despite our best efforts we are unable to again receive an offer as good as this one. Will your [friend/relative] reimburse you for the loss you suffered because you followed their advice?
>
> "Of course not; it's very easy to give advice when it isn't your own money. Your decision should be yours, not someone else's."

The Price-Cut Myth

Owners often will resist taking a reduction or become upset about having their price cut. You must explain that the list price simply reflects the owners' guess at a fair price. It is the market that finally decides. There is really no such thing as a price cut, because the buyers set the price.

Play the Percentage

For offers less than list price, compute the reduction as a percentage of the list price. Instead of talking about thousands of dollars apart, show the differences in percentages, which will not affect owners so emotionally. There are positive ways to express low offers:

"This offer provides you with over 92 percent of what you desired at the time of listing."

This description sounds much better than a reduction of thousands of dollars.

When the difference between what a seller wants and what a buyer wants to pay is slight, don't mention the purchase price, mention the difference.

"We are only two percent apart. The buyers want to give you 98 percent of what you asked. Are you willing to risk losing these buyers for only a two percent difference?"

The Cash Advantage

When you have either an all-cash offer or an offer where the buyers are willing to refinance and cash out the sellers, the offer is likely to be considerably less than list price. This is especially true if the owners had indicated a willingness to provide financing at a below-market interest rate. You can logically point out the advantage of the lower cash offer by this kind of reasoning:

"You wanted $200,000 for your home and indicated you would carry a second mortgage for $60,000 at nine percent. The buyers would then pay you $30,000 cash and assume the first mortgage of $110,000. After our brokerage fee is deducted, you would have $18,000 left plus the $60,000 mortgage at nine percent."

Write out the following:

$$\$60,000 \times 9 \text{ percent} = \$5,400 \text{ interest per year}$$
$$\$18,000 \times 14 \text{ percent} = \underline{\$2,520} \text{ interest per year}$$
$$\text{Total interest} = \$7,920 \text{ per year}$$

Explain that they could probably invest the cash at 14 percent interest in a good second mortgage. Get the owners to agree to this fact.

> *"Therefore, a sale at $200,000 would really mean $7,920 per year to you, is that correct?*
>
> *"The offer we have is for $175,000 cash. After paying off your $110,000 mortgage, it will leave you with $65,000. Deduct our brokerage fee and it comes to $54,500. Let us assume you invest the $54,500 at the same 14 percent in a good second mortgage. $54,500 times 14 percent equals $7,630. As you can see [write it out], a cash offer, even though for a lower price, can actually mean almost the same as a full-price offer where you finance the buyer at below-market interest."*

The Gamble

When a seller resists an offer because of a few thousand dollars, try this:

> *"You are obviously a gambler, [Mr./Mrs.] Jenkins."*

The owners's reaction usually will be, "What do you mean?"

> *"[Mr./Mrs.] Jenkins, you are betting $87,000, which is the offer you now have, in the hope of getting $3,000 more. I personally don't have the guts of a gambler. I wouldn't chance losing $87,000 I can have by just approving the offer, when it's only $3,000 more at stake. Those odds scare me. That's 87-to-three odds."*

"What Will You Pay for Your House?"

When owners refuse to accept an offer because of price, an extremely strong approach is then to ask:

> *"[Mr./Mrs.] Jenkins, what are you willing to pay for this house?"*

Your owners will typically ask what you mean. They don't want to buy the house; they already own it. They want to sell it.

> *"Whenever you turn down an offer to buy, you are really saying, 'No, the house is worth more to me than that.' By turning down an offer you are bidding against the buyer. If you accept the offer, you will have sold your house, but by refusing the offer, you become a bidder. What are you willing to pay for this house?" [Note that in selling we use the emotional term home, but now you want the owner less emotional so it becomes just a house.]*

If the owners still indicate they don't want to buy the house, ask:

> *"Then why are you bidding on it?"*

This approach makes sense. Often you will have to go through it a second time, explaining that when they turn down an offer, they are really buying it at the offered price themselves as a speculator, in hope of a quick resale at a higher price.

Case Histories

If an owner does not wish to accept a reasonable offer, give actual case histories—your broker should be able to give you several—of owners who refused offers only to later sell their properties for less than they had previously refused. Not only did they lose money by their refusals, they also had long and costly delays.

Family Separation

A job transfer can place great strain on a family relationship when one spouse has left or will have to leave the house. This can be an effective motivation to accept an offer:

> "I know that living apart has caused [or will cause] a great deal of strain and mental anguish. Right now we have an opportunity to solve your problems. Are you willing to subject your family to this pressure for a difference of opinion about value that amounts to only four percent?"

Keep in mind that value is not an absolute. It is only an opinion. The opinion of the buyer sets the market value.

Just a Signature Away

When owners are close to acceptance but not quite there, point out how easily they can settle the issue.

> "No matter how special or desirable a property is, it can't be sold without a buyer. Right now we have a buyer. You are only a signature away from selling your property."

Now hand the owners a pen or a second one if the one you handed them earlier isn't in their hands. I have handed over as many as a half dozen pens before one actually was used to sign the agreement.

Go to the Other Spouse

When only one spouse has voiced objections to what you believe is a good offer, an interesting tactic that is often successful is to go to the other spouse. (Usually, it seems to be the husband who voices strongest objection to price.)

> *"Mrs. Jones, just for a minute imagine you had to make a decision about this offer by yourself. Assume John was not here to give you advice. From the information I have provided you about other sales, would you accept my recommendation: that this is a fair offer and should be accepted?"*

If you get a positive answer (and the question is worded to elicit a positive response), there is a good chance the husband will accept. Remain silent after the wife says yes and wait for the husband to respond. Normally, he will go along with his wife.

Hesitation

If a husband and wife are hesitant, ask them if they would like you to leave the room so they can discuss the offer between themselves. This generally will be welcomed. It shows you are not using undue influence and reaffirms your sincerity. From experience, I have learned the usual result of the private talk will be acceptance. At worst you are now in a position to work on a counteroffer. However, before you hand them their counteroffer for signature, be certain to explain the effect of a counteroffer and try again to have the original offer accepted.

Feuding Owners

If spouses become antagonistic to each other during your presentation, it is actually a good sign. Spousal arguments are generally resolved by the parties and you need not get involved.

Limited-Use Property

If the owners of a limited-use property—a seven-bedroom home or a cold storage plant—are displeased with an offer, point out honestly that there is not a great deal of demand for properties of this type. Emphasize that you were very fortunate to find a buyer with these special needs.

In the event the owners make a counteroffer, let your prospective buyers know they were lucky to find a property that meets their specific needs. If they let this property go to some other buyer, it could take months or even years to find anything as suitable, and even then it would likely cost a great deal more.

Of course, both of these arguments are absolutely true, although they appear contradictory.

POWER STRATEGIES II:
OTHER OBJECTIONS

The Quick Offer

When an offer comes in shortly after the property has been listed, the owners may get the idea that finding buyers is easy and hold out for the full list price.

Even a quick, full-price offer may make the owners reluctant to accept it in the belief that they could have gotten more. It may seem strange, but when you get a quick offer, owners don't look at it as a great job. They believe it was a result of setting too low a price. Of course, when you don't sell quickly, owners don't then think the price is too high. Then it's because you are not doing your job.

Whenever you get a quick offer, do your homework. Have the comparables to show that the price is fair. Let the owners know how fortunate they are to receive an offer so quickly. Show your owners similar listings that expired unsold.

When you sell a home very quickly, owners will sometimes want a commission reduction. This is easy to turn around.

> *"Would it have made you happier if we had taken six months to sell your house? That is the average sale time in this market. Actually I feel we did one heck of a job for you. So good, in fact, that you should really be paying us more for such a quick sale."*

Commission Cutting

Some owners will refuse a good offer unless you materially reduce your commission. Call the owners' bluff (and it usually is a bluff) by taking this attitude:

> *"I am very sorry to hear that. I will inform the buyers that their offer has been rejected. I think you are making a serious mistake because I firmly believe this offer is advantageous to you. I don't*

believe in pressuring owners. If we find someone else who is interested in your property, we will of course do our best to sell it and perhaps we will be successful."

If you've mentioned that your buyers were interested in two properties but you directed them to this one, remind them:

"While I know Mr. and Mrs. Smith will be disappointed, I believe they will buy the other home at _____, which has three bedrooms."

Now the above is very strong and you may feel this position is too inflexible, but the owners agreed to pay you a stated percentage of a sale price. The owners are attempting to renege on their agreement with a take-it-or-leave-it attitude. You are simply saying you will leave it. Owners will seldom let you leave it.

Cutting commissions can create a very negative image of your firm. If you agree to reduce your fees, the owners will tell all their friends how they were able to save money by bluffing you. Other owners who paid your normal fees will feel cheated because you worked for others at a cut rate. Owners who know you cut commissions in the past will expect similar treatment when you sell their homes.

With owner financing, we are seeing many sales where there is little cash after closing. Many brokers realize that, in order to make a sale, some flexibility will be required. Some brokers will carry paper as their commission. Instead of receiving a commission in cash, they receive a promissory note that sets forth a payment schedule. If you must carry a note, it should be secured by a mortgage or trust deed on the property being sold or on some other property the seller owns. An unsecured note will leave you with nothing should the seller go bankrupt or become judgment-proof.

Taking paper will not negatively affect your image as will cutting commissions, but businesses need cash to survive. To sell the paper would require a substantial discount and borrowing on paper requires an interest rate in excess of the interest being received. Therefore, strive to obtain your commission in cash. If you insist on cash, owners will generally find the cash.

Low Down Payment

When an owner objects to the low down payment, a good response is:

"[Mr./Mrs.] Brown, when you purchased the house in 1962, how much of a down payment did you make?"

Chances are great that the present owners put down far less cash than the present buyers are offering. If there is a present FHA or VA loan, chances are excellent the owners paid very little or even nothing down. If the owners purchased with a low down payment, continue with:

> *"Buyers today are not much different than you were when you purchased the house. Most young people have two things: great expectations and the expense of starting a family. They are like you in that they don't have sizable savings. The fact that Mr. and Mrs. Smith have managed to set aside $5,000 in today's economy speaks highly of the fine people they are."*

Again, we try to turn negatives into positives.

If an offer provides for a very low down payment and the seller will not agree to finance the buyer with so little equity, there are many alternatives to suggest.

* In many states *land contracts*—where the seller retains title—provide for easy foreclosure should buyers default. The fact that the sellers retain title can convince many sellers to sell with low down payments.
* *Deferred down payments* by a series of balloon payments might also satisfy the sellers.
* If a buyer has other property, a *blanket encumbrance* using the other property as additional security will often interest a seller.
* A *lease-option arrangement* will favorably impress many sellers. Here, title does not pass until the buyers come up with an acceptable down payment. Perhaps part of the rent in the interim could apply toward the down payment.
* The sellers could milk needed cash out of the property by putting a small *second mortgage* on the property that the buyers could assume.

For a discussion of many other ways to handle low-down-payment buyers, I suggest you read my book, *Get Rich on Other People's Money: Real Estate Investment Secrets* (Arco, 1981).

Selling at a Loss

When accepting an offer would mean selling at a loss, the owners might not really dispute the fairness of the offer, but still resist the idea of losing money. Here is one way to deal with a loss situation:

"How long have you lived in this house, [Mr./Mrs.] Jenkins?

"If you accept the offer that is before you it will mean that you will have lived in the house for ten years for only $2,500. That's only $250 per year or about $20 a month. What is the value of the quality of life this house has provided? It would be hard to compute, but I am sure it would be considerable. You also had the tax advantage of having your interest and taxes as deductible expenses. No, I don't think you are taking a loss, [Mr./Mrs.] Jenkins. I think this house has been very good to you."

What we are trying to do is turn a negative into a positive. Owners feel they must make a profit, but nowhere is it written that home ownership always means a monetary profit. Profit can come in forms other than cash.

If owners are breaking even, treat it in a positive manner:

"You, in effect, have lived here for ten years for free. This house has been very good to you."

Owners often figure their investment in a property by adding up all they have spent on maintenance and repairs. Explain that repairs simply maintain value; they don't increase it. Only improvements increase value, and often by less than their full cost. When owners tell you how much they have invested in the property, ask questions if the figure seems high. Chances are they have added up everything from lawn seed to carpet cleaning.

"I Want To Think It Over."

If a seller wants time to consider an offer, explain *buyers' remorse* (page 182). By taking time to consider a reasonable offer, the owners run the risk of losing the sale. Even though an offer might provide several days for acceptance, buyers can revoke an offer any time prior to acceptance.

"The House Is Paid For; I Can Wait."

Many owners erroneously think that because they are not making house payments it isn't costing them anything to live in their home. Your approach to this reasoning should be:

"[Mr./Mrs.] Jones, because your house is paid for, you feel you can afford to wait for a better offer, is that correct?

"[Mr./Mrs.] Jones, would you consider a ten percent return on a cash investment to be a reasonable return today?

"[Mr./Mrs.] Jones, you own this home free and clear and it is worth at least $200,000, because that's the offer we have before

us. If you had $200,000 cash to invest, you would therefore expect $20,000 per year as a return on the investment. Let's see what that comes to per month. That's $1,666 per month. You are losing $1,666 every month because that's what you could be getting if you accepted this offer. In six months, your loss would be $10,000 and that isn't even considering your home costs of taxes, insurance and maintenance. Why, it's likely costing you $2,000 per month to live here—that's $24,000 per year. Now those are the true costs of ownership. Let's consider the offer we have again."

Return the Listing

Assume the listing is a little high and the owners absolutely refuse to accept what you consider to be a fair offer or to give a counteroffer. If you cannot get the buyers to increase the offer, a Power approach would be to return to the owners and ask them to accept the listing back and to sign a form releasing your firm of all further responsibility. (You should, of course, at the same time register your buyers under the safety clause of the listing in case the owners later sell directly to your buyers.)

The effect of this strong measure could be to make the owners realize they are being unreasonable.

WHEN TO RECOMMEND A COUNTEROFFER

For offers below fair price, you should not urge acceptance. This would be a breach of your fiduciary duties as the owners' representative. Be factual in your presentation and tell the owners their choices: rejection, acceptance or a counteroffer. Recommend that the offer not be rejected unless it is clearly frivolous. Point out that the price is below what you consider fair. Suggest a counteroffer, being careful to explain that a counteroffer acts to reject the original offer.

Owners will sometimes accept unreasonable offers for reasons of their own. A low price in your eyes may look good to an owner. Because of inflation, a California condominium purchased for $35,000 in 1972 could be worth $175,000 today. A ridiculous offer of $125,000 is still a $90,000 profit.

Chances are good the property was listed near the high edge of its fair market value range or even beyond it. The fair market value range is based upon actual recent sales of comparable properties, not other listing prices. Recommend a counteroffer in the lower area of the range using comparables to justify it. Such a counteroffer would appear to a prospective buyer as a significant price concession.

If you have brought a fair offer from the buyers, consider a counteroffer to be a last resort. It is an indication of failure. You must continue to strive for acceptance. However, there will be owners who refuse fair offers, even after you point out the advantages of acceptance. These owners are not likely to be highly motivated to sell.

Getting A Counteroffer

When you encounter owners who refuse to accept what you consider a fair offer even after you have pointed out all the advantages, inform them clearly what the consequences of their decision may be.

> *"An outright rejection of an offer usually ends the negotiation process. We have a serious buyer here and serious buyers are not that easy to come by. We can only sell when we have an offer and we have one now. I don't think you want to lose our buyers. A concession in the form of a counteroffer can keep the negotiation process alive. Do you have any suggestions on how an agreement can be reached?"*

Your objective is to get the owners to suggest counteroffer terms. If the terms are unrealistic, point out why and make suggestions for improvement. You want more than a counteroffer; you want a reasonable counteroffer that will be accepted. A sale is a two-way street that must offer benefits to both sellers and buyers. You are the catalyst helping to create that result; you are not trying to put anything over on anyone.

In arriving at an acceptable counteroffer, explain to the owners that price and terms are both important. Asking for better terms can actually make up for a lower price. Use your amortization tables to illustrate this:

> *"If you were willing to carry a $20,000 second mortgage at nine percent for fifteen years, the monthly payment would be $202.87. If you went to a 12 percent interest rate and cut the price by $3,000, you would get $212.31 per month on a $17,000 fifteen-year mortgage. Total payments received would be $9.44 more per month—a total of $1,699 more over the fifteen-year period."*

You can thus turn lowering the price into a positive feature. This approach is very effective with sophisticated sellers.

Should the owners insist on a price you think is too high, point out that you already tried to get the buyers to come up to $_____ but were unsuccessful. Suggest a lower figure.

If the owners are unwilling to make any concessions at all, explain to them that they should allow the buyers to save face. Even though their position is unrealistic, buyers must be allowed to feel that they received at least a minor concession through bargaining. Otherwise they may abort the sale. Explain that a minor concession is simply a shrewd negotiation technique. People like to be considered shrewd negotiators.

Splitting the Difference

When all logic fails, try an illogical technique: "Let's split the difference." There is no logic at all to this concept, but it smacks of fairness. People like to be considered fair. When one party is willing to go halfway, the other is often willing to meet them there. Every schoolchild has used the let's-split-the-difference technique.

When you bring a counteroffer back to the buyers and show them the sellers met them halfway (between list price and offered price), the sellers appear fair-minded and acceptance is likely.

A Counteroffer Switch

If you are unable to get what you consider to be a good offer accepted but the owners agree to a counteroffer, prepare the counteroffer on a separate offer form. You can now make one last attempt at getting the original offer signed. Hand the owners both the original offer and the counteroffer and a pen. Tell them:

> "[Mr./Mrs.] Jenkins, I want you to realize that with this counteroffer [point to the counteroffer] you will be rejecting this offer [point to the offer received]. The buyers then become deobligated [there's no such word, but it's effective]. By signing the counteroffer you are giving the buyers a second chance to decide if they want to own your house or someone else's house. Are you willing to take the risk of losing these buyers for a difference of only _____ percent? [Express the difference in a percentage rather than in dollars. The difference should be the difference between counteroffer and offer, not offer and list price.]

BACK TO THE BUYERS

Once an offer has been made, one of four events might take place:

1. The buyers can change their minds and revoke the offer.
2. The offer can be accepted.

3. The offer can be refused.
4. The owners can make a counteroffer.

This section shows tested ways of handling each situation.

The Buyers Revoke

If the buyers call you to revoke an offer, make an appointment to return the offer. This gives you another chance at selling the buyers. Often all that is needed is a little reassurance that they are doing the right thing as well as a reassurance of value. This is a good time to bring comparables with you. Be prepared to resell the buyers on all the benefits ownership will offer them.

The Accepted Offer

After an offer is accepted, don't call the buyers from the sellers' home. There is always the possibility that the buyers have had second thoughts and want to revoke their offer. Generally, an offer can be revoked at any time prior to acceptance. Acceptance does not take place until the buyers are notified, generally in writing. Mailing usually constitutes notification.

Buyers may also have second thoughts about other things, such as personal property they want. In one case, a salesperson called the buyers to tell them their offer was accepted and the owners got on an extension phone. The buyers asked if an item they wanted was being left in the house. The result was a telephone argument and no sale. Buyers and sellers are very skittish at the point of sale, so avoid any direct contact between them before the settlement.

If you cannot deliver the acceptance to the buyers immediately, mail it immediately. Mailing constitutes acceptance—once mailed, the buyers can no longer withdraw the offer. You should, of course, call the buyers immediately and tell them that the acceptance is in the mail. Congratulate them on having purchased a fine home. Give your buyers reassurance of value. Many sales crumble because buyers worry that they overpaid if their offer appears to have been accepted too quickly. Unless the offer was a full-price offer, never let the buyers feel that acceptance was easy. Point out the sellers' concerns and what you said to get the offer accepted for them. If they know you had to work to get their offer accepted they'll feel they got the best purchase possible. This reduces the likelihood of their backing out of the sale.

Buyers need tender loving care to keep them happy until closing. Salespeople who fail to reinforce the buyers lose sales before closing. If a comparable property is sold for more money, let the buyers know about it. It will reinforce their feelings that they made a wise purchase.

Often buyers' "friends" will tell them they paid too much. People with little knowledge of value and loose mouths have caused many good sales to never close. Your reinforcement of the buyers will protect you against this type of negative influence.

The Refused Offer

There will be times when, despite all your efforts, your owners will refuse not only to accept an offer, but also to grant any concessions at all in the form of a counteroffer. When you break this news to your buyers, you face the difficult—but not impossible—task of getting them to make a full-price offer.

Your approach here must aim at keeping the buyers from feeling that the owners are being arbitrary in their refusal to negotiate. You must make their insistence on a full-price offer appear reasonable.

> "[Mr./Mrs.] Broderick want very much to sell you their home. However, because they are serious sellers, they priced their property not at what other owners are asking, but at actual closing prices. They felt that by being realistic, they could obtain a quick sale. As you know, some owners list at outrageous prices, expecting to let the buyer negotiate and thus feel that he or she has gotten a bargain. That is not the case here. The property was fairly priced for a fair sale. I am sure the realistic pricing was one of the things that attracted you to this home. You would not have placed your offer if you didn't realize how well this home meets your needs. You know that this is the home for your family. I have prepared a new offer reflecting the price adjustment [hand the offer to the buyers]. For a difference of _____ percent, you don't want to risk losing your home. Priced as it is, we can be sure that it is going to sell."

If necessary, show the buyers comparables to prove that the price is indeed reasonable.

If the buyers refuse to make a full-price offer, make a definite appointment to show them further properties. Call the owners immediately to notify them that the prospects will not be making a new offer because they have decided to continue their search for a house. This might change the owners' attitude and result in their willingness to accept a compromise offer.

Presenting the Counteroffer

Your buyers should know when you are presenting the offer. You will have promised to contact them as soon as you have the news. Don't worry about disturbing them: They'll be waiting, no matter how late it is.

Don't call the buyers to tell them you have a counteroffer. Just say you must work out some details and will be right over. This avoids the problem of buyers building up emotional defenses.

Before you present the counteroffer, resell the virtues of the property. Next, point out the facts of your meeting with the owners. Let your prospective buyers know how hard you worked on their behalf.

Cover the points of agreement, then the points of disagreement. Refer to the disagreements as *adjustments*. Let your prospective buyers know why the sellers did not agree. Don't make their disagreements seem arbitrary.

Now point out the concessions you were able to get:

> *"While Mr. and Mrs. Jenkins felt the list price of $89,000 was fair and were unwilling to accept the $82,000 offered, I was able to convince them to accept $85,000. In doing so, they are meeting you more than halfway. I feel that at $85,000 the home is an excellent purchase. We are only $3,000 apart."*

In counteroffers, emphasize the relatively small difference in the amount:

> *"I think the home is well worth the $3,000 difference, don't you?"*

You can also show the difference as a cost per day using an amortization table and a pocket calculator:

> *"At ten percent interest the $3,000 difference only amounts to less than 88 cents a day. Isn't having your home worth 88 cents a day?"*

(Three thousand dollars amortized at ten percent over 30 years is $26.33 per month; divide by 30 to find the cost per day.)

When the parties are a few thousand dollars apart, you could say:

> *"Right now we are only $2,000 apart—that's just about one dollar per square foot. I don't think you should lose your home over such a small difference."*

Another approach would be:

> *"[Mr./Mrs.] Smith, am I right in assuming you expect to remain in this house at least ten years?"*

> *"Right now we are $5,000 apart. That's only $500 per year for ten years. Isn't this too small an amount to risk losing your home?"*

Show your buyers comparables. While their original offer may have been made largely on emotion, now logic will help. Your buyers want the house and chances are they want it more than before because the owners by their counteroffer are implying the buyers can't have it on their terms. Tell anyone they can't have something and they want it more. By showing them similar properties that sold for more money you reaffirm the buyers' sense of the house's value.

Emphasize that your buyers saved themselves *x* dollars by making their original offer. Congratulate them on being shrewd buyers. Now hand the buyers the counteroffer and a pen. Assume their approval:

> *"Approve where I have indicated. Your house-hunting days are now over."*

If your buyers still won't approve the sellers' counteroffer, many of the techniques you practiced for sellers can work on buyers, too. Again, point out the price difference as a percentage:

> *"You are now 96 percent of the way toward owning this home. Would you risk losing it for just a four percent difference?"*

The owners' counteroffer is really a price reduction. Point out that other salespeople in your office now know what the owner will actually accept, so the property is likely to go fast. The thought of someone else reaping the benefits of the buyers' efforts can move them toward acceptance very effectively. You can also use other Power techniques:

> *"If you didn't know that this was the home for you, you wouldn't have made an offer."*

> *"By accepting this counteroffer with these adjustments, you can relax knowing that you have purchased a home."*

> *"Right now we are only four percent apart. If you decide not to pay that four percent you could conceivably spend another five months looking for a suitable home and even then it might end up costing you more and not meet your needs as well as this one."*

If the sellers have to pay points, as with a new VA loan, explain that the sellers, by agreeing to pay these loan fees for them, are in fact receiving $_____ less. That they are not enriching the sellers as much as it seemed often softens buyers toward the counteroffer. Also explain other seller costs such as abstract or title insurance and termite inspections, which reduce net proceeds to the seller.

Counter to the Counter

If buyers are unwilling to accept a counteroffer, your next step is to obtain a counter to the counteroffer in the form of a new offer. You must get the buyers to make a concession. At times the final sale comes after a series of concessions by the buyers and sellers. Don't let the sale grow cold. Go back and forth between buyers and sellers without interruption, keeping both alert and expectant. Long delays encourage outside advice and other stumbling blocks.

The Second Try

When an offer is turned down, tell the buyers to consider making a new offer with just a little sweetener for submission in seven to ten days. The reason for this second attempt is that sellers often have second thoughts, especially if there is no activity on their home after they have refused an offer. The new, higher price offer (at least $1,000 more) also gives the sellers justification for holding out. It shows that this is about all the buyers can or will pay and helps the sellers realize that no one is trying to steal their home. The second try is worth the time and effort. I have found it to be successful more than 25 percent of the time.

When an offer is refused, keep in constant contact with the buyers and arrange other showings. During this period of time they are often dejected and likely to defect to other agents.

AFTER ACCEPTANCE

If the sellers are leaving the area, offer to help them in their new locale. Suggest that you can have a broker there contact them. This could mean an additional commission for you. Work through any of the national referral organizations, or call the real estate board in your sellers' new area.

Often agents sell homes and later find that their sellers purchased another home. Most sellers become buyers, so ascertain the sellers' needs.

Ask your sellers if any other neighbors are interested in selling. While their home was unsold they might not have wanted the competition, but now that their home is sold they may be very helpful. Referrals from a successful seller can go a long way toward obtaining a listing.

After acceptance, the sellers should be contacted on a regular basis. They should know what is happening regarding their sale and why. If any problems develop they should be immediately and fully informed. Don't try to keep bad news from one of the parties in the hope it will go away. Keep in mind that failure to communicate with buyers and sellers prior to closing could well result in no closing at all.

The buyers, too, need your continuing attention. After the acceptance, continue to assure them about what an excellent deal they made and what a fine home they purchased. Let both buyers and sellers know what is happening as the deal progresses. Salespeople lose a lot of sales because they don't monitor the details for the closing and fail to communicate with buyers and sellers.

Suggest lenders for your buyers. You might even want to keep loan applications on hand to give them. Suggest competitive lenders who have a good time record for processing loans. Many good sales fail to close because of lenders who are slow in processing loan applications.

Buyers at times indicate an interest in further property purchases. Don't show them other properties until the first sale has closed. If you do, they may think they've found a better deal and look for reasons not to complete their purchase.

It is essential to keep the buyers and sellers apart. All too often problems arise when one says something that upsets the other. Buyers and sellers are both nervous at this time and must be handled with care.

If the buyers want to take measurements prior to closing, handle it as if it were a showing. Have your owners prepare the property and leave the house. Be sure you accompany your buyers.

Don't allow buyers to make repairs prior to closing. They may find some real or imagined fault and become upset. The same holds true for buyers wanting early occupancy prior to closing. Suggest that they can get their wish by accepting an earlier closing.

The traps lurking in the preclosing period became dramatically clear to me at a broker friend's sixtieth birthday party. Among his guests were several clients including two doctors and their wives sitting at my table. One of the couples was selling a home to the other through the broker. As their host's liquor livened their spirits, the couples concocted a plan to cheat him out of his $15,000 commission. They would get their attorneys to find a loophole in their contracts—and it sounded as if they had several possible escapes. Then they would wait ninety days after the listing expired, as required by the ninety-day safety clause, and close the sale without a broker.

All that remained was to decide what to do with the ill-gotten loot. The wives described visions of carefree days sailing the ocean blue, and the husbands caught their excitement. I thought—naively, it turned out—that by the time Alka-Seltzer replaced the martinis, the couples would again listen to the promptings of their upright selves. Six months later our local newspaper's society page showed the couples living it up aboard a luxury Caribbean cruise ship.

Closing Plan

Have a timetable for closing with dates assigned for completing all required tasks. Constantly review the timetable and make certain that what has to be done is being done. Items included could be lender's appraisal, termite inspection, title report, existing loan balances and so forth. Some offices have elaborate visual boards that show at a glance what has been done and needs to be done prior to closing. A visual display reduces the likelihood of delays going unnoticed.

Unexpected Liens

You might come across a situation where a settlement is impossible because liens against a property and other settlement costs exceed the sale price. Don't assume the deal will be lost. There is something you can do. Contact the lienholder(s) and present your competitive market analysis. The lienholder is probably fully aware of the value of the property and the fact that the lien is not fully secured. Lienholders will often agree to release their liens in exchange for most or all of the proceeds of the sale. A sale allows a partial prepayment of the lien amounts. Lienholders might even be persuaded to carry the remaining indebtedness under an unsecured note, or waive the balance if they receive all the sale proceeds.

Take Care of the Little Things

Once you've gotten an accepted offer, the temptation is to relax and "don't sweat the small stuff". Unfortunately, little things can cause big problems, including a deal that falls apart. Keep both buyers and sellers informed right up to closing. If there are any problems, real or imagined, they must be solved to the satisfaction of both parties.

I remember a sale where the buyers were concerned about stained draperies. To satisfy the buyers, the offer stated, "The sellers shall have the living room draperies cleaned. If the present stain cannot be removed, the sellers shall replace the draperies with new ones of similar quality to be selected by the purchasers."

The stain could not be removed, so the buyers picked out some ready-made drapes at Sears that cost $80. The sellers refused to buy them because they felt $80 was too much. They would pay no more than $50. Rather than see a $30 difference blow over $2,000 in fees, I purchased the drapes for $80 and told the sellers I was able to get them for fifty. Everyone was pleased, and a "little thing" was prevented from ruining an otherwise clean and simple transaction.

AFTER CLOSING

Your activities don't end with a closing and a settlement check. During the sales process you should have developed a strong and favorable relationship with the buyers. They should have been impressed with your professionalism and your sincere interest in their needs. Nurture this relationship. Regular contacts with the buyers can provide a continuing source of strong referrals to their friends and associates. And when today's buyers become sellers, you want to represent them as their exclusive agent. Without inventory acquisition, or listings, your sales activity will come to a halt.

To help you become proficient in real estate listings I recommend my companion book, *Power Real Estate Listing.*

After Words

If you have read this far, you have acquired all the real estate sales knowledge you need to become as successful as you want to be. You have reached the point where words alone must make way for action: for motivation, for technical learning and for applying principles to real-life situations.

This book can now become just another how-to book on your shelf or it can become your working guide to a successful career. Many unsuccessful salespeople know very well what they should do, but their knowledge never leads to action because success takes too much work. If you want success you must give of yourself unsparingly. This means constantly practicing the techniques you have learned and constantly evaluating your successful and unsuccessful efforts to apply them in everyday situations.

It also means keeping in mind the basic idea of Power Selling: Power Selling is not the manipulation of people to make them do what you want them to—*that* is pressure selling. Power Selling is a way of helping people recognize their needs and the ways that property ownership can fulfill those needs. Power Selling is a natural selling technique that starts

215

with the first buyer contact and continues to and beyond the conclusion of the sale.

Power Selling is much more than just a way to locate property and to educate prospects about the purchase process that is most appropriate to their needs. Power Selling begins with helping prospective buyers recognize their needs and how to best meet those needs. It continues by reinforcing prospects' purpose and commitment so that they can become property owners.

By using Power Selling strategies you help owners and buyers improve the physical qualities of their lives. Even more importantly, you show them the way to attain a sense of well-being and security that is valuable far beyond any monetary measure.

Home ownership is a universal dream. You can help make that dream come true. If you use Power Selling to achieve success, you fulfill the needs and wishes of both yourself and your clients. Alfred Nobel didn't include real estate selling in the prizes he set up for great accomplishments, but perhaps he should have. Think about it for a moment. What is real estate selling but helping others to achieve a better way of life? Real estate selling is a noble profession well worth the work and attention it takes to succeed in it.

Remembering the worthwhile benefits of successful real estate selling will give you the motivation to work for it. Success is not an absolute. Success is whatever you want success to be. You and only you set your goals and measure their accomplishment. However you view success, to attain it you must know what you want. You must have a plan to reach your goals and you must work to follow your plan.

The old adage, "Plan your work and work your plan," can be the seven words that lead you to success.

Chances are good that while reading this book you said to yourself, "I can use that" or "I wish I had used that." As you read and reread the book and apply the lessons, you are likely to come up with variations, improvements or even entirely new concepts of your own. If so, I would like to hear from you. Just as you can use successful methods developed by others for your own success, you in turn can use your own success to help others. In the end, that is what real estate selling is all about.

If you would like to share listing or sales techniques with other agents, please send me your ideas. If they are included in a subsequent edition of *Power Real Estate Listing* or *Power Real Estate Selling*, you will receive appropriate credit.

Dr. William Pivar
75–496 Desert Park Drive
Indian Wells, CA 92210

Words and Phrases of
Power Selling

Everything you say to a prospective buyer should lead naturally toward the closing. In planning your presentation think not only about what you want to say but how you want to say it. Your choice of words can help create a positive emotional response in the buyer. When you describe homes and features, paint word pictures that will expand the prospect's visual impressions. The following language is a guide for helping you plan effective presentations, based on the individual features of the homes you will be showing.

For additional language, read my *Classified Secrets: Writing Real Estate Ads That Work* (Real Estate Education Company, 1988).

Air-Conditioning. *See*: Heating and Air-Conditioning

Alcoves. I am certain you will appreciate the intimacy of the music alcove.

> *Other Descriptive Terms:* Library alcove, reading alcove, sleeping alcove, sewing room.

219

Animals and Birds. There is at least one family of squirrels in that ancient oak tree.

> In the morning you can expect to see quail and doves at the
> well-frequented bird feeders.
>
> I understand that your nearest neighbors are a friendly fam-
> ily of raccoons.
>
> Don't be surprised to see a curious raccoon at your window
> at night.
>
> Deer have been seen on the property.
>
> The breakfast area overlooks the well-frequented hum-
> mingbird feeders.

Appliances. *Descriptive Terms:* Like-new, built-ins, built-in everything, Maytag appliances.

Architectural Styles.

Colonial. Currier & Ives would have loved this picture-book colonial.

> This home features colonial grace combined with modern
> comfort.
>
> [Mr./Mrs.] Jones, when you look at this home can't you see
> Tara, right out of *Gone with the Wind?*"
>
> [Mr./Mrs.] Jones, I think you will agree, this is truly a mon-
> umental colonial.
>
> This is a very pampered Dutch colonial.
>
> This is a much-sought-after but seldom available federal co-
> lonial.
>
> Don't you agree, [Mr./Mrs.] Jones, that this meticulous co-
> lonial exemplifies the elegance of southern charm?
>
> The design is obviously patterned after the noble houses of
> early Virginia.
>
> *Other Descriptive Terms:* Williamsburg-inspired colonial, a
> Quaker-village colonial, head-turning colonial, timeless
> colonial, impeccable colonial, clapboard colonial, Nan-
> tucket colonial.

Contemporary. Contemporary elegance—yes, but it also has the casual
flair of the Southwest.

> Have you noticed—the design has just a hint of oriental?
>
> The free-flowing contemporary design seems sculpted out
> of the stone and glass.
>
> Certainly it is sleek and sophisticated, but it is also warm and
> cheerful.

This home makes a statement as individual as you are.

The living area flows for entertaining yet maintains maximum privacy.

There is a fantastic feeling of openness and elegance in this .

Other Descriptive Terms: Exuberant design, exciting and spacious, open-concept planning, open-living design, provocative floor plan, excitingly different, innovative but not trendy, sophisticated contemporary, art deco.

English. This is reminiscent of an English country estate.

The home was patterned after the noble houses of England, where entertaining and hospitality were inseparable from a glorious tradition.

The home has a proper English design with muted elegance for truly civilized living.

[Mr./Mrs.] Jones, I am certain you will appreciate the timeless quality of classic Elizabethan design.

The home seems right out of "Masterpiece Theatre."

The home has an understated elegance that echoes the permanence of your achievements.

Other Descriptive Terms: Flawless Tudor, proper English brick, smashingly impressive, Cotswold manor, English country.

French. This French Regency home will surely be envied.

French Norman architecture has endured for almost 1,000 years.

The style is reminiscent of a Mediterranean villa, don't you agree, [Mr./Mrs.] Jones?

The ambiance of a French country home has been dramatically captured by the architect.

The French chateau style lends itself to entertaining on a grand scale or in small intimate groups, don't you agree, [Mr./Mrs.] Jones?

Other Descriptive Terms: French alpine, sassy French Provincial, sumptuous French country, Flemish cottage.

Italian. [Mr./Mrs.] Jones, don't you love the formality and grace of Italianate architecture?

The home is reminiscent of an ancient Roman villa.

Venetian Gothic combines the best of the Mediterranean influence with European elegance.

Other Descriptive Terms: Old-world Mediterranean, stately

Mediterranean, brick Italianate.

Spanish. The massive arches and tons of tile combine for a warmth and charm that only Spanish mission architecture can provide.

This home exemplifies the best of early California mission architecture.

With the flower-bedecked courtyard and bubbling fountain, you can almost hear the sound of a mariachi.

[Mr./Mrs.] Jones, wouldn't you love to have a Spanish theme party on this delightful patio?

Other Descriptive Terms: Adobe, hacienda, California Monterey, Presidio Spanish, Spanish colonial.

Traditional. While the design is traditional, there is just a touch of Spanish influence.

The home has the charm that only American traditional architecture can provide.

The home is an exciting blend of traditional and contemporary.

Other Descriptive Terms: English traditional, brick traditional, American bungalow, dignified traditional.

Victorian. [Mr./Mrs.] Jones, don't you agree, there is a certain charm and warm appeal that is found only in Victorian homes?

This is what a home was intended to be, don't you agree, [Mr./Mrs.] Jones?

Nooks and crannies for your collectibles, a wraparound front porch for summer evenings and just the feeling of space that doesn't have to serve two functions—that's why a Victorian home is my first choice for comfortable and gracious living.

Other Descriptive Terms: Turreted Victorian, gingerbread Victorian, Queen Anne Victorian, storybook Victorian.

Architect. This home was designed by _____. Don't you feel it captures the spirit of old New England?

This home was designed by the award-winning architect, _____.

The architect _____ was a disciple of _____. I think [he/she] has truly captured the essence of old Nantucket.

This home is an artistic masterpiece designed by the renowned _____.

Architecture. This_____ is magnificent in concept yet unique in design.

Don't you agree the architect has achieved a creative use of form and space?

The home has the aesthetic allure of classic design

Don't you agree, [Mr./Mrs.] Jones, that the architect has done a masterful job of blending the traditional with the timeless?

The home has a delightful European flair and style.

The home is dramatically different yet brimming with charm.

[Mr./Mrs.] Jones, doesn't this home break the monotony of the ordinary?

The architect has merged aesthetic form with the efficiency of function.

This home is the embodiment of simple elegance.

This is truly a home of unparalleled design in a setting of unsurpassed beauty.

The home was designed for flexibility and functionality.

The distinctive design creates the ambiance of a quiet European villa.

Don't you agree, there is a fantastic feeling of openness and elegance in this _____?

Don't you love the old-world character of this room?

There seems to be a charismatic blending of regal splendor with delicate charm.

Other Descriptive Terms: Distinctively designed, daringly designed, innovative design, a bold architectural statement, awe-inspiring design, free-flowing floor plan, innovative floor plan, exquisite architectural details, classical embellishments.

Bars. Your own pub room—wouldn't this be a great place to have a few close friends in for a Super Bowl party?

Having a wet bar allows for gracious entertaining. It is certainly much nicer than having to use the kitchen counter, don't you agree, [Mr./Mrs.] Jones?

Basements. Wouldn't this make a great rainy-day playroom?

The basement could easily be converted to an in-law suite or even a rental unit.

There is room here for at least two additional bedrooms.

Wouldn't this alcove make an ideal wine cellar?

There is plenty of room for a darkroom, a workshop as well as storage space in this exceptionally dry basement.

[Mr./Mrs.] Smith, how would you utilize all of this undeveloped basement space?

Baths. This master bath is almost sinfully sumptuous.

With the therapeutic whirlpool spa you have all the benefits of a health club right at home.

The opulence of this bath seems right out of the forties. All it needs is Rita Hayworth and a ton of bubbles.

This bath is bigger than the bedrooms in my first house.

Other Descriptive Terms: Sensuous master bath, Phoenician bath, Roman bath, garden bath.

Bedrooms. Whose room would this be, [Mr./Mrs.] Smith?

How would you arrange the furniture in this large master suite, [Mr./Mrs.] Jones?

A boy and his dog would love bunking in this rugged paneled bedroom.

Notice how the master suite is separated from the other bedrooms to give you maximum privacy.

Wait until you see the snuggle-up fireplace in the master suite.

A dormitory-size bedroom like this would be great for a children's slumber party.

The nursery is adjacent to the master suite.

The third bedroom, with its separate entrance, would be ideal for a home office or even a rental unit.

There is room for an additional bedroom in the _____.

The second master suite would make a teen suite that any teenager would love.

Carpeting. Not many owners put in all-wool carpeting such as this.

Genuine Berber carpeting certainly adds a feeling of excellence to a home, don't you agree, [Mr./Mrs.] Jones?

The neutral carpeting allows for a wide range of decorating possibilities. How would you decorate this room, [Mr./Mrs.] Smith?

The Karastan carpeting reflects the quality of the entire home.

Having small children, I am certain you will appreciate the fact that the carpeting is Dupont Stain-Master.

Other Descriptive Terms: Plush, sculptured, luxurious.

Ceilings. The 14-foot vaulted ceiling enhances the ambiance of the great room.

A soaring cathedral ceiling enhances the feeling of spaciousness, don't you agree, [Mr./Mrs.] Jones?

The feeling of spaciousness given by the vaulted ceilings takes this home out of the ordinary category. Don't you agree, [Mr./Mrs.] Jones?

Other Descriptive Terms: Illuminated, softly lighted, sky-lighted, cathedral, soaring, vaulted, beamed, open-beamed.

Clean. [Mr./Mrs.] Jones, after looking at a number of homes I am sure you find this home's immaculate condition a refreshing change.

The home certainly reflects caring owners.

From the condition of the home it's obvious the owners loved it.

The home is so clean you would think you were in a model that had never been lived in.

There is obviously nothing for you to do here but move in.

Other Descriptive Terms: Squeaky clean, flawless, impeccable, white-glove clean, pristine condition, superbly maintained, reflects owner's pride, move-in condition.

Closets. Aren't there more closets than you have ever seen?

You could get lost for days in these walk-in closets.

For the first time in your lives your closet problems are solved.

Colors. [Mr./Mrs.] Jones, would you make any changes to the general decor?

[Mr./Mrs.] Jones, don't you love the rich terra-cotta tones?

The warm, soft colors tend to set a California mood, don't you agree, [Mr./Mrs.] Smith?

The room is bathed in soothing pastels.

The neutral tones allow you great flexibility in decorating. How do you suppose you would decorate this room, [Mr./Mrs.] Jones?

Other Descriptive Terms: Soft terra-cotta tones, warm and rich color scheme, creamy beige, buttercup yellow, muted tones, soft tones, softly decorated, basic earth-tone decor, golden earth tones, warm earth tones, desert colors, California colors, cool and fresh, cool tones, bright and light, peaches-and-cream decor, a happy decor of _____, decorator-fresh, decorator-sharp, decorator-perfect.

Condominiums. I like having someone else cut my grass and shovel my snow—how do you feel about it, [Mr./Mrs.] Jones?

You really wouldn't even need a car. With this central location you can walk to everything. How far is your office, [Mr./Mrs.] Jones?

This is a home for a uniquely comfortable urban lifestyle.

It's sophisticated yet so comfortable, don't you agree, [Mr./Mrs.] Jones?

Isn't this an exciting alternative to apartment living?

There are all the amenities of a fine resort. Isn't this a sophisticated lifestyle?

This is more than just a place to live. With the recreational facilities it is a private world of fun and leisure.

With the soundproofing, you won't have to whisper anymore.

Other Descriptive Terms: Choice corner unit, private end unit, garden unit, upgraded Oxford model, upgraded beyond belief, strategic location, low monthly assessments.

Darkrooms. Wouldn't this be perfect for your home darkroom?

I'm sure you realize we were indeed fortunate to locate a home with a professional darkroom.

Decks. Isn't this the perfect spot for a barbecue? Do you enjoy cooking on a grill, [Mr./Mrs.] Jones?

A privacy deck is the perfect spot for afternoon sunbathing.

Sit down and relax for just a moment. Isn't this a pleasant spot for relaxation?

Sitting back and relaxing with a beautiful sunset view—this is really worth coming home to.

Other Descriptive Terms: Very private sun deck, sunrise deck, sunset deck, garden deck.

Dens. The separate entry makes the den ideal for a home office.

Isn't this the perfect sneak-away spot for quiet relaxation?

[Mr./Mrs.] Jones, would you use this as a home office, a music room or do you have some special use in mind?

Other Descriptive Terms: Study, home office, estate office, library, convertible den, music room.

Dining Rooms. What kind of dining room set do you have, [Mr./Mrs.] Jones?

Wouldn't you love to entertain your closest friends in this elegant formal dining room?

There is room here for a family reunion.

There is room here for your children and grandchildren as well. Isn't this a great place for a Thanksgiving or Christmas dinner?

Doors. Knock on the doors—these are solid-core doors, not light hollow doors used in some homes.

The sculptured entry doors are just a prelude to what awaits you inside.

Other Descriptive Terms: Massive hand-carved doors, sculptured entry doors, the French doors open to ____.

Entry. The stone archway enhances the charm of this _____.

The massive double doors will open onto a dramatic ____.

The impressive entry is just an introduction to what awaits you.

The handcrafted front doors provide a preview of the luxury and craftsmanship that await you.

The gates will open to your own private world.

Family Rooms. How would you furnish the family room, [Mr./Mrs.] Smith?

Would you use the room primarily for your children's play area?

Isn't this the perfect spot for informal gatherings of your close friends?

There is plenty of room here for a billiard table. Do you play pool, [Mr./Mrs.] Jones?

By using a convertible sofa, you could also use this room for guests.

Other Descriptive Terms: Drawing room, recreation room, salon, pub room, billiard room, leisure room.

Fencing. I think there is something very special about a white picket fence, don't you agree, [Mr./Mrs.] Jones?

Well-kept fences reflect an owner's pride in the property, don't you agree?

Other Descriptive Terms: Ranch-rail fencing, estate-rail fencing, fenced and cross-fenced.

Financing. We can offer extraordinary financial arrangements. Would you like to hear about them?

The net effect of the below-market owner financing is really the same as a tremendous price reduction.

Would you believe _____ percent financing? There is a _____ percent assumable loan for $_____.

Because the owner owns the property free and clear, we can likely finance the property to meet your particular needs.

If you can afford $_____ per month rent you can afford to own this fine home. Let me show you how.

Other Descriptive Terms: Payments are like rent, no-qualifying assumable loan, long-term assumable loan, the owner will handle the financing.

Fireplaces. Now this is a real corn-poppin' family fireplace.

I always wanted a snuggle-up bedroom fireplace.

Now this is a real toe-warming fireplace for those cold winter evenings.

[Mr./Mrs.] Jones, don't you love the warmth of a real wood fire on a cold evening?

A real old-fashioned orchard stone fireplace. Now this is the place to hang those Christmas stockings.

Incidentally, the seller will leave his wood pile. I'm sure you will appreciate that, [Mr./Mrs.] Jones.

Fixer-Uppers. [Mr./Mrs.] Jones, if you owned this home, how would you make it livable?

[Mr./Mrs.] Jones, how long do you think it would take to fix the floor and complete the painting?

How much paint do you suppose it would take to repaint the house? At, say, $12 per gallon, the paint would cost only $_____.

What do you expect the material would cost to fix up this home the way you would want it?

Would you do anything with the landscaping?

Would you panel this wall or repair the plaster?

Other Descriptive Terms: Quality construction but needs cosmetic surgery, presently livable, needs a few bushels of nails and barrels of paint, loaded with potential.

Flooring (Tile). The Mexican quarry tile flows through the entire home.

The sun-baked Mexican tiles have been sealed for easy care.

Real tile floors certainly add an air of warmth and elegance to a home, don't you agree, [Mr./Mrs.] Jones?

Other Descriptive Terms: Travertine tile, Portuguese tile, Italian tile, terrazzo, easy-care tile.

Flooring (Wood). I think pine plank flooring adds a warm feeling to a home, don't you agree?

Oak floors seem to fit any decor.

Gleaming parquet floors certainly add a feeling of elegance to a home.

Other Descriptive Terms: Authentic random-plank floors, pegged pine floors, heart oak floors, mellow maple floors, solid oak floors, soft-tone pine floors.

Furnished Homes. Don't you love the feeling of casual elegance that the decorator has achieved?

[Mr./Mrs.] Jones, would you make any major changes in the decor?

It was decorated by _____ _____, who decorated the _____ estate.

Price was obviously no object on these fabulous furnishings.

It is not just magnificently furnished but is fully accessorized as well. All you need is your toothbrush.

Other Descriptive Terms: Exciting accessories, extravagant appointments, lavishly appointed, decorator-furnished, designer-furnished, charmingly furnished.

Garages. There is plenty of room for bikes and trikes as well as a car and a station wagon in this _____.

There is room for both parents' and children's toys in this oversized garage.

Automatic door openers are certainly nice on those dark, rainy nights, don't you agree, [Mr./Mrs.] Jones?

[Mr./Mrs.] Jones, would you put your workshop in the garage or would you use the basement area?

Gardens. [Mr./Mrs.] Jones, would you put a family garden in this sunny spot?

[Mr./Mrs.] Jones, would you increase the size of the garden?

Isn't this a great spot for a family garden? Do you enjoy gardening, [Mr./Mrs.] Smith?

Other Descriptive Terms: English garden, organic garden, garden-size yard, family-size garden.

Golf. You're cart-distance from the course.

You're a _____ iron shot from the _____ fairway.

Would having a world-class golf course right in your backyard be hard to take, [Mr./Mrs.] Jones?

_____ is a golf-oriented community.

[Mr./Mrs.] Jones, have you considered which of the golf clubs you would join? You have a choice of _____ in the immediate area.

Heating and Air-Conditioning. [Mr./Mrs.] Smith, I am certain you will appreciate the fact that the furnace is a new high-efficiency gas model rated at over 90 percent efficiency. That means significantly lower heating costs than standard furnaces.

Because the house has zoned heating and cooling, you can turn down living areas at night for significant savings.

The state-of-the-art heat pump means significant savings on both heating and cooling.

The home is heated with economical natural gas.

The environment is totally climate controlled.

The owners' fuel bills indicate total heating costs for last year were only $_____.

With the wood furnace you can buy a chainsaw and heat your home for free.

The southwest window wall provides you with free solar heat.

The orientation of the house provides you with the benefit of passive solar heating, which simply means that nature pays part of your heating costs.

Homes (Bargain). It's priced at a fraction of its reproduction price.

You can't duplicate this home for $_____.

This is your opportunity to purchase a home below appraisal value.

At this price it is not going to last long.

Isn't this by far the best value you have seen?

Homes (Country). Your nearest neighbors are squirrels and a family of raccoons.

Don't you agree that this is a better place to raise a family?

What I like about country living is the peace of mind that comes from living close to nature and away from city problems. What attracts you to country living?

Don't you agree that a country home is really an investment in your family?

It is hard to realize but you can have all of this for the price of a mediocre city home.

It may seem different at first, being able to breathe clean air.

The charm is country and so is the quiet.

The country is right outside your door.

This is a true escape from the crime and grime of the city.

Other Descriptive Terms: A friendly lifestyle, an old-fashioned lifestyle, the security of country living, a happy alternative to city life.

Homes (Furnished). *See:* Furnished Homes

Homes (Large). With over _____ square feet the home still retains a feeling of warmth and intimacy, don't you agree, [Mr./Mrs.] Jones?

Will your children like having rooms of their very own?

There is room here for a family reunion with children and grandchildren as well.

Would you use this as a guest suite,[Mr./Mrs.] Jones?

Other Descriptive Terms: Texas-size, baronial size, family-size, tribe-size, magnificently proportioned, dramatically proportioned, embassy-size.

Homes (Low-Priced). This is your chance to escape the rental trap.

Wouldn't you like to take your landlord off your payroll?

At $_____ it's elegantly affordable.

Don't you agree renting is foolish when for the same money you can be an owner?

Isn't it better to build an equity in a home rather than collecting rent receipts?

Other Descriptive Terms: Easy to own, kiss your landlord good-bye, priced for you.

Homes (Luxury). This is truly a home that knows no compromise.

Isn't this what civilized living is all about?

There are all of the appointments one would expect in a home of this caliber.

Isn't this just a step above anything you have seen?

Although life seems filled with compromises, with this home you need compromise no more.

Once in a rare while a home such as this appears on the market.

This home reflects a gracious style of luxury that soon may no longer be available.

This is certainly one of this city's most envied homes.

This home provides the lifestyle that others can only hope to match.

This is truly a world-class residence.

This home speaks for itself and it says, "Success."

I feel that a home is the ultimate statement of one's success and this home says, "Success."

This is the home for one of the special few who can afford a truly spectacular residence.

Isn't this home the culmination of all your dreams?

If you promised yourself the best in life there is no better time than now to keep that promise.

Other Descriptive Terms: Magnificent estate, one of this city's great homes, understated elegance, muted elegance, a home that mirrors your achievements, truly an unparalleled home, a home for those who appreciate the fine art of living, a new definition of elegance.

Homes (New). This is one of the most exciting new homes I have seen.

There is still time to pick the colors and wall coverings.

I love the smell of freshness in a new home, don't you?

Everything's new and protected by warranty.

The home was built by _____, who is considered one of the finest contractors in the area.

Notice how the builder has fitted the home into the natural setting.

For the same price as old, doesn't a new home make sense?

Homes (Old). This home was bult when craftspeople still took pride in their work.

Doesn't it seem like you're stepping back in time to a more gracious period?

It seems to embody the charm and romance of a bygone era.

You can feel that special charm and warmth found only in older homes.

It reflects the pride of __ generations of family ownership.

This home remembers the time of fancy parasols and horse-drawn carriages.

Don't you agree, this home has an elegance unobtainable in the new homes of today?

This home offers a quality of life that only the past can provide.

This home brings back classic memories of workmanship and pride.

The opulence of yesterday certainly provides a refreshing atmosphere for gracious entertaining and family living, don't you agree, [Mr./Mrs.] Jones?

This eighteeth-century colonial reflects the time when the family home was the center of one's existence.

It truly represents the grandeur of the past with all the conveniences of tomorrow.

Imagine the opportunity—it's like living in a legend.

Other Descriptive Terms: Timeless elegance, ageless beauty, nineteenth-century perfection, antebellum, bed and breakfast potential, steeped in history, old-world charm.

Homes (Small). This is the home for mature adults who deserve a more luxurious lifestyle.

Isn't this the ideal alternative to apartment or condo living?

This home is designed for today's adult lifestyle.

Other Descriptive Terms: Intimate, sophisticated, retirement-size.

Homes (Vacation). *See:* Vacation Homes

Insulation. The state-of-the-art, energy-efficient construction will be appreciated when you pay your utility bills.

Six-inch sidewalls provide for maximum insulation and minimum heating and cooling costs.

The 12 inches of ceiling insulation means lower heating and cooling costs.

Kitchens. I'm certain, [Mr./Mrs.] Jones, that you will appreciate this state-of-the-art gourmet kitchen.

Don't you like a kitchen that's big enough for the whole family to eat in?

Notice how this rheostat controls the soft ceiling of light.

The Maytag appliances reflect the quality of the appointments in this _____.

The breakfast area catches the first morning sun. Don't you think a sunny kitchen and a good cup of coffee is the perfect way to start the day?

Other Descriptive Terms: Tribe-size kitchen, step-saver kitchen, one-step kitchen, country kitchen, French country kitchen, European kitchen, European-inspired kitchen, sun-drenched kitchen, European oak cabinetry, rich cherry cabinetry, cabinet-clad kitchen.

Lawns. This is likely the most beautiful yard in town.

[Mr./Mrs.] Jones, I am certain you will appreciate the low-maintenance landscaping.

The grounds have been professionally landscaped and maintained.

[Mr./Mrs.] Jones, don't you agree the grounds compliment the home?

The grounds feature exotic plantings from all over the world.

[Mr./Mrs.] Jones, would you make any changes in the landscaping?

Living Rooms. [Mr./Mrs.] Smith, how would you furnish a large room such as this?

Will you keep the same color scheme or will you make changes?

There is room for a grand piano in this entertaining-size living room.

This room was designed for casual elegance and I think they succeeded.

The glass walls seem to bring the outdoors in, making the room bright and cheerful for entertaining or quiet living.

The vaulted ceiling adds magnificent dimensions to the room, don't you agree?

This room was certainly designed for entertaining on a grand scale.

I think you will appreciate the intimate conversation area.

[Mr./Mrs.] Smith, don't you like the open concept planning?

Lofts. The southern exposure would make this a cheerful artist's studio.

The northern exposure makes this the ideal artist's studio because it offers diffused light without shadows.

The Swiss loft over the great room could be used for guests or it would make an ideal studio or home office.

Other Descriptive Terms: Sleeping loft, studio loft, library loft, balcony studio, artist's loft, Swiss loft.

Lot Size. *Descriptive Terms:* Estate-size, tribe-size, orchard-size, double-size, room for pool, room for tennis court.

Marble. Do you know that carrera marble is the sculptor's choice?

The master bath is sheathed in travertine marble.

The vanity tops are of genuine Grecian marble.

Notice the marble accents.

Mobile Homes. This _____ unit has been upgraded beyond belief.

This is really carefree living.

What I like about mobile home living is that you can just lock the door and leave for a weekend or weeks on end.

You are just a short stroll from the recreational facilities.

I think you will agree that this is one of the finest homes in the park.

The park has a five-star rating. Isn't this one of the finest parks you have seen in the area?

Other Descriptive Terms: Reasonable rent, space rent only $ _____, ground-level entrance, full skirting, established park.

Neighborhoods. You will be proud to give this _____ address.

This is an address that is sure to be envied.

A _____ address is an address of success.

I feel that this is the most prestigious street in _____.

I know you will agree that this is a very special neighborhood.

This is an area where neighbors maintain their property and your privacy.

This is probably the most coveted community in all of _____.

_____ is a pleasantly secluded and exclusive neighborhood of winding boulevards and intimate culs-de-sac.

The almost-no-traffic, tree-lined street preserves an almost rural atmosphere.

You will enjoy being able to walk to _____.

This is very much a family-oriented community.

Your home is less than ＿＿＿ minutes from ＿＿＿＿＿＿.

This is a very private community of fine homes.

＿＿＿＿＿＿＿＿＿ is an exclusive enclave of fine homes.

Other Descriptive Terms: Estate setting, country-like setting.

Paneling. Don't you love the look and feel of real wood paneling?

I feel that wood paneling adds warmth to a home, don't you agree?

There is certainly an air of masculinity about a wood-paneled den.

Notice that the paneling is solid cherry—not just a thin veneer.

Other Descriptive Terms: Courtroom paneling, warm wood paneling, imported hardwood paneling, solid walnut wainscoting.

Parking. There is room to keep a boat and motor home. Have you considered purchasing a boat or recreational vehicle?

The previous owners parked their recreational vehicle here—have you considered buying a recreational vehicle in the future?

Patio. Won't you enjoy entertaining your friends on this delightful flagstone terrace?

Notice how through the extensive use of glass the patio has become an extension of the living area.

Can't you picture yourself sipping a cool drink after work on this magnificent terrace?

Breakfast on the patio—isn't that an upbeat way to start your day?

Isn't this the perfect place for informal entertaining?

A barbecue for a few close friends—this is the perfect place for it, don't you agree?

Other Descriptive Terms: Breakfast patio, family patio, picnic-perfect patio, terrace, sun terrace.

Porches. Isn't this the perfect spot for a rocking chair?

When I was a child we all slept out on our porch on those hot summer nights. You know, those are some of the most pleasant memories that I have.

This is just the place to unwind and sip a lemonade—or would it be something stronger?

The porch seems as if it were just made for lazy summer days.

With a porch like this you really should get one of those old-fashioned porch swings.

Porches (Enclosed). [Mr./Mrs.] Smith, how would you furnish the solarium?

Isn't this the perfect spot for lots of green plants and white wicker furniture?

Other Descriptive Terms: Florida room, Arizona room, California room, Hawaiian room, conservatory, solarium, garden room, summer room.

Price. This home is realistically priced at $_____.

Priced to sell at $_____.

It's your home at $_____.

At $_____there should be no need for hesitation.

At $_____ you don't want this to slip by.

I believe it to be an obvious value at $_____.

This home is very well priced at $_____.

It's priced at $_____; don't you think it's worth every penny?

At $_____ this home is a solid value.

It is hard to believe, but it's priced at only $_____.

I believe it to be an uncommon find at $_____.

This is amazingly reasonably priced at $_____.

It is a very special home at $_____.

At $_____ you will never say you're sorry.

$_____ and you will call this home.

This is the home you deserve at $_____.

Don't pass up this rare offering at $_____.

The view is priced at $_____, but the house is free.

It's investment-priced at $_____.

It's a lot of home for $_____.

Most assuredly this fine residence could not be duplicated at its price of $_____.

This is a very special home at $_____.

You will think it's too good to be true. It's priced at only $_____.

It's going to sell quickly at $_____.

It's an unbelievable value at $_____.

Privacy. This is really your own world of privacy.
This offers a world of private elegance.
Notice the noise—that's the sound of silence.
There is nearly an acre of privacy.
There is no need to whisper here.
This is truly the ultimate in seclusion.
This is a home where privacy is absolute.
Isn't this a most rare private setting?
Wouldn't you love a very private end unit?
This home has end-of-the-road privacy.
Notice the very private sun porch.
Pampered privacy is what this home offers.
It has a very private garden.
This home is located in a very private corner of _____.

Remodeled. This home was thoughtfully remodeled to combine the best of the old with the new.
Don't you love the way the modern improvements complement the antique charm?
This home truly represents the grandeur of the past with all the modern conveniences of tomorrow.
Other Descriptive Terms: Unobtrusive improvements, dramatically updated, thoughtfully updated, nineteenth-century elegance combined with twentieth-century conveniences.

Renovated. *Descriptive Terms:* Handsomely renovated, masterfully renovated, museum-quality renovation, meticulous and imaginative renovation.

Restored. The home has been artistically restored to functional and aesthetic perfection.
The home was restored with antique lovers, such as yourselves, in mind.
The home has been meticulously restored to combine old-fashioned elegance with up-to-date amenities.
The home has been tastefully restored and updated to meet the living standards of the most discriminating.
Other Descriptive Terms: Museum-quality restoration, restored with imagination and elegance, restored to capture the aura of yesteryear, restorable, partially restored, restoration under way.

Roofs. Don't you love the mission tile roof?

> I think the hand-split cedar shake roof helps the home to blend in with the natural surroundings, don't you agree?
>
> The authentic slate roof will last for centuries, and is just a prelude to the quality that awaits us inside.
>
> *Other Descriptive Terms:* Spanish tile, French mansard, Dutch gambrel, Pennsylvania Dutch gambrel.

Schools. Over _____ percent of the graduates of _____

> High School go on to college. [Mr./Mrs.] Smith, isn't this the kind of peer pressure you would like influencing your children?
>
> Your children won't be late for school again. _____ is walking-close.
>
> With _____ Grade School only _____ blocks away, you won't have to play chauffeur anymore. I bet this is welcome news, [Mr./Mrs.] Smith.
>
> Is the quality of your [son's/daughter's] school important to you, [Mr./Mrs.] Smith?
>
> Your children would go to _____ Grade School, which I am certain you realize is considred one of the premier schools in the district.

Security. There is an ultrasonic security system for your peace of mind.

> The home features the latest in electronic security for worry-free living.
>
> You can stroll the streets at night in this gate-guarded enclave of prestigious homes.
>
> *Other Descriptive Terms:* Controlled-access community, monitored security, 24-hour security, video security, central security system.

Shutters. These are working shutters, not merely decorations.

> *Other Descriptive Terms:* Bermuda shutters, privacy shutters, plantation shutters, colonial shutters.

Siding. There is a substantial feeling about a brick home, don't you agree?

> It's built to last practically forever with its brick and stone exterior.
>
> A brick home offers maximum luxury yet minimum maintenance.
>
> Don't you agree the stone and cedar siding seems to blend right into the natural setting?

Other Descriptive Terms: Low-maintenance Masonite siding, no-maintenance aluminum siding, maintenance-free vinyl siding, western cedar siding, genuine cedar shakes.

Spas. *Descriptive Terms:* Hydrotherapy spa, titillating hot spa, tantalizing hot spa, sensuous hot spa, Jacuzzi, very private spa, therapeutic whirlpool spa.

Stairs. There is nothing more dramatic than a floating staircase. Any minute I expect to see an eighteenth-century maiden descending the stairs in an elaborate ball gown.

The circular staircase spirals up to the _____.

Note the intricately carved banisters.

Note the solid cherry balustrades.

[Mr./Mrs.] Smith, don't you agree this wonderful staircase adds an element of dramatic elegance to the home?

Other Descriptive Terms: Sweeping staircase, spiral staircase, center staircase, floating staircase, grand staircase, dramatic curved staircase.

Stone. There is something substantial about stone, don't you agree, [Mr./Mrs.] Jones?

Stone and massive wood beams provide a feeling of reality in an all-too-plastic world. Don't you agree, [Mr./Mrs.] Jones?

Other Descriptive Terms: Orchard stone, river rock, crab orchard stone, native stone.

Streets and Roads. Doesn't this street remind you of a quiet country lane?

I think this is the most prestigious street in _____.

On the best block of the most sought-after street in _____. Isn't this the neighborhood you deserve?

This home is tucked away on a quiet cul-de-sac for the ultimate in privacy.

Isn't this an elegant address?

Other Descriptive Terms: Tree-lined street, tree-canopied street, end-of-the-road seclusion, on a private lane, on a very special street, on the prettiest street and the friendliest neighborhood in _____, in a pleasantly secluded neighborhood of winding boulevards and intimate culs-de-sac, children-safe cul-de-sac.

Sunlight. Notice that the kitchen is flooded with the afternoon sunlight.

The kitchen is bright with the morning sun.

The southern window wall lets the sun pay part of your fuel bill with passive solar heat.

[Mr./Mrs.] Jones, don't you like a kitchen that is filled with the morning light?

There are _____ windows to welcome the sun.

Other Descriptive Terms: Sun-filled, sun-drenched, filled with sunlight.

Swimming Pools. With a pool like this you won't want to leave it for your vacation.

You can vacation right here in your own backyard.

How do you think your children will like having their own swimming pool?

Doesn't that pool look inviting?

The pool offers skinny-dipping privacy.

With a heated pool like this you will be able to keep fit and enjoy your exercise year-round.

I don't regard a pool as a luxury—to me it's an investment in your health. I don't know of a better way to keep fit, don't you agree with me, [Mr./Mrs.] Jones?

With the solar heater the sun pays for the heating. I bet that appeals to you, [Mr./Mrs.] Jones.

Other Descriptive Terms: Inviting pool, crystal-cool pool, dazzling pool, shimmering pool.

Taxes. Did you know, [Mr./Mrs.] Smith, _____ has the lowest tax rate in the county?

Last year the property taxes were only $_____. That's at least _____ percent less than they would be in _____.

With the street, curb, gutter and sidewalk all in and paid for, you won't be getting any expensive tax assessments for improvements.

Tennis. You are just steps to the courts.

Won't it be great to have your friends over to play at your own championship tennis court?

The tennis court will make keeping fit a lot of fun, don't you agree, [Mr./Mrs.] Jones?

There is plenty of room for your own tennis court.

Other Descriptive Terms: Illuminated court, championship tennis court, world-class tennis court.

Tile. Don't you love real ceramic tile?

I think Mexican tile adds a great deal of warmth to a home, don't you agree, [Mr./Mrs.] Jones?

Other Descriptive Terms: Floor-to-ceiling ceramic tile, sleek ceramic tile, flowing Mexican tile, sun-baked Mexican tile, Venetian tile, travertine tile.

Timeshares. You really only want your own cottage for two weeks each year, so why pay for fifty-two? Doesn't that make common sense, [Mr./Mrs.] Smith?

No matter what happens as far as the economy or inflation is concerned, you can lock in your future now with a one-time, full-price payment of only $_____.

I don't know if you realize it, but we belong to a vacation network. If you want a change you can exchange your two weeks for another location such as Hawaii, Tahiti, Florida or even Europe. Do any of those vacation places interest you, [Mr./Mrs.] Jones?

Other Descriptive Terms: Interval ownership, special shared ownership plan.

Trees. That is a great place for a hammock between those two tall walnut trees.

The hardwood trees will provide you with firewood forever.

Your children will love being able to cut your own Christmas tree in your private woods.

You should have bushels of fruit from the apple, pear and plum trees.

You can make your own maple syrup from the many sugar maples on your property.

You will love it here in the fall when the leaves turn to bright yellow and blazing orange.

Unfinished Area. Wouldn't this make the ideal artist's studio? [Mr./Mrs.] Jones, do either of you paint or write?

The walk-up attic could be easily converted to a studio or guest room, leaving plenty of space for storage.

You won't have to worry about storage space any longer when you see the full storage attic.

This would make a great hobby room or privacy studio. What would you use this space for, [Mr./Mrs.] Jones?

Utilities. Having natural gas is really appreciated most when it is time to pay utility bills.

The water is pure and cold from your own well—let me pour you a glass.

The utilities are all paid so there is no bond debt for you to assume.

No septic tank here—the home is connected to city sewers.

With underground utilities you have no unsightly and dangerous poles and wires. I think it makes for a much more pleasant community, don't you agree, [Mr./Mrs.] Smith?

Vacation Homes. How would you like to spend your summers here?

What kind of boat would you buy to keep at the dock, [Mr./Mrs.] Jones?

Wouldn't this be a great place for a family reunion?

Isn't this the perfect spot to slow down the tempo of your life?

Every day would be like a holiday living on the lake.

Would you eventually use this as a retirement home?

You are less than _____ from the golf course. Do you enjoy golf?

The fishing is great here—do you enjoy fishing?

How do you think you will like swimming and fishing in your own backyard?

Most of the neighbors have boats—do you enjoy boating?

I think the nicest part of owning a summer home is relaxing at the end of the day on the veranda and watching the sunset over the water.

There is nothing quite like the gentle sound of waves lapping at the shore to put you to sleep at night.

Other Descriptive Terms: Retreat, hideaway, lodge, weekend getaway, Currier and Ives setting, a happy alternative to city life, a place for a simpler life.

View. You can see forever and a little beyond.

Isn't this an unsurpassed view of _____.

Look—the entire city is spread out at your feet.

At night you will look down at a fairyland of flickering lights.

Where else can you go sightseeing right through your living room windows?

Imagine for a moment cocktails on the deck at sunset. Isn't that a relaxing thought?

The view alone is worth far more than the price and you get the house as well.

Nothing is more relaxing than a white-water view, don't you agree, [Mr./Mrs.] Jones?

This is truly a million-dollar view, at a price including the home of $_____. This is certainly a bargain.

Wall Coverings. Don't you love the decorator's lavish use of wall coverings?

Other Descriptive Terms: Designer wall coverings, imported wall coverings, marbleized wall coverings, trompe l'oeil wall coverings, imported grasspaper, richly textured wall coverings.

Windows. The soaring window walls seem to bring the outdoors right inside.

The clerestory windows bathe the room in warm natural light.

Other Descriptive Terms: Solar-bronze windows, window-wrapped solarium, wall of glass, Palladian windows, greenhouse windows, the living room windows frame _____, old-fashioned bay windows, intricately etched glass, stained glass, leaded glass, diamond glass, skylight.

Workshops. [Mr./Mrs.] Jones, do you think you could make good use of the workshop?

There is plenty of room here for your workshop.

The workshop is just waiting for your next project; what do you think it will be?

Index

250 *POWER REAL ESTATE SELLING*

Success Motivation Institute, 6
Summation closings, 168
Sunlight, describing, 241
Suppliers, as buyers, 45–46
Swimming pools, describing, 241
Syndication, getting into, 35–36
Syndicators, selling to, 35

T
Taking notes, 96
Taxes, describing, 241
Tax questions, 110
Tax Reform Act of 1986, 36
Teaching, and prospect leads, 44
Team approach, 5
Technical skills, 11–13
Telephone techniques, 49–61
Tenants, as prospects, 28–29
Tennis opportunities, describing,
  241–42
Three home showing approach,
  85–86
Tile, describing, 242
Time management, 15–16
Timeshares, 242
Toastmasters, 6
Tools of trade, 17–20

Trade courses, 11
Traditional styles, describing, 222
Training, of salespersons, 9–12
Trees, describing, 242
Trial closings, 159–60
Tying up prospects, 110–11

U–V–W
Under-list offers, 191–99
Unfinished areas, describing, 242
Unmarried couples, as prospects, 30
Unpriced sale, 177–78
Utilities, describing, 243
Vacation homes, describing, 243
Victorian styles, describing, 222
View, describing, 243–44
Vocabulary for sellings and closings,
  159, 219–44
Voice contact, 182
Wall coverings, describing, 244
Weddings, and prospect leads, 40
White elephants, 46
Windows, describing, 244
Word pictures, 122, 219–44
Workshops, describing, 244
Writing up the closing, 164–65